CRITICAL INSIGHTS
The Handmaid's Tale

CRITICAL INSIGHTS

The Handmaid's Tale

by Margaret Atwood

Editor
J. Brooks Bouson
Loyola University Chicago

Salem Press
Pasadena, California   Hackensack, New Jersey

Cover art by Fred Marcellino, 1987. ©Pulcinella Press, 2009.

Published by Salem Press

© 2010 by EBSCO Publishing
Editor's text © 2010 by J. Brooks Bouson
"The *Paris Review* Perspective" © 2010 by Jascha Hoffman for *The Paris Review*

All rights in this book are reserved. No part of this work may be used or reproduced in any manner whatsoever or transmitted in any form or by any means, electronic or mechanical, including photocopy, recording, or any information storage and retrieval system, without written permission from the copyright owner except in the case of brief quotations embodied in critical articles and reviews or in the copying of images deemed to be freely licensed or in the public domain. For information about the print edition address the publisher, Salem Press, P.O. Box 50062, Pasadena, California 91115. For copyright information, contact EBSCO Publishing, 10 Estes Street, Ipswich, MA 01938.

∞ The paper used in these volumes conforms to the American National Standard for Permanence of Paper for Printed Library Materials, Z39.48-1992 (R1997).

Library of Congress Cataloging-in-Publication Data
The handmaid's tale, by Margaret Atwood / editor, J. Brooks Bouson.
    p. cm. — (Critical insights)
Includes bibliographical references and index.
ISBN 978-1-58765-620-0 (alk. paper)
    1. Atwood, Margaret, 1939- Handmaid's tale. 2. Fantasy fiction, Canadian—History and criticism. I. Bouson, J. Brooks.
PR9199.3.A8H3163 2009
813'.54—dc22

2009026309

PRINTED IN CANADA

Contents

About This Volume, J. Brooks Bouson   vii

The Book and Author

On *The Handmaid's Tale*, J. Brooks Bouson   3
Biography of Margaret Atwood, Karen Carmean, Karen F. Stein,
　　and Earl G. Ingersoll   10
The *Paris Review* Perspective, Jascha Hoffman for *The Paris Review*   15

Critical Contexts

Margaret Atwood's *The Handmaid's Tale* (1985): Cultural
　　and Historical Context, Lisa Jadwin   21
Margaret Atwood's *The Handmaid's Tale*: Critical Reception,
　　Dominick Grace   42
"This Is the Way the World Ends": Margaret Atwood and the
　　Dystopian Impulse, Matthew J. Bolton   59
Feminism and *The Handmaid's Tale*, Jennifer E. Dunn   74

Critical Readings

The Handmaid's Tale, Coral Ann Howells   91
"Trust Me": Reading the Romance Plot in Margaret Atwood's
　　The Handmaid's Tale, Madonne Miner   112
"Just a Backlash": Margaret Atwood, Feminism, and
　　The Handmaid's Tale, Shirley Neuman   138
Alice in Disneyland: Criticism as Commodity in
　　The Handmaid's Tale, Chinmoy Banerjee   153
Selves, Survival, and Resistance in *The Handmaid's Tale*,
　　Elisabeth Hansot   175
"We Lived in the Blank White Spaces": Rewriting the
　　Paradigm of Denial in Atwood's *The Handmaid's Tale*,
　　Danita J. Dodson   196
Margaret Atwood's *The Handmaid's Tale*: Resistance Through
　　Narrating, Hilde Staels   227

v

A Body in Fragments: *Life Before Man* and *The Handmaid's Tale*,
    Eleonora Rao   246
Margaret Atwood's *The Handmaid's Tale*: Scheherazade
    in Dystopia, Karen F. Stein   261
The Handmaid's Tale as Scrabble Game, Joseph Andriano   276

Resources

Chronology of Margaret Atwood's Life	289
Works by Margaret Atwood	293
Bibliography	295
About the Editor	303
About *The Paris Review*	303
Contributors	305
Acknowledgments	308
Index	311

About This Volume

J. Brooks Bouson

An author who is part trickster, illusionist, and con artist, as she has often described herself, Margaret Atwood is also an author-ethicist with a finely honed sense of moral responsibility, as she sets out both to teach and to delight in *The Handmaid's Tale*. Although Atwood has sometimes had an uneasy relationship with the Professor Pieixoto type of critic she satirizes in the conclusion to *The Handmaid's Tale*, she does have an intense interest in her readers. "One of my university professors," Atwood recalls, "used to say that there was only one real question to be asked about any work, and that was—is it alive, or is it dead?" For Atwood a text is "alive" if it can "grow" and "change" through its interactions with its readers (140).

We can find evidence of just how "alive" *The Handmaid's Tale* is in the critical material brought together in this volume. Analyzing Atwood's novel from various critical and theoretical perspectives, these essays offer fresh insights not only on the sources of the novel, its critical reception, and its dystopian and parodic elements but also on its complicated feminist politics, its narrative strategies, and its literary and linguistic complexities. Lisa Jadwin, who deftly places *The Handmaid's Tale* in its cultural and historical contexts, shows how Atwood, as a "public intellectual," consciously engages with 1980s politics in telling Offred's story: with the rise of the conservative Moral Majority in the United States, which viewed women's rights as a threat to traditional cultural and family values, and with the cultural feminism of the 1980s, which celebrated women's "essential" difference from men and called for the creation of a separatist women's culture. In the "Historical Notes" section of the novel, which offers a "spoof" of an academic conference, Atwood engages with the culture wars that were beginning to erupt in the 1980s in the academy. For even though Atwood was aware that academics were intent on revealing "the extent to which political oppression can be perpetuated in language," as Jadwin explains, she also "detected a good deal of hypocrisy" in academic discourses and in the progressive agenda of a "politically correct" inclusiveness. Dominick Grace, who describes *The Handmaid's Tale* as a novel that has the "twin benefits of being a best seller and a novel with literary credibility," identifies three basic "strands" in the ongoing scholarly investigation of Atwood's work: the novel's connection to the dystopian tradition, its feminist politics, and its postmodern elements. Arguing that the "greatness" of Atwood's *Handmaid's Tale* "resides at least in part in its irreducibility to a single meaning or critical perspective," Grace comments that just as Atwood's novel refuses to offer "a conventional dystopian vision" or "a simple feminist solution to complex problems," so it insists "on questioning and subverting all orthodoxies, a trait closely linked to its affinities with postmodernism."

Offering examples of what Grace identifies as two of the major strands of criticism surrounding Atwood's novel, Matthew Bolton explores *The Handmaid's Tale*'s connection to the dystopian tradition, and Jennifer Dunn explores its link to twentieth-century feminism. Unlike modern dystopian novels such as Aldous Huxley's *Brave New World*, George Orwell's *1984*, and Ray Bradbury's *Fahrenheit 451*, which "displace Judeo-Christian notions of end-time onto an Almighty secular state," Atwood's two dystopian novels—*The Handmaid's Tale* and *Oryx and Crake*—"explicitly treat the religious element of dystopian literature," according to Bolton. Both novels dramatize the "role that religion can play in making of earth a heaven or a hell," for in *The Handmaid's Tale* Atwood "reimagines the Orwellian surveillance state as a Christian fundamentalist one" while in *Oryx and Crake* she shows how "man's hubris in playing God through genetic engineering reshapes the earth into a paradise . . . no longer fit for man himself." Finding "issues of biology, theology, and ethics" driving *The Handmaid's Tale* and *Oryx and Crake*, Bolton locates an "overarching moral" in both novels as Atwood, revealing the dangers of utopian thinking, shows how utopia becomes dystopia "precisely because the utopian thinkers are willing to sacrifice the basic human rights of the individual in order to bring about the perceived good of the many."

While Bolton focuses on the sacrifice of basic human rights in Atwood's dystopian society, Jennifer Dunn shows how "all the work of twentieth-century feminism has been utterly undone" in Atwood's fictional Gilead. "Lending itself to more than one feminist reading" as it engages with twentieth-century feminist thought, *The Handmaid's Tale* offers an explicit feminist critique of the objectifying male gaze and the binary logic that undergirds patriarchal society, and it also has affinities with the feminist projects that call for the recovery of lost and silenced female voices and the re-visioning of familiar stories as an act of resistance and survival. If in *The Handmaid's Tale* "language is shown to be a source of power, one as effective as the gaze," the "very elusiveness" of Offred's tale and its resistance to fixed meanings call attention not only to the "instability of language" but also to the "radical potential" of the acts of rewriting and retelling.

The critical readings included in this volume highlight the remarkable complexity of Atwood's widely taught and eminently readable and yet challenging, multilayered work in which Atwood, even as she addresses feminist concerns and offers a trenchant critique of sexism and the power politics of gender relations, also engages in a metafictional inquiry into the storytelling process. Focusing on the act of storytelling in *The Handmaid's Tale*, Coral Ann Howells argues that Offred's assertion of her right to tell her story is an act of resistance and survival. As Offred "claims the space to write about her body, her memories and her womanly desires," she becomes the "speaking subject" described by French feminist Hélène Cixous in her *écriture féminine*. Offred's tale, as it marginalizes the grand patriarchal narratives of the Bible and history, "effects a significant shift from 'history' to 'herstory'" and turns Offred into "the most important historian of Gilead." If the abrupt shift in the "Historical Notes" to the voice of Professor Pieixoto calls attention to the male historian's appropriation of Offred's story, Offred's tale not only shows the limits of Gilead's power over her but also defies the professor's act of appropriation. "By putting herself into the text, Offred has put herself 'into the world and into history,' challenging readers to connect her world with our own in the present in the hope of averting a nightmare like Gilead for our own future."

Whereas Howells describes the "transforming power of sexual desire" in Offred's account of her love affair with Nick, Madonne Miner argues against the common critical claim that love is a subversive force in Atwood's novel. Presenting the love plot as "potentially dangerous to women," *The Handmaid's Tale* shows how Offred, after she begins her affair with Nick, loses interest in the underground Mayday organization and in the possibility of escape. Thus, "whatever political commitment Offred might be capable of making vanishes in light of her commitment to romance." Through *The Handmaid's Tale*'s "highly qualified" treatment of the love plot, according to Miner, readers are led to a "critical assessment" not only of how they have "shaped love's plot" but also how it, in turn, has "shaped" them. Like Miner, Shirley Neuman questions the romance plot in *The Handmaid's Tale*, describing Offred's affair with Nick as "a relapse into willed ignorance." Focusing on the ways in which Offred's situation is a "fictional realization of the backlash against women's rights that gathered force during the early 1980s," Neuman argues against readings of the novel that conflate "Offred's desire to have 'everything back, the way it was' with Atwood's implicit utopia." The implicit women's utopia is not "'the time before,'" which, as the novel shows, was a time of "dangers, humiliations, inequities, and backlash" against women. Instead, the first step to utopia requires that contemporary women "'pay attention' and bear witness, as does Offred when she uses her uncertain freedom to tell her story."

Claiming that *The Handmaid's Tale* is based on a "media-generated awareness of the threat of Christian fundamentalism" that requires readers to forget the "immense gains" made by women as a result of the women's movement, Chinmoy Banerjee questions the "critical force" of Atwood's novel and states that Atwood's dystopian fantasy "is unlikely to scare a new generation of women into following in their mothers' footsteps." While *The Handmaid's Tale* is a "dystopia in its form," Atwood, through her insistent parody of Christian fundamentalism and her continual verbal play, "places side by side two possible modes of imagining the negative: the extension into horror and the reduction into absurdity." If the novel's horror seems "excessive and unmotivated," the play "seems comfortable and clever." A "parody of the Gothic" and a "pseudo-dystopia," *The Handmaid's Tale*, in Banerjee's view, uses the dystopian form "for consumption and enjoyment." To critics like Elisabeth Hansot and Danita J. Dodson, however, Atwood's futuristic tale is a serious work that offers a forceful critique of gender and power politics. For Hansot, the "genius" of *The Handmaid's Tale* is found in "the mundane and ordinary quality of the dystopian lives it depicts" as the Handmaids develop "hidden transcripts"—that is, hidden ways of critiquing the powerful—through their "short fragments of speech" and "small deviations in posture and glance." Offred also resists by elaborating "selves that reestablish some continuity with her discredited past and give some amplitude to her impoverished present." While the "precisely crafted selves" Offred constructs in solitude "offer no bridgework to the cruder arenas where Moira and Ofglen act," the "provisional and precarious selves" she crafts as she resists the regime "do survive to tell Offred's story."

For Dodson, who, like many commentators, draws a connection between Gilead and the past, present, and potential future of the United States, Atwood rewrites the story of the Puritans in *The Handmaid's Tale* by focusing on the "violent legacy" of the Puritans and their "divine mission" in the founding of America. Invoking the "rawness and originality of the slave narrative" in telling the story of Offred's "forced servitude," Atwood develops "her major American genre reenactment" in *The Handmaid's Tale*: "the narrative of the enslaved black mother." Even as Atwood illuminates the "confusing reality that domestic imperialism and enslavement" have characterized an America established on the utopian principle of "liberty and justice for *all*," she also reveals that "the most important movement toward achieving decolonization and ending oppression is to give voice to suppressed histories."

Also focusing on Atwood's insistence on the need to give expression to women's silenced voices and suppressed histories, Hilde Staels describes how Offred "defies the strict rules" of Gilead's "authoritative discourse" as she speaks from the margins of society and tells her story. In Gilead, where the "governing discourse" is an "artificial, so-called Biblical speech," the "aesthetic, creative use of language" is outlawed and "all dangerous personal, irrational and emotional elements that escape calculation" are censored. Offred, however, "breaks through the discursive Law of the theocracy" by expressing her "inner feelings and bodily sensations," and she "revives the capacity for individual spiritual and emotional life" by disrupting the sacred word. If Offred, through her poetic discourse, reactivates "the lost potential of language and the conditions for the production of meaning," the male historians who later transcribe Offred's tale, ironically enough, mirror the "authoritative word of Gilead" through their search for a "univocal, transparent meaning."

Whereas for Staels Offred's poetic speech "reactivates the lost potential of language," for Eleonora Rao, who describes *The Handmaid's Tale* as an example of "historiographic metafiction," the "gaps and ambiguities in Offred's tale and its emphasis on being a 'story' suggest the impossibility of full representation." Drawing on Lacanian psychoanalytic theory, which locates a "connection between bodily fragments and the dissolving ego," Rao argues that the "fragmentation, discontinuity and contradictions" of Atwood's narrative "suggest a sense of a lack of a rationalizing and unifying entity at work in the text." Thus, for Rao, the novel's fragmented structure suggests the fragmented nature of subjectivity.

Offering a more hopeful reading of Offred's fragmented narrative, Karen F. Stein, in her "critic's tale that rereads and reinterprets the novel," examines the complexities of Offred's narrative, which is "a game, a story, an inscription of the self." A "Scheherazade of the future," Offred, through her storytelling, "grows more politically aware and self-conscious" and, in her storytelling, she creates both "a self and an other, a listener." As she tells her tale, Offred "deconstructs it" with her wordplay and metafictional interventions, and yet storytelling remains a "paradoxical project," for though it "appears to provide some degree of control and agency for the teller," to be "fixed in words" is to be "less free than those who live in the gaps." Even as Atwood "tells a good tale" she also, in *The Handmaid's Tale*, "engages in metafictional commentary on the storytelling process"; indeed, by the time the critic reads the novel, "Atwood has already told and retold the story, questioned and hedged, changed the context, deconstructed and reconstructed the narrative" and so readers and critics "join Atwood in the process she has already begun, the project of reinscribing the text."

Offering an example of the kind of gamelike enjoyment provided by Atwood through her complex verbal play in the novel, Joseph Andriano argues that the game of Scrabble—featured in the scenes in which Offred and the Commander play Scrabble together—is a "pervasive controlling metaphor" in Atwood's novel. "To make a play in Scrabble is to attempt to gain an advantage with words, to counteract, to cross. It is a game of text/countertext." If to Gileadean society the Word has a single monolithic meaning, Offred undercuts the Word not only through her constant wordplay but also through the forbidden game of Scrabble she plays with the Commander, which provides an image of the ultimate collapse of Gilead as "the monolithic Word, the tablet of stone, crumbles into Scrabble tiles, a scattering of letters that form a myriad of words having only accidental semantic and syntactic elements." Although Professor Pieixoto, the third player in the Scrabble game, undercuts Offred's speech, his "Historical Notes" are "like the last play of a loser in a Scrabble game," as Andriano astutely observes, since the actual winner of the Scrabble game is "the fourth player—Margaret Atwood."

Work Cited

Atwood, Margaret. *Negotiating with the Dead: A Writer on Writing*. New York: Cambridge University Press, 2002.

THE BOOK AND AUTHOR

On *The Handmaid's Tale*
J. Brooks Bouson

An internationally acclaimed writer and literary celebrity, Canadian author Margaret Atwood is perhaps best known for her 1985 futuristic dystopian novel *The Handmaid's Tale*, which envisions what life might be like in the United States if the ultraconservative Religious Right were to seize control of the government and establish a totalitarian society based on a fundamentalist reading of the Bible. An award-winning and best-selling novel, *The Handmaid's Tale* has reached a wide international audience in the years since its publication; indeed, it has been translated into French, German, Spanish, Italian, Danish, Finnish, Norwegian, Greek, Polish, Portuguese, Slovenian, Croatian, Japanese, Chinese, and Korean, among others. Not only has it become a staple in literature and women's studies courses in colleges and universities, but it also has been the subject of book-club discussions and various study guides as well as countless critical investigations as readers, students, teachers, and scholars have grappled with the plight of Atwood's Handmaid, Offred, who serves as a breeder in the Republic of Gilead, a fundamentalist theocracy formed in the United States after the violent overthrow of the government.

Vintage Atwood and a virtuoso performance, *The Handmaid's Tale* has been canonized as a feminist classic for its trenchant critique of the power politics of gender relations and its dire warnings against the antifeminist backlash that began in the conservative 1980s. Just as Atwood, in the years since the publication of *The Handmaid's Tale*, has come to be regarded as a revered Canadian writer who "touches on 'global' concerns that transcend national borders" in her works, so *The Handmaid's Tale* has come to be read not only as a global feminist fable for the twenty-first century but also as a "political fable for our time, as if the present is rushing in to confirm Atwood's dire warnings about birth technologies, environmental pollution, human rights abuses, religious fanaticism, [and] extreme right-wing political movements" (Moss 28, Howells 94).

The Handmaid's Tale is a work that continues to compel and disquiet women readers who find chilling evidence in the contemporary twenty-first century world that the future depicted in Atwood's cautionary fable "is a too logical extension of many dimensions of the present" and that Atwood's novelistic "account of the creation of a fascist and totalitarian state" could, with some minor changes in detail, provide "a plausible future scenario for readers in Asian, African and Middle Eastern nations" (Staines 21, Jacob 31). Yet while Atwood has been lauded as a prophetic writer for her feminist dystopia, when she first started thinking about the novel, as she recalls, she avoided writing it because it "seemed too hopeless a task and too weird a concept" ("Introduction" 3). When, in 1984, she finally began writing the novel in West Berlin on a rented electric typewriter, the "irony" of the year was "not lost" on her: "How could I be so corny as to start a dystopia in the year scheduled for George Orwell's? But the thing could no longer be avoided: it was that novel or none" ("Introduction" 4). Although she wrote *The Handmaid's Tale* "with some trepidation," fearing it might be viewed as "stupid" or "silly" and end up being the "worst failure" one could "possibly imagine" (Hancock 114), she persisted working on it and finished writing it in the spring of 1985. Published in 1985 in Canada and England and in 1986 in the United States, *The Handmaid's Tale* was also made into a film; the film version of the novel, which was scripted by Harold Pinter and directed by Volker Schloendorff, premiered in the two Berlins in early 1990, soon after the Wall fell late in 1989. If Atwood feared when she was writing the novel that others might find the work "silly," she instead has ended up being taken very seriously indeed, not only by women readers but also by members of the conservative Religious Right who have tried to get the novel banned from high school reading lists because of what they describe as its "sexual content" and "obscenity" (see Wood 199). Once when she was asked about the American reaction to the novel, Atwood replied,

"Oh, banned in high schools, death threats at the time of the movie," her tone suggesting, as one commentator notes, that she took "a kind of pride in these incidents," as if being the target of censorship was "a mark of recognition of her accomplishment as a writer" (Cohen 50).

Describing *The Handmaid's Tale* as "speculative fiction of the George Orwell variety," Atwood insists that her novel is "based on actuality or possibility" (Meyer 161). "All fictions begin with the question *What if*," Atwood explains, and the "*what if*" of *The Handmaid's Tale* is "*what if* you wanted to take over the United States and set up a totalitarian government . . . ? How would you go about it? What conditions would favor you?" ("Writing Utopia" 97, 98). In Atwood's dystopian scenario, right-wing religious fanatics stage a military takeover of the government of the United States by assassinating the president and machine-gunning the Congress, and then they establish a fundamentalist regime that harks back to seventeenth-century American Puritanism. As Atwood comments, the "future society" that she proposes in *The Handmaid's Tale*, like Puritan New England, takes the form of a theocracy "on the principle that no society ever strays completely far from its roots" ("Writing Utopia" 97).

In the patriarchal and theocratic Republic of Gilead, women are consigned to various classes according to their functions: the Wives, who are married to the ruling elite; the Handmaids, who serve as breeders for the regime and give up their children to the Wives; the Marthas, who work as domestic servants in the homes of the elite; and the Aunts, who indoctrinate and train the Handmaids. Because fertile women are viewed as a natural resource in a world of mass sterility and birth defects—a result of widespread environmental devastation caused by the overuse of pesticides, by toxic waste leakages from stockpiles of chemical and biological weapons, and by nuclear power accidents—the Handmaids are treated as property of the male leaders and turned into sexual commodities to be exploited by the state. Concerned, as she has remarked, that the gains made by women as a result of the feminist movement may be "precarious" (Langer 133), Atwood addresses a postfeminist generation of women in *The Handmaid's Tale*. In chilling detail, she delineates the virtual enslavement of the Handmaids, who are reeducated by the Aunts and then assigned to the households of the Commanders of the regime—members of the ruling elite whose Wives are infertile—where they are forced to undergo a monthly impregnation ritual. In telling the story of Offred, a thirty-three-year-old Handmaid—whose proprietary and patronymic name identifies the Commander to whom she temporarily belongs, for she is "Of Fred"—Atwood lays bare the inherent misogyny of patriarchal culture. Stripped of their individuality and used for breeding purposes as they are forcibly enlisted in the regime's project of reversing the precipitous decline in the Caucasian birthrate, the Handmaids, as Offred remarks, are "containers," "two-legged wombs . . . sacred vessels, ambulatory chalices" (124, 176). Those Handmaids who do not capitulate to the regime are brutally punished or executed.

"Ordinary," the Handmaids are told, "is what you are used to. This may not seem ordinary to you now, but after a time it will" (45). A "refugee from the past," Offred recalls her pre-Gilead life in a society where women felt as if they were "free to shape and reshape forever the ever-expanding perimeters" of their lives (294). Offred is part of the "transitional" generation. "For the ones who come after you," she is told, "it will be easier. They will accept their duties with willing hearts." They will freely submit, Offred recognizes, because "they will have no memories, of any other way" (151). "In the days of anarchy, it was freedom to. Now you are being given freedom from. Don't underrate it," the Handmaids are told (33). Yet even as they are promised "freedom from" the sexual degradation and violence—the pornography and rape—that existed in the pre-Gilead world, they are forced to undergo the sexual humiliation of the monthly insemination ritual, which is based on the biblical story of Rachel and Bilhah, in which the barren Rachel tells her husband Jacob to have sexual relations with her handmaid so that she might "have children by her" (Genesis 30:3). As Offred lies between the legs of the Commander's wife, the Commander services her. "What he is fucking is the lower part of my body. I do not say making love, because this is not what he's doing. Copulating too would be inaccurate, because it would imply two people and only one is involved" (121). In Gilead, as the Commander tells Offred, women are "protected" so that they "can fulfill their biological destinies in peace" (284). The pre-Gilead years—that is, contemporary society—in the Commander's view, "were just an anomaly, historically speaking. . . . All we've done is return things to Nature's norm" (285). What lies behind the patriarchal ideal of protected womanhood, as Atwood's novel insists, is a rigid belief in the male use and control of female sexuality.

"*Blessed are the silent*," according to the revised Gileadean Bible (115). In Gilead, men have "the word" while women like Offred, who are not allowed to read or write or speak openly to others, are rendered speechless (114). Commenting that a novel is "always the story of an individual, or several individuals" and not "the story of a generalized mass," Atwood recalls that the "real" problem she confronted when writing *The Handmaid's Tale* was figuring out "how to make the story real at a human and individual level" ("Writing Utopia" 100). Like Atwood's other fictional characters, Offred is, above all else, a compelling storyteller. In *The Handmaid's Tale* we hear, through the voice of Offred, Atwood's characteristic voice, which ranges from the serious and poetic to the wryly ironic and deeply sardonic. Atwood's Handmaid not only tries to hold on to her memories of her pre-Gilead past—that is, our present—through her storytelling, but she also attempts to retain a sense of her individual identity and her connection with imagined others. "I wait. I compose myself," she says. "My self is a thing I must now compose, as one composes a speech" (86). In the "Historical Notes" appended to Offred's tale, readers learn that her narrative is really an oral diary, a transcription of some thirty cassette tapes. For Offred, to compose her story is to rebel against the Gileadean regime, which relegates women to silence. It is also an act of individual assertion and survival as she communicates to an imagined listener. "By telling you anything at all I'm at least believing in you, I believe you're there, I believe you into being. Because I'm telling you this story I will your existence. I tell, therefore you are" (344).

To Atwood, if novel reading has "any redeeming social value," it is that it forces readers "to imagine what it's like to be somebody else" ("Writing the Male" 430). But the twenty-second-century male historian who transcribes Offred's tapes—Professor Pieixoto—is a "bad" reader of Offred's text, as critics have long observed. Atwood's fictional professor reveals his moral obtuseness not only in his refusal to pass judgment on Gileadean society but also in his cold, academic dissection of Offred's story. A male historian who is obsessed with problems of authentication and with establishing the identities of the people described in Offred's tale, Professor Pieixoto is incapable of empathizing with Atwood's Handmaid or of reacting to what is so palpable to Atwood's readers as they respond to the story of her Handmaid—Offred's desperate need to tell her story and to be heard and understood. As Atwood reads and interprets women's lives in *The Handmaid's Tale*, she emphasizes the survival value of the act of storytelling. To Atwood, not only is story essential to the novel, but story also must have what she calls "the Ancient Mariner element, the Scheherazade element: a sense of urgency. *This is the story I must tell; this is the story you must hear*"; indeed, story "must be told with as much intentness as if the teller's life depended on it" ("Reading Blind" 75; see also "In Search" 175). If Atwood's fictional professor seemingly has interpretive authority as he comments on Offred's tale, we may hear in his final words—"Are there any questions?" (395)—the voice of Atwood herself anticipating the ever-proliferating questions asked by critics and readers alike as they grapple with the interpretive and emotional complexities of *The Handmaid's Tale* and its Scheherazade-like storyteller, who, condemned to a life of silence, tells her story as an act of resistance and survival.

Works Cited

Atwood, Margaret. *The Handmaid's Tale*. Toronto: McClelland and Stewart, 1985. Boston: Houghton Mifflin, 1986. New York: Ballantine/Fawcett Crest, 1987. London: Vintage, 1996.

_____. "In Search of *Alias Grace*: On Writing Canadian Historical Fiction." *Writing with Intent*, 158-76.

_____. "Introduction: Part One, 1983-1989." *Writing with Intent*, 3-5.

_____. "Reading Blind: *The Best American Short Stories, 1989.*" *Writing With Intent*, 68-79.

_____. "Writing the Male Character." *Second Words: Selected Critical Prose*. 1982. Boston: Beacon Press, 1984. 412-30.

_____. "Writing Utopia." *Writing with Intent*, 92-100.

_____. *Writing with Intent. Essays, Reviews, Personal Prose: 1983-2005*. New York: Carroll & Graf, 2005.

Cohen, Mark. *Censorship in Canadian Literature*. Montreal: McGill-Queen's University Press, 2001.

Hancock, Geoff. "Tightrope-Walking over Niagara Falls" (Interview). Ingersoll 90-118.

Howells, Coral Ann. *Margaret Atwood*. 2nd edition. New York: Palgrave Macmillan, 2005.

Ingersoll, Earl G., ed. *Waltzing Again: New and Selected Conversations with Margaret Atwood*. Princeton, NJ: Ontario Review Press, 2006.

Jacob, Susan. "Woman, Ideology, Resistance: Margaret Atwood's *The Handmaid's Tale* and Third World Criticism." *Margaret Atwood: The Shape-Shifter*. Ed. Coomi Vevaina and Coral Ann Howells. New Delhi: Creative Books, 1998. 26-43.

Langer, Beryl. "There Are No Texts Without Life" (Interview). Ingersoll 125-38.

Meyer, Bruce, and Brian O'Riordan. "The Beaver's Tale" (Interview). Ingersoll 153-63.

Moss, Laura. "Margaret Atwood: Branding an Icon Abroad." *Margaret Atwood: The Open Eye*. Ed. John Moss and Tobi Kozakewich. Ottawa: University of Ottawa Press, 2006. 19-33.

Staines, David. "Margaret Atwood in Her Canadian Context." *The Cambridge Companion to Margaret Atwood*. Ed. Coral Ann Howells. New York: Cambridge University Press, 2006. 12-27.

Wood, Ruth. "Called to Be a Handmaid: Defending Margaret Atwood." *Censored Books II: Critical Viewpoints, 1985-2000*. Ed. Nicholas Karolides. Lanham, MD: Scarecrow Press, 2002. 199-205.

Biography of Margaret Atwood
Karen Carmean, Karen F. Stein, and Earl G. Ingersoll

Achievements

Early in her career, Margaret Atwood received critical recognition for her work. This is particularly true of her poetry, which has earned her numerous awards, including the E. J. Pratt Medal in 1961, the President's Medal from the University of Western Ontario in 1965, and the Governor-General's Award, Canada's highest literary honor, for *The Circle Game* in 1966. Twenty years later, Atwood again won this prize for *The Handmaid's Tale*. Atwood won first prize in the Canadian Centennial Commission Poetry Competition in 1967 and won a prize for poetry from the Union League Civic and Arts Foundation in 1969. She has received honorary doctorates from Trent University and Queen's University. Additional honors and awards she has received include the Bess Hoskins Prize for poetry (1974), the City of Toronto Award (1977), the Canadian Booksellers Association Award (1977), the St. Lawrence Award for Fiction (1978), the Canada Council Molson Prize (1980), and the Radcliffe Medal (1980). *The Blind Assassin* won the 2000 Booker Prize, and Atwood received Spain's Prince of Asturias literary prize for 2008.

Biography

Margaret Eleanor Atwood was born in Ottawa, Ontario, Canada, on November 18, 1939, the second of Carl Edmund Atwood and Margaret Killam Atwood's three children. At the age of six months, she was backpacked into the Quebec wilderness, where her father, an entomologist, pursued his special interests in bees, spruce budworms, and forest tent caterpillars. Throughout her childhood, Atwood's family spent several months of the year in the bush of Quebec and northern Ontario. She did not attend school full-time until she was twelve.

Though often interrupted, Atwood's education seems to have been more than adequate. She was encouraged by her parents to read and write at an early age, and her creative efforts started at five, when she wrote stories, poems, and plays. Her serious composition, however, did not begin until she was sixteen.

In 1961, Atwood earned her B.A. in the English honors program from the University of Toronto, where she studied with poets Jay Macpherson and Margaret Avison. Her M.A. from Radcliffe followed in 1962. Continuing graduate work at Harvard in 1963, Atwood interrupted her studies before reentering the program for two more years in 1965. While she found graduate studies interesting, Atwood directed her energies largely toward her creative efforts. For her, the Ph.D. program was chiefly a means of support while she wrote. Atwood left Harvard without writing her doctoral thesis.

Returning to Canada in 1967, Atwood accepted a position at Sir George Williams University in Montreal. By this time, her poetry was gaining recognition. With the publication of *The Edible Woman* and the sale of its film rights, Atwood was able to concentrate more fully on writing, though she taught at York University and was writer-in-residence at the University of Toronto. In 1973, Atwood divorced her American husband of five years, James Polk. After the publication of *Surfacing*, she was able to support herself through her creative efforts. She moved to a farm near Alliston, Ontario, with Canadian novelist Graeme Gibson; the couple's daughter, Eleanor Jess Atwood Gibson, was born in 1979. In 1980, Atwood and her family returned to Toronto, where Atwood and Gibson became active in the Writers' Union of Canada, Amnesty International, and the International Association of Poets, Playwrights, Editors, Essayists, and Novelists (PEN).

Analysis

For Margaret Atwood, an unabashed Canadian, literature became a means to cultural and personal self-awareness. "To know ourselves," she writes in *Survival*, "we must know our own literature; to know ourselves accurately, we need to know it as part of literature as a whole." Thus, when she defines Canadian literary concerns she relates her own as well, for Atwood's fiction grows out of this tradition. In her opinion, Canada's central reality is the act of survival: Canadian life and culture are decisively shaped by the demands of a harsh environment. Closely related to this defining act of survival, in Atwood's view, is the Canadian search for territorial identity—or, as literary theorist Northrop Frye put it, "Where is here?"

Atwood's heroines invariably discover themselves to be emotional refugees, strangers in a territory they can accurately label but one in which they are unable to feel at home. They are alienated not only from their environment but also from language itself; for them, communication becomes a decoding process. To a great degree, their feelings of estrangement extend from a culture that, having reduced everything to products, threatens to consume them. Women are particularly singled out as products, items to be decorated and sold as commodities, though men are threatened as well. Indeed, Canadian identity as a whole is in danger of being engulfed by an acquisitive American culture, though Atwood's "Americans" symbolize exploitation and often turn out to be Canadian nationals.

Reflective of their time and place, Atwood's characters are appropriately ambivalent. Dead or dying traditions prevent their return to the past, a past most have rejected. Their present is ephemeral at best, and their future inconceivable. Emotionally maimed, her heroines plumb their conscious and unconscious impressions, searching for a return to feeling, a means of identification with the present.

Atwood often couches their struggle in terms of a journey, which serves as a controlling metaphor for inner explorations: The unnamed heroine of *Surfacing* returns to the wilderness of Quebec, Lesje Green of *Life Before Man* wanders through imagined Mesozoic jungles, Rennie Wilford of *Bodily Harm* flies to the insurgent islands of Ste. Agathe and St. Antoine. By setting contemporary culture in relief, these primitive sites define the difference between nature and culture and allow

Atwood's heroines to gain new perspectives on their own realities. They can see people and places in relation to each other, not as isolated entities. Ultimately, however, this resolves little, for Atwood's novels end on a tenuous note. Although her heroines come to terms with themselves, they remain estranged.

Supporting her characters' ambivalence is Atwood's versatile narrative technique. Her astringent prose reflects their emotional numbness; its ironic restraint reveals their wariness. Frequent contradictions suggest not only the complexity of her characters but also the antagonistic times they must survive. By skillful juxtaposition of past and present through the use of flashbacks, Atwood evokes compelling fictional landscapes that ironically comment on the untenable state of modern men and women. Still, there remains some hope, for her characters survive with increased understanding of their world. Despite everything, life does go on.

From *Critical Survey of Long Fiction* (3d Rev. Ed.). Pasadena, CA: Salem Press, 2010. Copyright © 2010 by Salem Press, Inc.

Bibliography

Bloom, Harold, ed. *Margaret Atwood*. Philadelphia: Chelsea House, 2000. Collection of essays by literary critics provides analyses of Atwood's major novels. Includes brief biography, chronology of Atwood's life, and an informative editor's introduction.

Brown, Jane W. "Constructing the Narrative of Women's Friendship: Margaret Atwood's Reflexive Fiction." *Literature, Interpretation, Theory* 6 (1995): 197-212. Argues that Atwood's narrative reflects the struggle of women to attain friendship and asserts that Atwood achieves this with such reflexive devices as embedded discourse, narrative fragmentation, and doubling.

Cooke, Nathalie. *Margaret Atwood: A Biography*. Toronto: ECW Press, 1998. Although this is not an authorized biography, Atwood answered Cooke's questions and allowed her access, albeit limited, to materials for her research. A more substantive work than Sullivan's biography *The Red Shoes* (cited below).

Howells, Coral Ann. *Margaret Atwood*. New York: St. Martin's Press, 1996. Lively critical and biographical study elucidates issues that have energized all of Atwood's fiction: feminist issues, literary genres, and her own identity as a Canadian, a woman, and a writer.

_____, ed. *The Cambridge Companion to Margaret Atwood*. New York: Cambridge University Press, 2006. Collection of twelve excellent essays provides critical examination of Atwood's novels as well as a concise biography of the author.

McCombs, Judith, ed. *Critical Essays on Margaret Atwood*. Boston: G. K. Hall, 1988. Indispensable volume comprises thirty-two essays, including assessments of patterns and themes in Atwood's poetry and prose. Discusses her primary works in chronological order, beginning with *The Circle Game* and ending with *The Handmaid's Tale*. An editor's introduction provides an illuminating overview of Atwood's writing career. Includes a primary bibliography to 1986 and a thorough index.

Stein, Karen F. *Margaret Atwood Revisited*. New York: Twayne, 1999. Presents a thorough overview of Atwood's writings in all genres. Includes references and a selected bibliography.

Sullivan, Rosemary. *The Red Shoes: Margaret Atwood, Starting Out*. Toronto: HarperFlamingo Canada, 1998. Biography focuses on Atwood's early life, until the end of the 1970's. Attempts to answer the question of how Atwood became a writer and to describe the unfolding of her career.

Wilson, Sharon Rose. *Margaret Atwood's Fairy-Tale Sexual Politics*. Jackson: University Press of Mississippi, 1993. One of the most extensive and thorough investigations available of Atwood's use of fairy-tale elements in her graphic art as well as her writing. Covers her novels up to *Cat's Eye*.

_____, ed. *Margaret Atwood's Textual Assassinations: Recent Poetry and Fiction*. Columbus: Ohio State University Press, 2003. Collection of scholarly essays examines Atwood's work, with a focus on her writings published since the late 1980's. Includes discussion of the novels *Cat's Eye, The Robber Bride, Alias Grace,* and *The Blind Assassin*.

The *Paris Review* Perspective
Jascha Hoffman for *The Paris Review*

We can't live without a mother to deliver us. So perhaps it is natural that writers of speculative fiction have long been preoccupied with man's efforts to control the way we are born. By taking on the subject of infertility, Margaret Atwood's harrowing novel *The Handmaid's Tale* has a prominent role in this tradition. What is different about Atwood's work is that it manages all the satire of science fiction without resorting to any high-tech menaces. Her cautionary tale may as well be set in the Dark Ages.

Writers looking to the future have tended to pin their fears and hopes on scientific breakthroughs. In *Brave New World*, published nearly half a century before the first successful in-vitro fertilization, Aldous Huxley imagined a world in which children bred in test tubes were taught to enjoy sterile sex. Sarah Hall's recent *Daughters of the North* raised the prospect of universal chastity belts that can be disabled only by the government. Films like *Gattaca* and *Code 46* presented scenarios in which the genetic screening of babies leads to a society stratified by a new sort of eugenics. And science is catching up to science fiction. Artificial wombs, featured in such outlandish distractions as *Star Wars* and *The Matrix*, are now under development at Cornell.

The Handmaid's Tale, however, builds its dystopia on nothing more sophisticated than the missionary position—coupled with the threat of force. The novel is set in Cambridge, Massachusetts, in the late twentieth century, after the far-right Protestant theocracy of Gilead has taken over New England and enslaved women as servants and surrogate mothers in apparent response to an epidemic of infertility. We observe this monstrous society through the eyes of Offred, one of the few women left who might still be fertile. She has been forced into the role of a surrogate mother, or handmaid. Each month she must rest her head on the belly of her master's sterile wife to be used as little more than a womb with legs.

In many ways *The Handmaid's Tale* resembles historical fiction more than it does science fiction. The men who founded the repressive state of Gilead are modeled less on contemporary Christian conservatives than on Atwood's own Puritan ancestors, she has commented, and the novel can therefore be read as a potent distillation of some old-fashioned prejudices against women. The sense of looking back into a dark time is confirmed in the epilogue, which reveals that the whole story has been reconstructed from a lost audio diary by male historians in 2195.

Atwood returned to a similar mode of cautionary satire in her novel *Oryx and Crake*, set in a near-future filled with genetically engineered hybrid animals, blood sport posing as entertainment, and rampant child pornography. Like that book, *The Handmaid's Tale* is undeniably meant as social commentary. But to read it mainly as a warning against patriarchal repression would be to miss the moral ambiguity that lies at its heart.

Even as she earns a bit of leverage with her master, Offred does not grow into the role of a heroine. Rather, she adapts to the daily humiliations, learns to protect herself by betraying others, and seldom hesitates to sacrifice her dignity for fleeting comfort. Over time it becomes harder to see Offred as a victim. Her memories of life as a free woman only highlight how complicit she has become in her own imprisonment. In the end, Atwood gives us neither the satisfaction of a daring escape nor the pathos of a tragic death at the hands of the regime. Instead, the handmaid does what she's always done. She gropes for a path that will allow her to survive.

At one point Offred recalls that her mother, a radical feminist who was presumably assassinated by the government, tried to pass on a small piece of wisdom from an earlier era: "Truly amazing what people can get used to," she said, "as long as there are a few compensations." It is Offred's fate—and mankind's shame—that the daughter proves the mother right.

Copyright © 2008 by Jascha Hoffman.

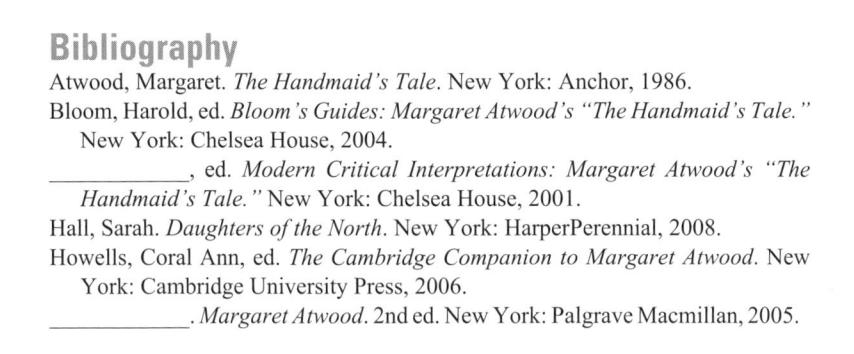

Bibliography

Atwood, Margaret. *The Handmaid's Tale*. New York: Anchor, 1986.

Bloom, Harold, ed. *Bloom's Guides: Margaret Atwood's "The Handmaid's Tale."* New York: Chelsea House, 2004.

_____, ed. *Modern Critical Interpretations: Margaret Atwood's "The Handmaid's Tale."* New York: Chelsea House, 2001.

Hall, Sarah. *Daughters of the North*. New York: HarperPerennial, 2008.

Howells, Coral Ann, ed. *The Cambridge Companion to Margaret Atwood*. New York: Cambridge University Press, 2006.

_____. *Margaret Atwood*. 2nd ed. New York: Palgrave Macmillan, 2005.

CRITICAL CONTEXTS

Margaret Atwood's *The Handmaid's Tale* (1985): Cultural and Historical Context_____

Lisa Jadwin

Margaret Atwood's novel *The Handmaid's Tale* has been both controversial and influential in the decades since its publication. The novel reached best-seller status in the mid-1980s and has continued to sell well in North America and abroad and has been translated into more than thirty-five languages, including Chinese and Serbo-Croatian ("Poised"). *The Handmaid's Tale* has been made into a feature-length film, an opera, a full-cast radio adaptation, and a stage play. Perhaps most important, it has been introduced to many young readers in secondary and postsecondary English and language-arts curricula across the United States and Canada. *The Handmaid's Tale* has been compared favorably to some of the greatest dystopian works of all time, including Yevgeny Zamyatin's *We* (1921); the early-twentieth-century works of Franz Kafka; Aldous Huxley's *Brave New World* (1932); and George Orwell's *Nineteen Eighty-Four* (1949). At the time of the novel's publication, *Publishers Weekly* decreed that *The Handmaid's Tale* "deserves an honored place on the small shelf of cautionary tales that have entered modern folklore." Its sternest critics, including conservative taxpayers seeking to ban the novel from school curricula and liberal writers dismayed by its critique of feminism, have admitted that Atwood's novel derives its power from an accurate, if disturbing, critique of contemporary cultural norms. Furthermore, the cultural issues Atwood explores in *The Handmaid's Tale*—religious fundamentalism, feminism, consumerism, environmental decline, and rampant technology—have become more intensely debated since the mid-1980s, making the novel seem increasingly prescient and relevant. Atwood herself has said, "The thing to remember is that there is nothing new about the society depicted in *The Handmaid's Tale* except the time and place. All of the things I have written about have—as noted in the 'Historical Notes' at the end—been done before, more than once." She adds, "History proves that what we have been in the past we could be again" ("A Note to the Reader").

In nearly a dozen interviews and essays, Margaret Atwood has discussed the events and ideas that inspired *The Handmaid's Tale*. Readers who remember the era will recognize the novel as a cultural roman à clef teeming with thinly disguised ideas and personalities from the mid-1980s. Decoding their identities is one of the pleasures of linking the novel to its historical roots. Atwood notes that her own lifetime has been characterized by political upheavals and radical social change. The Nazi Holocaust began just before her birth in 1939, and World War II dominated her early childhood. A controversial act of mass destruction ended the Second World War when the allied forces deployed atomic bombs on the Japanese cities of Hiroshima and Nagasaki in August 1945. Though Atwood may have been too young to comprehend these events, her sense of political injustice intensified as she matured. She was intensely aware of the anti-Communist purges of the 1950s, and as a teenager she devoured Arthur Koestler's *Darkness at Noon* and Orwell's *Nineteen Eighty-Four*. The political was also personal: "As a college student," she has said, "I was a volunteer worker with immigrants wishing to improve their English, and my charge was a woman doctor who'd escaped from Czechoslovakia. She was a wreck. I got an earful" ("Note to the Reader.") The horrors of atomic warfare have evidently so permeated Atwood's epistemology that she uses a nuclear metaphor to characterize the act of creating *The Handmaid's Tale*:

> Every book is a sort of mushroom cloud thrown up by a large substance of material that has been accumulating for a lifetime. I had long been interested in the histories of totalitarian regimes and the different forms they have taken in various societies; while the initial idea for *The Handmaid's Tale* came to me in 1981, I avoided writing it for several years because I was apprehensive about the results—whether I would be able to carry it off as a literary form. ("Note to the Reader")

Atwood's family, with its dietitian mother and entomologist father, moved frequently throughout Margaret's childhood. Some years they lived in cities such as Toronto and Ottawa; for long stretches, they lived in spartan accommodations in the remote forests of Quebec as the family moved to accommodate her father's career. Although Atwood did not attend school full-time until the age of eleven, she was an early, voracious reader, absorbing everything in sight, including textbooks, best sellers, classics, and popular fiction. She has credited her unconventional upbringing with having given her an abiding respect for both wilderness and education as well as a strong sense of her identity as a Canadian. She began her prolific career as a writer with five books of poetry, one of which (*The Circle Game*) won the coveted Governor-General's Award in 1966. While continuing to write poetry, she also turned her hand to fiction, publishing her first novel, *The Edible Woman*, in 1969. Since then, Atwood has published dozens more novels, collections of short stories, and poetry anthologies as well as numerous articles and reviews. Having settled in Toronto with her spouse Graeme Gibson and their daughter, she has sustained a long career as one of Canada's best-known intellectuals. She has occasionally held short-term university teaching positions and has lectured widely throughout the world.

The "mushroom cloud" of experience that generated *The Handmaid's Tale* began to take shape in the early 1980s, when Atwood says she felt "increasingly alarmed by statements made frequently by religious leaders in the United States; and then a variety of events from around the world could not be ignored, particularly the rising fanaticism of the Iranian monotheocracy" ("Note to the Reader"). Her sense that religious fundamentalism—at home and abroad—was a threat to freedom was heightened after she made a brief stopover in Afghanistan in 1978. There she and her family observed the rise of Muslim fundamentalism. At that time, Afghanistan was undergoing a transformation; decades of civil war and a ruinous war with the Soviet Union had left the country devastated and vulnerable to religious fundamentalists.

In Iran, the Ayatollah Ruhollah Khomeini was coming to power and beginning to spearhead a coup d'état designed to oust the shah. While in Afghanistan, Atwood was unsettled when men spoke exclusively to her partner instead of addressing her directly. She marked the absence of women in the streets and marketplaces ("When Afghanistan" 204-6). But her strongest impression arose when, indulging her curiosity, she purchased a purple chador, the full-length "veiling" garment that is compulsory attire for some fundamentalist Muslim women who appear in public. Atwood knew that the chador was more than just a garment.

> I . . . knew that clothing is a symbol, that all symbols are ambiguous, and that this one might signify a fear of women or a desire to protect them from the gaze of strangers. But it could also mean more negative things, just as the color red can mean love, blood, life, royalty, good luck—or sin. ("When Afghanistan" 206)

Though Atwood hoped the chador would give her a sense of freedom—acting as a kind of fantasy "cloak of invisibility" that would endow her with "the power to see without being seen"—instead she found it alienating:

> Once I put it on, I had an odd sense of having been turned into negative space, a blank in the visual field, a sort of antimatter—both there and not there. Such a space has power of a sort, but it is a passive power, the power of taboo. ("When Afghanistan" 207)

In subsequent years, Atwood's fears of rising totalitarianism intensified when war broke out in several Middle Eastern countries and there was a sharp increase in anti-Western political rhetoric by Muslim dictators and their followers. "[*The Handmaid's Tale*] was conceived," sums up reviewer Joyce Carol Oates, "out of Atwood's alarm at the frequency with which she heard, from her American friends, the facile expression 'It can't happen here' in response to Atwood's accounts of 'excursions into the darker side of religious fanaticism in Iran and Afghanistan'" (Oates).

In the early 1980s, Atwood began compiling a file of newspaper clippings documenting the rise of fundamentalist theocracies around the world, including those theocratic movements in the United States that sought to dissolve the traditional boundary between church and state. These clippings, which grew into a commodious "file of stories supporting the contentions in the book," became her quarry for *The Handmaid's Tale*. Ultimately, Atwood argues, there was literally nothing in the novel "that was not based on something that has already happened in history or in another country, or for which actual supporting documentation is not already available" ("Interview"). The clippings enabled Atwood to document the rise of totalitarianism around the world and to begin to imagine specific techniques that governments might use to implement greater controls on their citizens. As Orwell had predicted in *Nineteen Eighty-Four*, language was used as a tool to control understanding. In the Philippines, for example, the word "salvaging" became the government-endorsed euphemism for the officially sanctioned murders of political dissidents. And the control of citizens in general was epitomized by the control of women's bodies. In Romania, dictator Nicolae Ceauşescu's government took control of women's fertility, outlawing birth control and abortion. At the same time, Atwood noted that China's "one child" policy legislated the opposite effect. "I'd followed events in Romania, where women were forced by the Ceauşescu regime to have babies, and also in China, where they were forced not to" ("Interview").

By 1984, when Atwood began to shape *The Handmaid's Tale*, the North American cultural climate had become markedly more conservative. In anticipation of celebrating Orwell's *Nineteen Eighty-Four* in the year 1984, social critics busied themselves evaluating the growth of totalitarianism in the world since the 1949 publication of Orwell's novel. With dismay, they reported that the world was still plagued by oppressive governments and that neither the capitalist empires of the "First World" nor the communist countries of the "Second World" had managed to achieve the climates of peace and social justice that many had hoped would follow World War II. And the "Third World"—the nations we now call "developing countries"—continued to be plagued by economic and political chaos that was the perfect incubator for despotism. Fittingly, Atwood started work on *The Handmaid's Tale* in West Berlin, a setting that perfectly expressed the impasse between political worlds. In the spring of 1984, she notes, she had no way of knowing that "in five years the Wall would topple and the Soviet Union would disintegrate" ("Interview").

In the early 1980s, the United Kingdom, Commonwealth countries (which include Canada and Australia), and the United States all experienced conservative "revolutions" in which new governments defined themselves in opposition to their liberal predecessors. In 1984, Canada's longtime liberal prime minister Pierre Eliot Trudeau, who had served since 1968, was ousted by the Progressive Conservative Brian Mulroney, who achieved enormous parliamentary majorities in the two subsequent elections. The new Canadian conservatism of Mulroney, however, was relatively mild compared to the Tory government of Margaret Thatcher, the United Kingdom's first female prime minister and prime architect of a conservative movement that was to challenge many of England's socialist institutions and dominate the United Kingdom from 1979 to 1990 (and, through the government of her protégé John Major, from 1990 to 1997). Thatcher inherited a troubled economy, deindustrialization, and a burgeoning welfare economy. Her reforms of her predecessors' policies included a return to supply-side economics; increased privatization of previously government institutions; new limitations on welfare benefits; a hawklike, isolationist foreign policy; and attacks on trade unions.

The "Reagan revolution" in the United States roughly paralleled the rise of the Thatcher and Mulroney governments in the United Kingdom and Canada. Like Thatcher, Ronald Reagan, a former movie star who had been governor of California, inherited a troubled economy, a deindustrializing culture, and an increase in the cost of governmental entitlements. Unlike Thatcher, however, Reagan was elected indirectly because of the rise of one of the Muslim theocracies Margaret Atwood had been watching for more than a decade: the fundamentalist Islamic coup d'état in Iran. For decades, Iran had been ruled by the wealthy and dictatorial Mohammad Reza Shah Pahlavi, who had been installed in 1953 and was supported by the American Central Intelligence Agency. On November 4, 1979, a group of students, incited by the long-exiled fundamentalist religious authority Ayatollah Ruhollah Khomeini, took over the U.S. embassy in Tehran, seizing fifty-two hostages. (Six American diplomats managed to escape by hiding out in the Canadian embassy and securing Canadian passports in a rescue engineered by Canadian ambassador Ken Taylor that has now become known as "the Canadian Caper.") The taking of the American hostages, who were held for 444 days, was viewed worldwide as a violation of diplomatic tradition. During this period, the United States itself was effectively "held hostage" as the world was subjected to the anti-Western rhetoric of Iranian leaders. The national prestige of the United States was further damaged when "Operation Eagle Claw," a secret rescue effort ordered by Democratic president Jimmy Carter, ended in failure in April 1980. The public humiliation of the United States, intensified by the failed rescue mission, ensured Carter's defeat in the 1980 presidential election, paving the way for the Reagan revolution. It is important to note that Reagan secured the release of the hostages six minutes after his inauguration on January 21, 1981. It was later revealed that Reagan had obtained the hostages' release by agreeing to provide arms to the anti-U.S. Iranian government.

 Margaret Atwood has expressed a strong sense of Canadian identity and has always striven to preserve a certain detachment from Canada's dominating neighbor to the south. Yet Atwood, like most of her countrymen and -women, finds it impossible to ignore the influence of the United States. The 1980 presidential election was also affected by the rise of what was called the "Moral Majority," an evangelical Christian political action committee that purportedly delivered two-thirds of the white evangelical vote to Ronald Reagan. While this voting bloc was instrumental in helping to defeat Carter, its growth and strength also revealed a burgeoning transformation of the U.S. cultural climate. Founded by evangelical preacher Jerry Falwell in 1979, the Moral Majority promoted an agenda that included outlawing abortion, opposition to state recognition and acceptance of homosexuality, opposition to the Equal Rights Amendment (ERA), enforcement of a "traditional" (that is, patriarchal) vision of family life, and censorship of media outlets that promoted what the movement perceived as an "antifamily" agenda.

The Moral Majority was not the only force in American society that defined itself in opposition to what had come to be called "women's rights." The 1973 U.S. Supreme Court decision in the case of *Roe v. Wade*, which had legalized most abortions in the United States, had also provided a target for opponents of feminism. Since the 1970s feminists had defined "the right to choose"—that is, women's control of their own fertility—as a key underpinning of women's rights. Now many opponents of abortion focused on abortion as a "litmus test" for conservative political candidates. Many conservatives who defined themselves as "pro-choice" rather than "pro-life" were targeted by political action committees for political defeat, and opposition to abortion became a major "plank" in Republican political platforms. Abortion opponents emphasized the "rights of the fetus" rather than the "rights of women" or the "right to choose." As Kristen Luker argued in her pathbreaking study *Abortion and the Politics of Motherhood*, evangelical Christian political action groups succeeded in defining opposition to abortion as a key part of Republican identity, effectively drawing all conservatives into their circle of influence.

Women's rights had experienced many advances from the 1920s (when the Nineteenth Amendment to the U.S. Constitution gave women the right to vote) through the 1970s (when labor and consumer laws were updated to eliminate some kinds of gender discrimination). At the beginning of the 1980s, women's rights, which had once been framed in terms of simple equality and fairness, were now perceived by some in the United States as a threat to "traditional" cultural values and especially to the "Christian" family, which was pictured as comprising a breadwinner father, a stay-at-home mother, and several children. The Equal Rights Amendment to the U.S. Constitution, which would have established that "equality of rights under the law shall not be denied or abridged by the United States or by any State on account of sex," was rejected in 1979, when a majority of states failed to ratify it (including some who rescinded earlier ratifications in response to political pressure). Opponents argued that the ERA would mandate taxpayer-funded abortion and legalize same-sex marriage—issues that have become political "hot potatoes" for conservative and liberal politicians alike. A Supreme Court challenge to the defeat of the ERA in 1982 failed to reinstate it, and though it has been reintroduced in every Congress since 1984, it has never received sufficient support for ratification.

Meanwhile, President Reagan, who had promised during his presidential campaign to reduce both federal taxes and federal spending, began to implement a series of cuts to the federal budget. Though the defense budget emerged untouched, programs that served primarily women, though they comprised less than 10 percent of the federal budget, accounted for fully one-third of the total number of federal budget cuts during the Reagan administration. As the national murder rate declined, reported incidents of domestic violence increased by 160 percent. Nationwide, government support for rape crisis workers, victim advocacy, and battered women's shelters declined. Challenges to *Roe v. Wade* became commonplace at the state and local levels, and Medicare support for abortion was eliminated. Meanwhile, the power of evangelical political action committees increased. M. G. "Pat" Robertson, founder of the Christian Coalition, has described feminism as a threat to society. In a fund-raising letter opposing a state equal rights amendment (quoted in the *Washington Post* in August 1993), Robertson wrote, "The feminist agenda is not about equal rights for women. It is about a socialist, anti-family political movement. Feminists encourage women to leave their husbands, kill their children, practice witchcraft, destroy capitalism and become lesbians."

Atwood's exploration of feminism—from both conservative and liberal viewpoints—in *The Handmaid's Tale* is clearly a response to these phenomena. She does not limit her critique to conservative thought. Instead, Atwood confronts the issue from both sides:

> This is a book about what happens when certain casually held attitudes about women are taken to their logical conclusions. For example, I explore a number of conservative opinions still held by many—such as a woman's place is in the home—and also certain feminist pronouncements—women prefer the company of other women, for example. ("Interview")

At the time of the book's inception, the feminist movement was experiencing serious internal conflict, not simply about abortion rights but also about the politics of inclusion and the rise of "essentialism"—the celebration of women's sexual difference, in a sort of positive take on Sigmund Freud's maxim that "anatomy is destiny." With characters like the Aunts, who embrace their duties as enforcers of patriarchal law, and Offred's memories of her feminist-activist mother, Atwood brings up what critic Lorna Sage has called "the tendency in present-day feminism towards a kind of separatist purity, a matriarchal nostalgia . . . [that] threatens to join forces with right-wing demands for 'traditional values'" (307). Atwood does not hesitate to mock contemporary trends in gender politics. Early in the novel, Offred reminisces about a conversation with her college friend Moira:

> What's your paper on? I just did one on date rape.
> Date rape, I said. You're so trendy. It sounds like some kind of dessert. *Date rapé*. (38)

Lois Feuer concludes that *The Handmaid's Tale* reveals "costs at both ends of the spectrum in the essentialist debate: the 'woman's culture' that Offred's mother envisioned has eventuated in the oppression she thought she was fighting in burning pornographic magazines." She continues:

> Atwood looks explicitly at the thesis that we are our own enemies; the fundamentalist conservatives who create Gilead by overthrowing American democracy use as a guide a CIA pamphlet on destabilizing foreign governments produced by that very democracy. In like manner, the essentialism of Offred's mother and her "woman's culture" unintentionally supports the essentialism of the fundamentalist right. (89)

The novel's famous dichotomy between "freedom to" and "freedom from" focuses on the sexual freedoms of women contested by feminists and evangelical conservatives. At one end of Atwood's spectrum is Gilead, where women have few freedoms, but their fertility is respected and they are free from the threat of sexual violence in the streets. At the other end is the "before" society, where women enjoyed sexual freedoms but were often sexually exploited and violated. Atwood undermines the appeal of Gileadean "freedom from," however, at the end of the novel, when Offred and the Commander go to Jezebel's. Offred meets Moira and learns that mutilation and forced prostitution are Gilead's standard punishment for female disobedience.

Because it engages politics, biology, philosophy, and history, human fertility is the source of the precipitating crisis of Gileadean society. In Atwood's imaginary world, a marked decrease in human fertility, apparently brought on by environmental pollution and degradation, has decimated the birthrate, especially among the highest levels of Gileadean society. By forcibly restoring the Old Testament traditions of concubinage and plural marriage, Gileadean leaders hope to increase the number of births, and they rationalize a series of Draconian rules that rigidly sort women according to their biological fertility. As was typical of twentieth-century dictatorships, crisis makes totalitarianism possible because societies will accept extreme injunctions to prevent catastrophe. In the mid-1980s, populations of some animals, notably amphibians, began to decline inexplicably; scientists posited that there might be documented evidence of decreasing fertility among a number of species. This sterility or decreased fertility might be caused by increasing environmental damage (waste from nuclear power generation, pollution, effects of heavy metals). In addition, among humans, population rates in industrialized countries as well as some developing countries (like China) began to decline steadily. These declines were attributed to a number of factors, including increased access to family planning, with couples deciding not to have children or to limit the size of their families; infertility issues caused by women waiting to begin families until their thirties, when fertility naturally begins to decline; and environmental factors. Though Gilead is technologically sophisticated—for example, using advanced forms of surveillance to control its citizens—it is still unable to control this basic biological function. Atwood reminds us that, though each Handmaid receives the finest health care, a nutritious diet, plenty of exercise, and no drugs or alcohol, conception and successful parturition are unlikely, especially in a patriarchal culture that is unwilling to accept "unbabies" (babies with disabilities) or to entertain the idea that a Commander himself might be sterile.

"Freedom to" and "freedom from" are also intimately related to what Atwood perceives is an essential hypocrisy embedded in the ideals of American democracy. Though *The Handmaid's Tale* takes place in an unspecified historical period, Atwood deliberately set the novel in a futuristic version of Cambridge, Massachusetts, where she lived while pursuing a graduate degree in English literature from Harvard under Perry Miller, the expert on Puritan culture to whom the novel is dedicated. At the time, she notes,

I took a particular interest in the Salem witchcraft trials. What sorts of conditions produce a group mentality that so blatantly violates justice and defies common sense, in the name of God and righteousness? What sorts of people benefit from egging such things on? I've always remembered the words of one New England divine, who preached a sermon of repentance after they'd all realized how badly they'd been bamboozled: "The Devil was indeed among us, but not in the form we thought." ("For God and Gilead")

Her "exile" at Harvard made Atwood aware of the degree to which the United States, with its ostensible philosophy of freedom and equality, has a paradoxical history of oppression and imperialism.[1] As Danita J. Dodson has argued:

> *The Handmaid's Tale* illuminates the deplorable irony that a nation established upon the utopian principle of "liberty and justice for all" has also been a dystopia for those humans sequestered and tortured because of differences from mainstream culture. As casualties of a patriarchal-based empire within the national borders, Native Americans, African Americans and women are all examples of peoples who have been historically locked away from the utopian American Dream. (66)

American history, she notes, "is built upon the huge myth that the U.S.A. is anti-imperialistic because of its documented opposition to the totalitarianism of 'evil empires' around the world" (66). Atwood uses *The Handmaid's Tale* to suggest that "progress toward global human rights will never be possible until nations of 'freedom' face their own incarcerated dystopian realities" (Dodson 66).

As a public intellectual, Atwood was conscious of engaging with contemporary politics, the history of ideas and events, and literary tradition. She acknowledges that *The Handmaid's Tale* is indebted to earlier dystopian writers, indebted to "a tradition," she notes, "that can be traced back to Plato's *Republic*, through Sir Thomas More's *Utopia* and the horse's paradise of Swift's *Gulliver's Travels*, and then through the many literary utopias and dystopias of the 19th and early 20th centuries" ("For God and Gilead"). Like her predecessors, Atwood is preoccupied with the effects of war, industrialization, and environmental devastation, and the alienation of individuals from each other. In their imaginary worlds, surveillance and propaganda allow states to control their citizens, and daily life becomes quantified, rigidly scheduled, and choreographed. Work is efficient but meaningless, and humans live in engineered environments that isolate them from nature and the natural aspects of their existence, including sexuality. Yevgeny Zamyatin's *We* (1921), written in response to the author's experiences of the Russian revolutions of 1905 and 1917, was a major inspiration for Orwell's *Nineteen Eighty-Four*, also written in the aftermath of war and fascist revolution. Atwood notes that, while these texts strongly influenced her conception of *The Handmaid's Tale*, her enterprise differs in one key way:

> The majority of dystopias—Orwell's included—have been written by men, and the point of view has been male. When women have appeared in them, they have been either sexless automatons or rebels who've defied the sex rules of the regime. They've acted as the temptresses of the male protagonists, however welcome this temptation may be to the men themselves. Thus [Orwell's] Julia, thus the cami-knicker-wearing, orgy-porgy seducer of the Savage in *Brave New World*, thus the subversive femme fatale of Yvgeny Zamyatin's . . . seminal classic *We*. I wanted to try a dystopia from the female point of view—the world according to Julia, as it were. ("George Orwell" 291)

Yet, though the novel is presented through a female perspective, it is more than simply a feminist dystopia, except, as the liberal-feminist Atwood has said, "insofar as giving a woman a voice and an inner life will always be considered 'feminist' by those who think women ought not to have these things" ("George Orwell" 291). Like Orwell, Atwood is very interested in the ways in which language can be used to control thought and, by extension, individual action. Orwell's "insistence on the clear and exact use of language," said Atwood, is central to his enterprise. "Euphemisms and skewed terminology should not obscure the truth" (292). Thus, in *The Handmaid's Tale*, women are not permitted to learn to read and write. Signs feature icons rather than words; reading in the home is restricted to the locked Bible; "old world" language becomes so profane (and thus paradoxically sacred) that Offred and the Commander feel titillated when they enjoy a secret game of Scrabble. Linguistic coinages such as "Particicution" and "Prayvaganza" echo modern coinages like the word "electrocution," which is a compound of "electric" and "execution." As in Orwell's text, euphemisms control perception; an execution of a dissident is reframed as a "Salvaging," and biblical allusions enforce the equation of Gilead and the patriarchal world of the Bible (the grocery store is "Loaves and Fishes," the handmaids' boot camp is the "Rachel and Leah Center," and the sadistic female sergeants are "Aunts").

Offred, who is forced to speak rather than write her memoir, still remembers the previous world, where she learned to love language, something we learn about when she plays Scrabble with the Commander and slyly generates such complex words as "zygote." In her everyday activities, Offred resists Gilead's propagandistic vocabulary by using blunt, deliberately uneuphemistic language. In one often-quoted scene, she reframes the ostensibly sacred "Ceremony" by trying to find an accurate term for what is happening to her:

> My red skirt is hitched up to my waist, though no higher. Below it the Commander is fucking. What he is fucking is the lower part of my body. I do not say making love, because this is not what he's doing. Copulating too would be inaccurate, because it would imply two people and only one is involved. Nor does rape cover it; nothing is going on here that I haven't signed up for. (93)

Though her diction is crude, Offred is careful to choose the verb that best describes her position as an object rather than a participant—even the kind of unwilling participant that would be characterized by the word "rape."

"At the end of *The Handmaid's Tale*," writes Atwood, "there's a section that owes much to *Nineteen Eighty-Four*. It's the account of the symposium held several hundred years in the future, in which the repressive government described in the novel is now merely a subject for academic analysis. The parallels with Orwell's essay on Newspeak should be evident" ("George Orwell" 292). The "Historical Notes," however, do not outline a theory of language. Instead, they critique the "discourses" of academia, which in the mid-1980s was beginning to become the primary battleground of the "culture wars" over the progressive agenda of "political correctness." Politically correct or inclusive language adheres to the principles advanced by the Sapir-Whorf hypothesis, the linguistic theory that language possesses the power to shape thought and action. While Atwood was aware that academics were attempting to reveal the extent to which political oppression can be perpetuated in language, she detected a good deal of hypocrisy in their discourses. Thus, as Arnold Davidson has suggested, while "the historical notes with which *The Handmaid's Tale* ends provide comic relief from the grotesque text of Gilead," "in crucial ways, the epilogue is the most pessimistic part of the book," since "the intellectuals of 2195 are preparing the way for Gilead again." The academic world, by "recreating the values of the past," also creates "the values of the future" (120).

The "Historical Note" is a spoof of an imaginary academic conference in 2195 at the University of Denay in Nunavit. (While Nunavut is the newest and northernmost territory in Eastern Canada, the pun "deny none of it" is part of the joke here.) Evidently, North American life has changed very little in two centuries. After sifting through several pages of tendentious academic posturing, the reader learns that Offred's "diary" is in fact a construction rather than the carefully ordered diary of a known individual. Professor James Pieixoto, director of archival research at Cambridge University, has transcribed and ordered thirty audiotapes that were discovered in such far-flung places as Seattle and Syracuse. The "tale" of fifteen sections and forty-six chapters is essentially his re-creation of what might have been. Instead of being filled with excitement about the diary, however, Pieixoto seems to have little respect for the text he has "constructed." As David Hogsette has argued:

> The professor completely misreads Offred's text. He does not understand her perspective; nor does he make any effort to join the audience of her autobiography. Even though *The Handmaid's Tale* is a speculative or science fiction novel, the flesh-and-blood audience of this novel must attempt a reading dynamic appropriate for more "realistic" works of fiction. We see that in the epilogue, Pieixoto, a fictitious reader of a fictitious autobiography, does not become a member of Offred's audience. The epilogue enables Atwood to reinforce a proper reading of her novel, a reading that involves avoiding Pieixoto's blind scholarly reading pattern and extending beyond our subjective frames of reference, thus simultaneously becoming a member of Atwood's and Offred's respective audiences. (275)

Though he "owns" Offred's text to the extent that he is its re/constructor, Pieixoto holds it fundamentally in contempt. He proves himself hostile to feminism and feminist literary criticism when he makes disparaging remarks about the diary. He expresses a frisson of sexist delight in the homophone "tale"/"tail" and talks salaciously about the duties required of Offred as a Handmaid. He makes off-color jokes about his female counterpart on the panel: The "charming Arctic char that we all enjoyed last night," he says, is the equivalent of the current "Arctic Chair" that we are now enjoying (312). At this moment, Arnold Davidson has argued, Professor Pieixoto has effectively demoted his female colleague, Professor Maryann Crescent Moon, to the status of "'handmaid' to Pieixoto's 'central text'" (119).

Atwood, who has had extensive experience working within university settings, piles on details that contribute to the verisimilitude of her portrayal of a 1980s academic conference. Signs of politically correct inclusiveness abound: While Professor Gopal Chatterjee, a philosopher from India, talks about "Krishna and Kali in State Religion of Gilead," the session on *The Handmaid's Tale* is chaired by Professor Crescent Moon, of the Department of *Caucasian* Anthropology at the University of Denay. Yet when Professor Pieixoto concludes his talk by saying, "As all historians know, the past is a great darkness, and filled with echoes. Voices may reach us from it; but what they say to us is imbued with the obscurity of the matrix out of which they come; and try as we may, we cannot always decipher them precisely in the clearer light of our own day," the reader is meant to experience a sense of ironic dislocation. Though the words sound progressive, expressing humility and respect, we know that Professor Pieixoto means none of it.

Note

1. During the 1979-80 hostage crisis, one of the hostage takers emphasized this when he told Bruce Laingen, chief U.S. diplomat in Iran at the time, that Americans had no right to complain because they had effectively taken the whole country of Iran hostage in 1953.

Works Consulted

Atwood, Margaret. "For God and Gilead." *The Guardian*, March 22, 2003. http://www.guardian.co.uk/music/2003/mar/22/classicalmusicandopera.fiction. Accessed October 8, 2008.

_____. "George Orwell: Some Personal Connections." In Atwood, *Writing with Intent*, pp. 287-293.

_____. *The Handmaid's Tale*. Toronto: McClelland and Stewart, 1985; Boston: Houghton Mifflin, 1986.

_____. *Second Words: Selected Critical Prose*. Toronto: Anansi, 1982.

_____. *Survival: A Thematic Guide to Canadian Literature*. Toronto: Anansi, 1982.

_____. "When Afghanistan Was at Peace." In Atwood, *Writing with Intent*, pp. 205-7.

_____. "Writing Utopia." In Atwood, *Writing with Intent*, pp. 92-104.

_____. *Writing with Intent: Essays, Reviews, Personal Prose 1983-2005*. New York: Carroll & Graf, 2005.

"Comment: 'Handmaid's Tale' Characterized Unfairly by Its Opponents: An Open Letter to the Judson Independent School District from Canadian Novelist Margaret Atwood." *San Antonio Express-News*, April 12, 2006. http://www.mysanantonio.com/opinion/MYSA041206_2O_atwoodcomment_116e42b9_html. Accessed October 10, 2008.

Davidson, Arnold E. "Making History in *The Handmaid's Tale*." In *Margaret Atwood: Vision and Forms*, ed. Kathryn VanSpanckeren and Jan Garden Castro. Carbondale: Southern Illinois University Press, 1988, pp. 113-21.

Dodson, Danita J. "An Interview with Margaret Atwood." *Critique* 97.2 (Winter 1997): 96-104.

_____. "'We Lived in the Blank White Spaces': Rewriting the Paradigm of Denial in Atwood's *The Handmaid's Tale*." *Utopian Studies* 8.2 (1997): 66-87.

Ehrenreich, Barbara. "Feminism's Phantoms." *The New Republic* 194.11 (March 17, 1986): 33-35. Interprets the novel as a warning about feminism's repressive tendencies.

Evans, Mark. "Versions of History: *The Handmaid's Tale* and Its Dedicatees." In *Margaret Atwood: Writing and Subjectivity*, ed. Colin Nicholson. New York: St. Martin's Press, 1994, pp. 177-88. Discusses Puritanism in the novel.

Feuer, Lois. "The Calculus of Love and Nightmare: *The Handmaid's Tale* and the Dystopian Tradition." *Critique* 97.2 (Winter 1997): 83-95.

Filipczak, Dorota. "Is There No Balm in Gilead? Biblical Intertext in Margaret Atwood's *The Handmaid's Tale*." *Literature and Theology* 7 (1993): 171-85.

Freibert, Lucy M. "Control and Creativity: The Politics of Risk in Margaret Atwood's *The Handmaid's Tale*." In *Critical Essays on Margaret Atwood*, ed. Judith McCombs. Boston: G. K. Hall, 1988, pp. 280-91.

Garlick, Barbara. "*The Handmaid's Tale*: Narrative Voice and the Primacy of the Tale." In *Twentieth-Century Fantasists. Essays on Culture, Society and Belief in Twentieth Century Mythopoeic Literature*, ed. Kath Filmer and David Jasper. New York: St. Martin's Press, 1992, pp. 161-71. Explores how the novel's treatment of utopia is supported by its structure.

Gibson, Graeme. "Travels of a Family Man." *Chatelaine*, March 1979, pp. 36, 38, 132-3, 135-7.

Grace, Dominick M. "*The Handmaid's Tale*: 'Historical Notes' and Documentary Subversion." *Science-Fiction Studies* 25 (1998): 481-94.

Greene, Gayle. "Choice of Evils." *Women's Review of Books* 3.10 (July 1986): 14. Compared to works by Marge Piercy and Doris Lessing, *The Handmaid's Tale* critiques radical feminism.

Greenwood, Herbert N. Foerstel. *Banned in the U.S.A.: A Reference Guide to Book Censorship in Schools and Public Libraries*. New York: Greenwood Press, 2006. Notes how *The Handmaid's Tale* was challenged in high school curricula in Richland, Washington (1998), Tampa, Florida (1999), and Upper Moreland, Pennsylvania (2000) for being "an anti-Christian tract," "age-innappropriate" and "sexually graphic" (pp. 229-230).

Hammer, Stephanie Barbé. "The World as It Will Be? Female Satire and the Technology of Power in *The Handmaid's Tale*." *Modern Language Studies* 20 (1990): 39-49.

Hogsette, David S. "Margaret Atwood's Rhetorical Epilogue in *The Handmaid's Tale*: The Reader's Role in Empowering Offred's Speech Act." *Critique* 38.4 (Summer 1997): 262-278.

"Interview with Margaret Atwood." Random House (Atwood's American publisher). http://www.randomhouse.com/resources/bookgroup/handmaidstale_bgc.html#interview. Accessed October 11, 2008.

"Judson Board Set to Write Final Chapter on Sci-Fi Book." *San Antonio Express-News*, March 21, 2006. http://www.mysanantonio.com/news/MYSA032206_01A_book_ban_86b7db6_html. Accessed October 10, 2008.

Kane, Patricia. "A Woman's Dystopia: Margaret Atwood's *The Handmaid's Tale*." *Notes on Contemporary Literature* 185 (November 1988): 9-10.

Kaplan, Amy. "Left Alone with America: The Absence of Empire in the Study of American Culture." In *Cultures of American Imperialism*, ed. Amy Kaplan and Donald Pease. Durham, NC: Duke University Press, 1993, pp. 3-21.

Larson, Janet. "Margaret Atwood and the Future of Prophecy." *Religion and Literature* 21 (1989): 27-61.

Malak, Amin. "Margaret Atwood's *The Handmaid's Tale* and the Dystopian Tradition." *Canadian Literature* 112 (Spring 1987): 9-16. Examines how Atwood's feminist focus distinguishes her novel from dystopian classics like Huxley's *Brave New World* and Orwell's *Nineteen Eighty-Four*.

Neuman, Shirley. "'Just a Backlash': Margaret Atwood, Feminism, and *The Handmaid's Tale*." *University of Toronto Quarterly* 75.3 (Summer 2006): 857-868.

"Novel Solution in Judson: Board Reinstates Sci-Fi Book." *San Antonio Express-News*, April 13, 2006. http://www.mysanantonio.com/news/MYSA032406_01A_banned_book_1ce7575_html. Accessed October 10, 2008.

Oates, Joyce Carol. "Margaret Atwood's Tale." *New York Review of Books* 53.17 (November 2, 2006). http://www.nybooks.com/articles/19495. Accessed October 10, 2008.

"Objections to the Use of *The Handmaid's Tale* in a High-School Class of Minors." www.sibbap.org/handmaidstale.html. Accessed October 10, 2008.

"Poised for International Stardom." CBC Radio Archives. February 14, 1986. http://archives.cbc.ca/arts_entertainment/literature/topics/1494-10062. Accessed October 10, 2008.

Sage, Lorna. "Projections from a Messy Present." *Times Literary Supplement* (March 21, 1986): 307.

Stein, Karen F. "Margaret Atwood's Modest Proposal: *The Handmaid's Tale*." *Canadian Literature* 148 (Spring 1996): 57-73.

_____. "Margaret Atwood's *The Handmaid's Tale*: Scheherazade in Dystopia." *University of Toronto Quarterly* 61 (1991): 269-79.

Stillman, Peter G., and S. Anne Johnson. "Identity, Complicity, and Resistance in *The Handmaid's Tale*." *Utopian Studies* 5.2 (1994): 70-86.

Stimpson, Catherine R. "Atwood Woman." *The Nation* 242 (May 31, 1986): 764-67.

Sullivan, Rosemary. "What If? Writing *The Handmaid's Tale*." *University of Toronto Quarterly* 75.3 (Summer 2006): 850-6.

Tomc, Sandra. "'The Missionary Position': Feminism and Nationalism in Margaret Atwood's *The Handmaid's Tale*." *Canadian Literature* 138 (Fall 1993): 73-87.

VanSpanckeren, Kathryn, and Jan Garden Castro, eds. *Margaret Atwood: Vision and Forms*. Carbondale: Southern Illinois University Press, 1988.

Wagner-Lawlor, Jennifer. "From Irony to Affiliation in Margaret Atwood's *The Handmaid's Tale*." *Critique* 45.1 (Fall 2003): 83-96.

Margaret Atwood's *The Handmaid's Tale*: Critical Reception

Dominick Grace

The Handmaid's Tale, Margaret Atwood's sixth novel, was published in 1985. It was immediately successful, spending fifteen weeks on *The New York Times* best-seller list in hardback in 1986, selling "within the first year of its publication well over a million copies" (Phoebe Larmore, quoted in Loudermilk). The novel won the Canadian Governor-General's Award for fiction in 1985 and the 1987 Arthur C. Clarke Award (given to the best work in science fiction published in Britain in a given year), and it was nominated for the Booker Prize (the major award for fiction published in the British Commonwealth or Ireland and one of the most prestigious literary awards in the world), the Nebula Award (one of the major awards given to works of science fiction), and the Prometheus Award (given to libertarian science-fiction novels, though describing *The Handmaid's Tale* as "libertarian" requires some bending of the term). It was also a featured alternate selection from the Book-of-the-Month Club. A major film adaptation was released in 1990, and the novel has also been adapted into an opera, which premiered in 2000, a radio adaptation for BBC radio in the same year, and a stage version, which premiered in 2002. *The Handmaid's Tale* has been in print consistently since it was published and is widely taught in high school and college courses; a survey of college-level courses in science fiction published in *Science-Fiction Studies* in 1996 lists *The Handmaid's Tale* as the eleventh most frequently assigned work, appearing in more than forty such courses ("Addendum"). Numerous study guides (e.g., from Coles Notes, CliffsNotes, and enotes) as well as books geared for teachers of the novel (e.g., those by Gagliardi and by Wilson, Friedman, and Hengen, listed below) further reflect its widespread popularity in the classroom. It has been the subject of numerous articles and of a few essay collections and book-length studies. In short, the novel was and remains hugely popular, and it has generally, though not universally, been highly praised by critics and scholars. This essay will explore the early reactions to the novel and then trace the range and development of subsequent responses.

Initial Responses

The Handmaid's Tale was widely reviewed in newspapers and in magazines of various kinds, from those targeted specifically at women (such as *Glamour, Ms., Chatelaine*) to newsmagazines (*Time, Newsweek*) and political magazines (*The New Republic, New Statesman, The Nation*), as as well as in literary and academic journals. The range of review venues reflects the novel's wide appeal and the range of topics it addresses, though any new book by an established author will garner wide reviews. Reviews were generally positive. Marni Jackson described the novel as "a grim and brilliant fable" (4); the *Publishers Weekly* review called it "astonishing" and said it "deserves an honored space on the small shelf of cautionary tales that have entered modern folklore" ("*The Handmaid's Tale*," 45); Gayle Greene noted not only the novel's "horrific vision" but also its "complex structure" and "delicate interplay of wit and horror" (14) and found its greatest value in "its power to disturb" because "it does not offer easy solutions" (15). Catherine R. Stimpson praised Atwood's skill with language in the novel, calling her "a rhetorical marvel." Such terms of praise can be found in many of the early reviews.

However, the novel also received negative responses. One of the most notable critical reviews was also in one of the most prominent publications. In her review in *The New York Times Book Review*, Mary McCarthy called the book "very readable" (1) but criticized the "thin credibility of the parable" (35). (Many other commentators have also objected to Atwood's minimal explanation of how Gilead came about.) For McCarthy, Atwood does not convincingly depict a future plausibly extrapolated from the contemporary real world. How Gilead could conceivably come to be, she argued, is not clear in the novel. She also found the characterization "in general . . . weak" (35). In contrast to Stimpson, she even criticized Atwood's "inability to imagine a language to match the changed face of common life" (35). William French also found the novel implausible, though for somewhat different reasons; he objected to how it intermingles several different warnings without reconciling them:

> We're not clear what we're being warned against. Is it the danger of a fanatical religious group taking control of the United States and imposing a tyranny similar to that in Iran? Or the possibility of our poisoning the atmosphere with chemical and nuclear pollutants to the point at which a normal birth is a rarity, and infertility threatens the survival of the race? Or the danger of the feminist cause over-reaching itself, resulting in a repressive male backlash? (D18)

Interestingly, perhaps, given French's listing of alternate possibilities in his critique, the novel itself challenges the validity of thinking in terms of either/or. Nevertheless, French was not alone in finding too many strands woven together; Paul Gray's review, for instance, concludes with a similar observation that the novel "warns against too much: heedless sex, excessive morality, chemical and nuclear pollution" (84), a list that does not fully duplicate French's and so actually multiplies the different subjects raised by the novel. The novel's ending was problematic for some readers (it was changed in the film version: Offred acts rather more like a hero, and her final fate is made explicit), with Maria Margaronis offering perhaps the most succinct critique of it as "silly" (738). The novel's conclusion has generated so much attention that there is almost a separate critical tradition responding to the conclusion, as we will see below.

The early reviews also began to identify the contexts in which the novel would be studied more intensively. Many reviews other than the *Publishers Weekly* one, for instance, noted the novel's debt to dystopian traditions. William French invoked Aldous Huxley's *Brave New World* while Paul Gray and Gayle Greene invoked both that novel and George Orwell's *Nineteen Eighty-Four* (84; 15), and Peter Prescott went so far as to say that Atwood is a better novelist than Orwell or Huxley (70). By contrast, Barbara Ehrenreich contrasted *The Handmaid's Tale* with the more prevalent feminist utopian tradition (33), thereby noting the novel's connections with a specific genre as well as with a specific ideological perspective. Indeed, the novel's complex treatment of feminism drew comment from many early reviewers (e.g., Chieco, Greene, and Updike, though Updike perhaps dismissively preferred to see the novel's concerns as "feminine" [121] rather than feminist).

Reviewers also addressed the novel's interest in language and in narrative strategies and genres, in addition to those already mentioned. Victoria Glendinning, for instance, noted its gothic elements, which mesh somewhat with the elements of bedroom farce noted by Stimpson; the gothic mode carries the seeds of both romance and sexual farce, both of which Atwood plays on in her novel. Stimpson also links the book to the protest novel and the psychological novel. Indeed, the novel deliberately invokes and mixes different literary genres. Beneath these generic nods is the novel's deeper interest in the process of narrative itself, a process repeatedly fascinating to Offred and one that underlies studies that locate the novel in the postmodernist tradition.

Critical Interpretation

The Handmaid's Tale has the twin benefits of being a best seller and a novel with literary credibility; it is both popular and serious fiction. This relatively unusual status may help explain not only the amount of critical commentary the novel has generated and continues to generate but also the rapidity with which the novel became the subject of serious and protracted study. The first academic articles on *The Handmaid's Tale* were published within a year of its publication, which is remarkable. Not surprisingly, many of these early studies addressed obvious aspects of the work, such as its connections with feminism and with the dystopian tradition. Early articles include Jacques Leclaire's "Féminisme et dystopie dans *The Handmaid's Tale* de Margaret Atwood," Amin Malak's "Margaret Atwood's *The Handmaid's Tale* and the Dystopian Tradition" (first published in 1987), Janet L. Larson's "Margaret Atwood and the Future of Prophecy," David Ketterer's "Margaret Atwood's *The Handmaid's Tale*: A Contextual Dystopia," and Chris Ferns's "The Value/s of Dystopia: *The Handmaid's Tale* and the Anti-Utopian Tradition," among others. In the decades since it was published, the novel has generated considerable attention from several perspectives, but the most notable of these address its dystopianism, feminism, and postmodernism, or some combination thereof. The following sections address each of these major strands.

The Handmaid's Tale and Dystopianism

Atwood vehemently denies that *The Handmaid's Tale* is science fiction; when asked, her response is, "No, it certainly isn't science fiction" ("Interview" 393). However, she goes on to acknowledge that the book is "speculative fiction in the genre of *Brave New World* and *Nineteen Eighty-Four*" (393). As the novel's awards and nominations listed above indicate, Atwood is drawing something of a false distinction, since fiction in the utopian or dystopian mode is widely accepted as belonging to the larger genre of science fiction. The utopian mode is rooted in Thomas More's *Utopia*, a word he coined from the Greek, punning on two possible meanings: *eu-topos*, or good place; and *ou-topos*, or no place. The name acknowledges that the ideal state does not really exist, and utopian fiction generally functions satirically by imagining an ideal state the qualities of which are implicitly (or explicitly) contrasted with the real world. The term "dystopia" was coined on the model of More's *Utopia* to describe not an ideal place but rather the opposite, a bad place. Again, dystopian fiction imagines a much worse alternative to the reality against which the author contrasts it, and as with utopian fiction, dystopian fiction usually has a satirical or at least political or didactic aim. Plot and characterization often take a backseat to social or political commentary in such fiction. Atwood's explicit association of her novel with classic examples of the dystopian novel encourages critical readings of the novel in relation to the genre, though readers hardly needed Atwood's acknowledgment to make the connection or to begin to analyze the novel in relation to the conventions of dystopian literature.

Amin Malak established the basis for dystopian readings of the novel by noting the numerous traits of such fiction it invokes, such as a desire to forewarn readers of dire possibilities; a depiction of the dangers of power, notably totalitarian power; a central interest in patterns of binary opposition; and a focus on ideological rather than psychological exploration, reflected in the generally flat and undeveloped nature of characters in such works (4-6). Malak also notes, however, that "the novel offers two distinct additional features: feminism and irony" (10). As Barbara Ehrenreich had already noted, feminism had before *The Handmaid's Tale* more frequently generated utopian visions (though Atwood's novel is far from the first feminist dystopia; it is merely the first one to achieve widespread and mainstream recognition), and the genre is usually too serious to tolerate the humorous and self-reflexive influences of irony. The importance of these aspects of the novel will be discussed in more detail below.

Many commentators on the novel, however, critique its dystopian vision because Atwood does not devote sustained attention to one of the most significant of science-fiction conventions: extrapolation. Atwood does briefly explain how the Gileadean regime came to power, and she does even gesture toward conventional science-fiction tropes by linking the rampant infertility that justifies the suppression of women with pollutants and contaminants produced by science/technology, so there is a (very minimal) scientific underpinning to one of the novel's major conceits. However, science fiction is often concerned with detailed and plausible extrapolation from the world of the "now" to the future world, and Atwood is not. Critics such as Tom O'Brien and Chinmoy Banerjee (among others) critique what they see as the novel's failure on this front. O'Brien specifically criticizes the novel's failure to consider industrial and economic realities that would be "difficult to tame into cooperative roles in any planned economy" (252). Banerjee suggests that "Atwood is concerned with the aesthetic enjoyment of a particular kind of victimization, and not with a critical examination of its determinant relations" (80). Such points are valid (excepting Banerjee's invocation of "enjoyment," perhaps) if one expects the novel to conform to all the conventions of dystopian fiction, but Atwood's interests are not merely dystopian, or if they are dystopian, they have other bases as well. The novel's feminist and postmodernist inclinations militate against the logical and linear underpinnings of conventional science fiction. Feminism, for instance, challenges dominant patriarchal assumptions about what is important, while postmodern literature challenges the very idea that meaning is determinable, so it is perhaps not surprising that the novel "fails" to devote much attention to rationalizing its vision. The "Historical Notes" section should make this point clear, in its implicit criticism of the scholarly wish that rather than preserving her personal narrative, Offred had instead preserved data that would have help answer questions about such things as Gilead's economy or its "determinant relations."

The most interesting discussions about the novel's utopian/dystopian agenda have tended to focus on its conclusion. Whereas Gilead is easily recognized as a dystopian nightmare, the end of the novel proper and its coda, set in 2195, some two hundred years after the main action, have inspired much debate. The end of Offred's narrative, with her perhaps being rescued and stepping "up, into the darkness within [the van]; or else the light" (368), frustrated many readers with its refusal to determine Offred's fate, and the coda makes clear that Offred's ultimate fate remains a mystery. The film version explicitly resolves the question by providing a final image of the escaped Offred pregnant with her child, and it eliminates the "Historical Notes" entirely. The novel, by contrast, offers in the notes section a presentation at an academic conference, in which Professor Pieixoto discusses Gilead and Offred's narrative while noting that nothing about Offred, even her real name, can be known. Some scholars challenge this conclusion, noting that the novel leaves open the possibility that Offred's real name was June, and a few studies even insist on referring to the protagonist as June rather than Offred (Ildney Cavalcanti, for instance, refers to her as Offred/June) in what seems an ironic duplication of Pieixoto's imposition of meaning on the narrative.

The key debate about this coda is whether it provides some sort of relief by showing that Gilead did not last (a reading Atwood has encouraged) or whether it is a darkly ironic final warning that the Gilead lesson has not been learned. In an interview with Geoff Hancock, Atwood asserts that the "Historical Notes" should be compared to the afterword of *Nineteen Eighty-Four*, which shows that Big Brother's reign came to an end (142). However, many readers of the novel find the "Historical Notes" section just as dystopian as the rest of the book. Jamie Dopp sees the "Historical Notes" as nothing less than a despairing assertion of patriarchal repression, which is perhaps the most extreme response to the notes, but many other commentators reject the idea that the Nunavit of the future provides a positive alternative to Gilead. Harriet F. Bergmann, for instance, notes echoes between the dystopia of Gilead and the surviving sexism in Nunavit in, for instance, Pieixoto's cannibalistic punning, and she finds the coda deeply ironic (854), while Ken Norris finds the future scholars' Gileadean role-playing disturbing (363).

Other readers, however, suggest that the "Historical Notes" section does in fact offer hope, albeit not in the form of a utopian space. While simple opposition between the ideal and the horrifying is a frequent strategy in dystopian fiction, Atwood works at a more complex level. Sharon Rose Wilson points out, for instance, that despite the resemblances between the world of Nunavit and the world of the 1980s, which would suggest that it could breed a new Gilead, there are key differences as well. Canadian readers especially will recognize that the name Nunavit is very similar to Nunavut, the name of a territory for Dene and Inuit people that did not in fact exist when the novel was written; that it exists in the novel's future world suggests the emancipation of some repressed peoples (291-92). (Canada in fact created a territory called Nunavut in 1989.) Critics of the novel have come to see the notes section as presenting neither a utopian alternative nor a despairing affirmation of eternal patriarchal repression but rather, and in keeping with the monitory function of dystopian literature, a continued warning of the need to remain vigilant and to keep questioning dominant discourses; as Ildney Cavalcanti asserts, "The 'Historical Notes' cause readers to become critical, suspicious" of the claims Pieixoto makes about the clearer vision of his own day (172). It is certainly no accident that the final words of the novel are "Are there any questions?" (388).

The Handmaid's Tale and Feminism

The dystopian vision of *The Handmaid's Tale* clearly depicts Gilead as a patriarchal (even misogynist) state, and the novel has been linked with feminism since its first publication. Though there are various branches of feminism, in its broadest and most basic sense feminist thought concerns itself with the role and treatment of women in society from perspectives more or less critical of the dominant historical assumptions about women's place. Insofar as feminism advocates for the equal treatment of women, Atwood identifies herself as feminist, but she is reluctant to link herself with more activist definitions of the term and prefers not to be identified as an activist writer. It is therefore not surprising, perhaps, that despite being recognized and even hailed in some quarters as a feminist text, *The Handmaid's Tale* has also been the subject of debate and controversy in feminist circles. Even initial reviewers of the novel (e.g., Ehrenreich, Greene, McCarthy) found troubling the fact that the novel's depiction of Offred's mother and of feminist tactics such as book burning suggested that feminism itself shared some of the blame for Gilead. Even within Gilead, female complicity in the oppression of women is an important element in the maintenance of the state. Atwood is not interested in idealizing women or in treating them merely as tragic victims, and scholars such as Tara J. Johnson have offered insightful readings of the depiction of a repressive rather than a liberating feminine model in the novel.

Further aspects of the novel, such as Offred's passivity and complicity, or the novel's ultimate invocation of romance clichés, lead some readers (e.g., Banerjee and Dopp) to question the novel's commitment to feminism. Unlike other characters, such as Ofglen or Moira, Offred engages in no active resistance to the Gileadean regime and finally surrenders even the hope of escape, preferring her romance with Nick. She is very much like the heroine of a romance novel, and many feminist responses to the novel either regret or try to accommodate this troubling facet of the book. Sandra Tomc, for instance, notes "Atwood's sheer reliance on the contrivances of women's junk fiction to structure the plot of *The Handmaid's Tale*" (85) and lists some of the key examples:

> Offred is the innocent heroine who finds herself imprisoned in a menacing world over which she has no power, and indeed seeks to gain none for fear of compromising her womanly integrity. She falls in love with a man . . . who is an attractive, ambiguous figure, stereotypically characterized by his roguish cynicism, his silence and his ability to melt the heroine with his ways in bed. . . . The ambiguous lover turns out to be her saviour, the knight who rescues her from the menace. (85-86)

Though Tomc argues that Atwood invokes such clichés to subvert them, she also notes that the novel's strategies "propose models of autonomy for women that many feminists would consider too dangerously androcentric and heterosexist to be of much value" (91).

Madonne Miner also discusses the novel's invocation of romance, identifying Offred as the culprit in relying on romance clichés: "Because Offred so much wants to believe in the fairy tale, she closes off other plot options" (166), and because Offred closes them off, they are closed off to the reader, as well, Miner suggests. Therefore, the novel does not offer a feminist alternative to Gilead, an absence that Miner and others regret. Indeed, Tae Yamamoto asks, "How can a feminist read *The Handmaid's Tale?*" as part of the title of her article on the novel, and she concludes that the novel does not provide a clear answer.

Nevertheless, such readings point to the complexities of Atwood's ironic and satiric invocation of superficially antifeminist motifs and toward a response to the novel that accommodates its interrogation not only of patriarchy but also of feminism. Feminist readings of the novel have ultimately had to come to terms with the fact that "Atwood seems ambivalent about feminism as a political movement" (Loudermilk 124). Indeed, some commentators have come to recognize in the novel a critique of feminism, or of aspects of it. As Fiona Tolan concludes in her study of the novel as a critique of second-wave feminism:

> *The Handmaid's Tale* gives no easy solutions and, indeed, ends with its protagonist stepping into an unknown fate. This irresolution reflects the position of mid-1980s feminism. In articulating the potential danger of certain directions in which the movement had been heading, the novel can only advise its readers to err on the side of caution, and defend liberty before ideology. (31)

Just as the novel does not offer a conventional dystopian vision, neither does it offer a simple feminist solution to complex problems. It insists on questioning and subverting all orthodoxies, a trait closely linked to its affinities with postmodernism.

The Handmaid's Tale and Postmodernism

Like feminism, postmodernism includes many elements and branches and is therefore difficult to define quickly or simply. In broad terms, though, and in terms especially relevant to *The Handmaid's Tale*, postmodernism describes an artistic (and theoretical) movement that challenges any and all notions of hierarchy or absolute value systems; meaning is subjective and relative, and language is not a tool we use to represent or describe the real but creates a reality of its own, the only reality we can grasp. That is, postmodernism argues that meaning is entirely a subjective matter; it is not inherent in things themselves but is a function of perception. The same thing can have as many different meanings as there are perceptions of it, and no one meaning is privileged over the others. Postmodern literature, therefore, tends to be highly self-conscious, to draw attention to its status as literature and to how it is constructed. That is, postmodern literature tends to be highly metafictional, or fiction in which the making of fiction is itself part of the subject. Postmodernism's antihierarchical perspective also leads not only to literary experimentation that subverts conventional expectations but also to the mixing and combining of different genres, including forms conventionally viewed as "high" and "low" art (e.g., the sort of junk fiction referred to by Tomc).

We have already seen some indications of how *The Handmaid's Tale* is postmodern. Offred frequently draws attention to the fact that she is constructing narratives about herself, even constructing herself as a conglomeration of words: "I compose myself. My self is a thing I must now compose, as one composes a speech. What I must present is a made thing, not something born" (82). (The punning evident here is not only a frequent device in the novel but also a popular postmodern technique; the much-reviled pun has been rehabilitated by postmodernism because of the ways punning foregrounds how multiple meanings can be embedded in a single term.) Offred thinks of the story she is telling in terms of story, as defined by the conventions of fiction as much as by the conventions of biography—indeed, the novel suggests that there is little difference between the two. She narrates multiple versions of some events, for instance, and asserts that each version is equally true—and equally untrue (see, for instance, pp. 128-31, when Offred offers the different stories she believes about the fate of her husband). And of course, the "Historical Notes" section completely redefines the narrative we have just read, forcing us to reconsider it in multiple ways.

The novel therefore foregrounds its own postmodern elements, and critical responses to it have frequently addressed it in postmodern terms. Not surprisingly, such considerations often overlap with feminist and genre-based readings, since issues of genre are frequent postmodern preoccupations and since feminist challenges to conventional wisdom mesh well in some respects with postmodern ideology. Magali Cornier Michael, for instance, links feminism and postmodernism in her reading of the novel by focusing on the novel's social critiques, specifically its critiques of "traditional views on relations of power as static fixed systems" (147) and its presentation instead of the idea "that subjectivity is in part a function of relations of power" (148). The differences between Gilead and the United States of the 1980s, when the novel was published, are superficial, Michael argues, and the novel uses its fictional construction not so much to create a plausible future vision (thereby challenging critiques of the novel's implausibility) as to use fictional devices to represent and subvert the real (see, for instance, pp. 152ff.).

Postmodernist readings of the novel are of course especially interested in what the novel has to say about language. In contrast to Mary McCarthy's criticism of Atwood's failure to come up with an appropriate new language in the novel, critiques from a postmodern perspective foreground the novel's complex and sophisticated use not only of literary devices but also specifically of language itself. As Michael points out:

Offred is a very self-conscious narrator, who questions language and the possibility of telling a story accurately even as she attempts to tell her own story. Although she is aware of the impermanence of oral tales, she rejects the notion that writing is more *real* or *true* than speech, since language and subjectivity render mimesis impossible. As a narrator, she demonstrates a postmodern sensibility in her rejection of the dichotomy between reality and fiction, in her emphasis on the gaps in language, and in her investigation of the constructed quality of language. (157)

Hilde Staels discusses the novel's contrast between the "singular and final" system of meaning imposed by Gilead, one in which "ambiguity of meaning and variety of experience are excluded" (15), with the "personal, multivocal tale" of Offred (122). Such readings suggest that the concerns expressed by readers such as Tome do not take into account the novel's postmodern strategies. Here again, the "Historical Notes" section is crucial to an understanding of the novel in postmodern terms. The "Historical Notes" section foregrounds the difficulties of reading and determining meaning by satirizing the complacent academic response of Pieixoto. The key point is that Offred is "'off-read' or mis-read" by Pieixoto (Lacombe 7). Most commentators on the "Historical Notes" section recognize its irony. The point of that irony is to encourage readers not to accept the narrative or its ready-made reading at face value but rather to engage themselves with the text. The job of the postmodern reader is to be an active, critical participant in the gleaning of meaning from a text. Again, it is no accident that the final words of the novel are "Are there any questions?"

Conclusion

Since its publication, *The Handmaid's Tale* has been the subject of ongoing and evolving critical attention. The novel's complexities and ambiguities have encouraged constant rereading and reevaluation. Its refusal to treat the generic conventions it invokes (notably those of dystopian fiction but also those of other fictional modes such as romance and the gothic) conventionally has challenged readers to explore its generic limits. Its similar refusal to offer a straightforward feminist dystopia but rather to critique feminism as well as misogyny has provided fertile ground for feminist responses to the novel, both critical of its lack of conformity to feminist doctrine and respectful of its questioning of feminist orthodoxy. The novel's postmodern refusal to hierarchize meanings, to privilege one possible reading over any other, has further encouraged protracted and productive responses. More than twenty years after its publication, *The Handmaid's Tale* continues to engage and trouble readers. As with many great novels, its greatness resides at least in part in its irreducibility to a single meaning or critical perspective.

Note
Thanks to Katy Johns for research assistance.

Works Cited
"Addendum: The Works Most Widely Assigned." *Science-Fiction Studies* 23.3 (1996).
Atwood, Margaret. *The Handmaid's Tale*. 1985. Toronto: Seal, 1986.
_____. "An Interview with Margaret Atwood on Her Novel *The Handmaid's Tale*." In Atwood, *The Handmaid's Tale*. 393-98.
Banerjee, Chinmoy. "Alice in Disneyland: Criticism as Commodity in *The Handmaid's Tale*." *Essays on Canadian Writing* 41 (Summer 1990): 74-92.
Bergmann, Harriet F. "'Teaching Them to Read': A Fishing Expedition in *The Handmaid's Tale*." *College English* 51 (1989): 847-54.
Bloom, Harold, ed. *Margaret Atwood's The Handmaid's Tale*. Philadelphia: Chelsea House, 2001.
Cavalcanti, Ildney. "Utopias of/f Language in Contemporary Feminist Literary Dystopias." *Utopian Studies* 11.2 (2000): 152-80.
Chieco, Kate R. "*The Handmaid's Tale*." *Affilia* 2 (1987): 81.
Dopp, Jamie. "Subject-Position as Victim-Position in *The Handmaid's Tale*." *Studies in Canadian Literature* 19.1 (1994): 43-57.
Ehrenreich, Barbara. "Feminism's Fantasms: *The Handmaid's Tale* by Margaret Atwood." *The New Republic* 194 (March 17, 1986): 33-35.

Ferns, Chris. "The Value/s of Dystopia: *The Handmaid's Tale* and the Anti-Utopian Tradition." *Dalhousie Review* 69.3 (1989): 373-82.
French, William. "Pessimistic Future: *The Handmaid's Tale*." *Globe and Mail* (October 5, 1985): D18.
Gagliardi, Elizabeth. *The Handmaid's Tale by Margaret Atwood*. London, ON: Althouse Press, 2002.
Glendinning, Victoria. "Lady Oracle." *Saturday Night* 101 (January 1986): 39-41.
Gray, Paul. "*The Handmaid's Tale*." *Time* 127 (February 10, 1986): 84.
Greene, Gayle. "Choice of Evils." *Women's Review of Books* 3.10 (July 1986): 14-15.
Hancock, Geoff. "Interview with Margaret Atwood." *Canadian Fiction Magazine* 58 (1986): 113-43.
"*The Handmaid's Tale*." *Publishers Weekly* 228 (December 13, 1985): 45.
Jackson, Marni. "Critic's Choice." *Chatelaine* 58 (October 1985): 4.
Johnson, Tara J. "The Aunts as an Analysis of Feminine Power in Margaret Atwood's *The Handmaid's Tale*." *Nebula* 1.2 (2004): 68-79. http://www.nobleworld.biz/images/Johnson.pdf. Accessed August 7, 2008.
Ketterer, David. "Margaret Atwood's *The Handmaid's Tale*: A Contextual Dystopia." *Science-Fiction Studies* 16.2 (1989): 209-17.
Lacombe, Michele. "The Writing on the Wall: Amputated Speech in Margaret Atwood's *The Handmaid's Tale*." *Wascana Review* 21.2 (1988): 3-20.
Larson, Janet L. "Margaret Atwood and the Future of Prophecy." *Religion and Literature* 21.1 (1989): 27-61.
Leclaire, Jacques. "Féminisme et dystopie dans *The Handmaid's Tale* de Margaret Atwood." *Etudes Canadiennes/Canadian Studies* 21.1 (1986): 299-308.
Loudermilk, Kim A. *Fictional Feminism: How American Bestsellers Affect the Movement for Women's Equality*. New York: Routledge, 2004.
McCarthy, Mary. "Breeders, Wives and Unwomen." *The New York Times Book Review* (February 9, 1986): 1, 35.
Malak, Amin. "Margaret Atwood's *The Handmaid's Tale* and the Dystopian Tradition." Bloom 3-10.
Margaronis, Maria. "The Good Mother." *The Nation* 243 (December 27, 1986): 738.
Michael, Magali Cornier. *Feminism and the Postmodern Impulse: Post-World War II Fiction*. Albany: State University of New York Press, 1996.
Miner, Madonne. "'Trust Me': Reading the Romance Plot in Margaret Atwood's *The Handmaid's Tale*." *Twentieth Century Literature* 37.2 (1991): 148-68.
Norris, Ken. "'The University of Denay, Nunavit': The 'Historical Notes' in Margaret Atwood's *The Handmaid's Tale*." *American Review of Canadian Studies* 20.3 (1990): 357-64.
O'Brien, Tom. "Siren's Wail." *Commonweal* 113 (April 25, 1986): 251-53
Prescott, Peter S. "No Balm in This Gilead." *Newsweek* 107 (February 17, 1986): 70.
Staels, Hilde. "Margaret Atwood's *The Handmaid's Tale*: Resistance Through Narrating." Bloom 13-26.
Stimpson, Catharine R. "*The Handmaid's Tale*." *The Nation* 242 (May 31, 1986): 764-67.

Tolan, Fiona. "Feminist Utopia and Questions of Liberty: Margaret Atwood's *The Handmaid's Tale* as Critique of Second-Wave Feminism." *Women: A Cultural Review* 16.1 (2005): 18-32.

Tomc, Sandra. "'The Missionary Position': Feminism and Nationalism in Margaret Atwood's *The Handmaid's Tale*." Bloom 81-91.

Updike, John. "Expeditions to Gilead and Seegard." *The New Yorker* 62 (May 12, 1986): 118-26.

Wilson, Sharon Rose. *Margaret Atwood's Fairy-Tale Sexual Politics*. Toronto: ECW Press, 1993.

Wilson, Sharon Rose, Thomas B. Friedman, and Shannon Hengen, eds. *Approaches to Teaching Atwood's "The Handmaid's Tale" and Other Works*. New York: Modern Language Association, 1996.

Yamamoto, Tae. "How Can a Feminist Read *The Handmaid's Tale*? A Study of Offred's Narrative." *Margaret Atwood: The Open Eye*. Ed. John Moss and Tobi Kozakewich. Ottawa: University of Ottawa Press, 2006. 195-205.

"This Is the Way the World Ends":
Margaret Atwood and the Dystopian Impulse
Matthew J. Bolton

> This is the way the world ends
> This is the way the world ends
> This is the way the world ends
> Not with a bang but a whimper.
> —T. S. Eliot, "The Hollow Men"

Humanity seems to have a primal impulse to imagine the worst. Our morbidity may be a naturally selected trait, the legacy of our lemurlike ancestors' faculty for picturing just how bad the next trip to the watering hole could be. The primate who brooded for a moment before climbing down from the canopy of the treetops readied himself for the dangers to come; because he had pictured his own end, he was prepared to avoid it. Or perhaps this is a culturally determined impulse, rooted in the disparate religious practices that would evolve into the Greek tragedies and the Teutonic myths of Ragnarok and the Old Testament vision of a lost Garden of Eden. If the paradise of the Old Testament is lost to the past, the New Testament promises that man can choose, through his thoughts and actions, paradise or damnation in times to come. This Judeo-Christian dichotomy between Heaven and Hell may be the framework that undergirds the seemingly nonreligious tradition of the modern dystopian novel. Aldous Huxley's *Brave New World*, Yevgeny Zamyatin's *We*, George Orwell's *Nineteen Eighty-Four*, Ray Bradbury's *Fahrenheit 451*, and Anthony Burgess's *A Clockwork Orange*, among others, are works of contemporary social criticism rooted in biblical prophecy. Each author is a figurative voice in the wilderness, crying "prepare." Yet whereas these midcentury dystopian novels displace Judeo-Christian notions of end-time onto an Almighty secular state, Margaret Atwood's two dystopian novels explicitly treat the religious element of dystopian literature. In *The Hand-*

maid's Tale, Atwood reimagines the Orwellian surveillance state as a Christian fundamentalist one, in which Big Brother is not a totalitarian God-substitute but a shared notion of God himself. Nearly two decades later, Atwood created an equally prescient dystopia in *Oryx and Crake*, where man's hubris in playing God through genetic engineering reshapes the earth into a paradise fit for his evolutionary successors, but no longer fit for man himself. Atwood's dystopian novels explore the role that religion can play in making of earth a heaven or a hell.

The Republic of Gilead, the Christian fundamentalist police state of *The Handmaid's Tale*, is disturbing not because it is so different from modern America but because it is on a continuum with it. This police state has been achieved within a single generation, and its citizens and subjects therefore still remember their former lives in an America very much like our own. When Offred first meets the Commander's wife, for example, she realizes she has seen the older woman before: She was once a televangelist named Serena Joy. Serena was a gospel-singing soprano who could "smile and cry at the same time" (16). While Serena's role on her television gospel hour is a familiar one to most readers—she might call to mind Tammy Faye Bakker—her role in the military coup that was to come takes us into unfamiliar territory. Offred remarks, cryptically, "It was after that she went on to other things" (16). Because Offred knows full well the connection between the rise of the televangelists and the fall of America, she can laconically draw a connection between her memories of a young Serena Joy and the old woman who sits before her in the Commander's house, talking of "the things we fought for" (16). Offred's first encounter with the Commander's wife is an encounter with history itself, for the gulf between the young Serena Joy and the stout, wrinkled woman who confronts Offred in the sitting room is the gulf between our present time and Offred's.

The members of Offred's generation are the vital link between past and future, for they carry with them memories of life in an America that is essentially our own. For the generations to come, the United

States will be ancient history and life in Gilead will seem the norm rather than a deviation from that norm. Offred, however, has the historical perspective that allows her to see the hypocrisy and perversion inherent to Gilead. In *Oryx and Crake*, Crake, who has given much thought to extinction, identifies the importance of continuity across the generations. "All it takes," he observes, "is the elimination of one generation. One generation of anything. Beetles, trees, microbes, scientists, speakers of French, whatever. Break the link in time between one generation and the next, and it's game over forever" (223). Offred, like the Commander and the Commander's wife, is one of these links in time. What she sees around her now calls to mind memories of her former life, and so her narrative constantly shuttles across time, as she reflects on the process by which that former life was taken away from her.

Though the foment that led to the overthrow of the United States was a long time in the making, the act by which the extremists seized power was swift and brutal: They machine-gunned Congress and the president, declared martial law, and suspended the Constitution. Not surprisingly, the Gileadeans immediately distanced themselves from this act by blaming the massacre on Islamic extremists. One of the central ironies of the Gileadeans' rise to power, therefore, lies in one group of fundamentalist religious extremists blaming another for endangering the American way. Once the Gileadeans have suspended the Constitution, they are able to reshape society incrementally through a series of economic, legal, and military dictates. In the name of safety and order, one human right and civil liberty after another is stripped away. This is a prescient point in a novel written some fifteen years before the September 11, 2001, attacks and the consequent global war on terror. Out of fear and uncertainty, the Americans of Atwood's future sacrifice liberty for security, only to find too late that the walls going up around them are meant to keep them in rather than to keep their enemies out.

Gilead seizes power by presenting itself as a bulwark against anti-American forces abroad and at home. Yet the false dichotomy that Gilead sets up by positioning itself against Islamic extremism ultimately collapses into itself. For Gilead, by the time in which the novel is set, is strikingly similar to an Islamic theocracy. In the epilogue that frames the novel—the transcript of an academic conference held some two hundred years after Offred's time—one of the professors' studies is titled "Iran and Gilead: Two Late-Twentieth-Century Monotheocracies, as Seen through Diaries" (300). The encounter between Offred, accompanied by her fellow Handmaid, Ofglen, and a group of Japanese tourists drives home this point. Offred and her companion are garbed in the crimson robes and white wimples that mark them as Handmaids, a mandated form of dress that suggests a Christian version of the Muslim burka. Whereas a nun takes on the habit as a voluntary act (and note that Roman Catholic nuns rarely wear habits in the wake of Vatican II), Offred wears her garment under orders of the state. Her encounter with the foreign women in Western garb is disconcerting on several levels. At first, Offred sees these women as alien, as radically different from herself. Then, after a moment, she realizes that they are now what she was once:

> We are fascinated, but also repelled. They seem undressed. It has taken so little time to change our minds, about things like this.
> Then I think: I used to dress like that. That was freedom.
> *Westernized*, they used to call it. (28)

Here, then, is another moment in which past and present collide in the historicizing vision of a woman who has survived a cataclysmic period of change. The visiting women, exercising a freedom that Offred and Ofglen no longer possess, ask the Handmaids whether they are happy. There can be, of course, only one answer:

> Ofglen says nothing. There is silence. But sometimes it's as dangerous not to speak.
> "Yes, we are very happy," I murmur. I have to say something. What else can I say? (29)

The scene is also disconcerting for the reader, whose sympathies and vantage point lie not with the women living in a more or less free and secular society but with the ones who aver that they are happy despite the fact that they are wearing the restrictive dress mandated by a fundamentalist state. We know that Offred is not, in fact, happy, and that her reply is predicated on fear of retaliation. This knowledge therefore challenges the notion of cultural relativism, by which one might argue that while the state of Iran, for example, mandates that women wear the burka, one should respect that society's right to align itself according to different lights from one's own. Atwood's scene suggests that women living in a repressive state are not necessarily able to speak for themselves, and that it is therefore a mistake to attribute state-sanctioned misogyny to culturally specific practices.

Nor is this the only instance in which cultural relativism proves to be a less than satisfactory worldview. The book's epilogue, "Historical Notes on *The Handmaid's Tale*," suggests that a return to a secular and enlightened pre-Gilead state is not enough to remedy the plight of women in other places. Much of the world seems to have become, by 2195, progressive and inclusive, as the names and places of origin of the academics attest. Yet in looking back on the state of Gilead and putting Offred's journal into context, Professor Pieixoto comes close to apologizing for the oppressive nature of the Gileadean state:

> In my opinion we must be cautious about passing moral judgment upon the Gileadeans. Surely, we have learned by now that such judgments are of necessity culture-specific. Also Gileadean society was under a good deal of pressure, demographic and otherwise, and was subject to factors from which we ourselves are happily more free. Our job is not to censure but to understand. (302)

The professor's "editorial aside" is greeted with applause from his colleagues (302). Offred's plight has become the stuff of academia: human suffering and injustice parsed in clinical and scholarly language.

The prefatory comments that precede the professor's speech, in which a conference organizer updates the attendees about plans for a fishing trip and an "Outdoor Period-Costume Sing-Song," further trivializes Offred's narrative. What seems to be Atwood's narrative device for concluding and further contextualizing Offred's story is, in fact, one more instance of social criticism. Rational discourse may not be enough to ensure that justice prevails, and as idyllic as the 2195 society seems to be, it might well profit from some modicum of the Gileadeans' moral convictions. In rationalizing the institution of the Handmaid, the professor perpetuates the notion that women's rights are culturally determined rather than inherent.

The Handmaid's Tale is prophetic, therefore, in that it invokes the future—two futures, to be specific—to critique the present. The Old Testament prophet was not a fortune-teller or a palm reader but a fierce social critic who brought his moral presence to bear on the judges and kings who led the Israelites. His eyes were as much on the present as on the future, and his voice was meant to speak truth to power. Likewise, the New Testament promise of salvation and threat of damnation is always predicated on actions and beliefs in the present moment. Atwood's novel takes issue with the oppression of women here in the present day and with the complicity inherent in regarding women's rights as culturally determined. Yet her focus is also on trends in American life that suggest the erosion of hard-won women's rights: the backlash against feminism, the blurring of lines between church and state, the exploitation of women in pornography and in advertising, and the bombing of abortion clinics in the name of saving lives. It is perhaps this last development that most clearly animates Atwood's vision of the future.

Offred's status as a Handmaid is the reductio ad absurdum of state control of reproductive rights. In Atwood's vision of the future, the violence against abortion providers that was a crime in the 1980s has become a state-sanctioned event in the intervening decades. Offred comes upon the corpses of three men who have been executed and hanged from the walls of the city:

> The men wear white coats, like those worn by doctors or scientists. . . . Each has a placard hung around his neck to show why he has been executed: a drawing of a human fetus. They were doctors, then, in the time before, when such things were legal. (32)

The abortion provider and the abortion-clinic bomber have changed roles: Crimes have become obligations and obligations, crimes. Offred's status as a Handmaid—one compelled by biblical precedent to bear the child of a Commander whose own wife is infertile—represents the complete state control of her reproductive life. It is totalitarianism as inscribed on the female body. In the years between our time and Offred's, the movement to keep women from having the means to prevent or end a pregnancy has become a movement to compel women to have one.

In Gilead, biblical precedent and religious dogma have been turned into apparatuses of the totalitarian state. Whether the union of Christianity with the police state represents a monstrous perversion of the gospel or its logical conclusion is something each reader must decide for him- or herself, for Offred and Atwood alike are ambiguous on the subject. Living in a society in which religion has become a form of systematic and institutional oppression, Offred must locate the sacred elsewhere: in her memories of the past and in her faith that Luke, her husband, is still alive and well. Her meditations on Luke, whom she sometimes imagines alive and sometimes dead—but dead from a quick and painless end—may be a form of prayer. These remembered and imagined scenes of domestic life in a free world are Offred's vision of a paradise lost.

* * *

Issues of biology, theology, and ethics likewise drive Atwood's more recent dystopian novel, *Oryx and Crake*. Like *The Handmaid's Tale*, this story is framed not in a single future setting but in a pair of settings. In the present time of the novel, a lone human survivor of a viral apocalypse, who was once named Jimmy but now goes by the name Snowman, keeps watch over a tribe of humanoids who have been genetically designed to thrive on an earth no longer fit to sustain man. Snowman is in a wretched state. The sun burns him, the flies bite him, the fauna threatens him. Yet there is a strange beauty to this post-apocalyptic Eden, a brave new world in which seabirds nest in the shattered office towers that rise from a lagoon. Hungry, half-naked, and profoundly lonely, Snowman casts his mind back on his lifelong relationship with the genius Crake, who destroyed the old world in order to bring this new one into being.

Before the apocalypse, Jimmy and Crake's America was a place in which consumerism and corporate culture had run rampant. Atwood envisions a terrible but carnivalesque future that is presaged by a cohort of present-day ills: runaway pollution and consequent climate change, the growing gap between the rich and the poor, the rise of the gated community and the exurb, the proliferation of Internet pornography and violence, the threat of terrorism, the emergence of genetic engineering of crops and animals as a lucrative field, and the dumbing-down of language and culture. Given some fifty or a hundred years to percolate, these disparate trends lead to a dystopia in which the well-to-do live in corporate compounds while the rest of the world struggles to survive in a decidedly hostile global economy and environment. Genetic splicing has allowed men to create animals like the pigoon, an oversized hog whose body grows multiple human organs that may be harvested for transplantation. The notion that humans may control and improve on nature through genetic manipulation seems, in this society, to be part and parcel of their disregard for the climate and the environment. When Jimmy worries that a new crossbreed called the wolvog—an animal with the appearance of a house pet but the savagery of a wolf—could get out of the lab and start breeding in the wild, Crake replies, "Nature is to zoos as God is to churches" (206). Jimmy challenges the point, saying, "I thought you didn't believe in God." Crake's reply is telling: "I don't believe in Nature either . . . or not with a capital N" (206). For Crake, nothing is sacred: not art, not nature, and not God.

In a dedicated laboratory complex called Paradice, Crake works secretly on two related projects: a germ that will wipe out mankind and a race of genetically modified people who can take man's place. The name Crake has chosen for his lab suggests not only the paradise of Eden but also a "pair of dice," the element of chance involved in natural selection and evolution. In creating this new race of men, Crake becomes a God who, unlike the God of Einstein, does indeed play at dice. Through a series of experiments, he builds into his new race the defenses and adaptations that will allow them to survive in the overheated and ozone-depleted world outside his air-conditioned laboratory. But his genetic engineering is not purely of a physical nature; his greatest concern lies with social engineering. He wants to breed out of these new men and women the violence and cupidity that he sees all around him. Rewiring their sexuality, for example, so that they go into heat every three years eliminates the sexual compulsions that lead to prostitution and pornography. Crake, always the cerebral scientist to Jimmy's romantic wordsmith, sees desire itself as an undesirable quality. Jimmy recalls Crake's attempts to isolate another neurological trait, "the G-spot in the brain," the belief in the divine (157). In Crake's analysis, belief in God, like sexual desire, is the cause of war and misery.

It is ironic, therefore, that in the postapocalyptic world, Crake's progeny view him as a God and Snowman as a prophet. The Crakers, despite their maker's genetic interventions, are full of questions. Snowman has dutifully answered them, spinning out an ersatz cosmology in much the same spirit in which he once wrote copy for pharmaceutical products he knew to be little more than snake oil. He defends his storytelling by reasoning, "He'd had to think of something. . . . *Crake made the bones of the Children of Crake out of the coral of the beach, and then he made their flesh out of a mango*" (96). Because Snowman is so different from them physically, and because he has access to knowledge closed to them, the Crakers view him as an intermediary between God and themselves. He has become their holy man: "Above his head flies the invisible banner of Crakedom, of Crakiness, of Crakehood, hallowing all he does" (96). Snowman wears—however uncomfortably—the mantle of the prophet.

The implications of the Crakers' gradual deification of their maker and elevation of Snowman to visionary status are profound, suggesting that believe in God is not merely a cultural construct but a deep-seated biological drive. Just as the wolvogs and the pigoons did indeed slip their pens and proliferate in the wild, so do the Crakers' thoughts turn to the cosmos and to the fundamental questions of where they came from and why they came into being. Nature is thriving after the destruction of the zoos, and God after the destruction of the churches. Snowman knows what his friend would have thought of this development: "Crake was against the notion of God, or of gods of any kind, and would surely be disgusted by the spectacle of his own gradual deification" (104). Snowman also knows that his own status among the Crakers is becoming as fixed and inviolable as Crake's. They remember what he has told them already, and he must now work within the confines of the cosmology he has established: "At first he'd improvised, but now they're demanding dogma: he would deviate from orthodoxy at his peril" (104). Snowman has locked himself into a role that he will never be able to escape, and because the Crakers mature rapidly, reaching adulthood by four years of age, he will presumably see several generations pass during which his semicoherent improvisations will become a rigid theological framework.

The other central figure in Snowman's cosmology is Oryx, who in real life was Jimmy and Crake's one true love. If the boyhood friends were of the "haves," the privileged compound set, she was the product of the desperate "have-nots," a peasant girl sold into child slavery and prostitution. Captivated, as was Jimmy, by a picture of her (or of someone who looked very much like her) on an Internet pornography site, Crake locates Oryx and brings her to Paradice to train the members of his new race in how to deal with plants and animals. In later times, therefore, the Crakers associate Oryx with nature. Snowman's creation myths posit a divine order founded not on monotheism but on dualism: a god who made man in his image and a goddess who made all of the plants and animals on which man depends. The women, in particular, have taken to Oryx and talk of "consulting" her. Snowman muses on this religious communion:

> They must perform some kind of prayer or invocation, since they can hardly believe that Oryx appears to them in person. Maybe they go into trances. Crake thought he'd done away with all that, eliminated what he called the G-spot in the brain. God is a cluster of neurons, he'd maintained. It had been a difficult problem, though: take out too much in that area and you got a zombie or a psychopath. But these people are neither.
> They're up to something though, something Crake didn't anticipate: they're conversing with the invisible, they've developed reverence. (157)

Crake thought he had remade man as a static being, a ruminant species that would be content simply to *be*. But the Crakers are *becoming* something: they are developing before Snowman's eyes the rudiments of mythology, religion, and culture.

Nor is art slow to follow religion. Returning from a days-long foraging expedition to the ruined Paradice, Snowman finds that the Crakers have made a simulacrum of him in his absence. "*Watch out for art*," he recalls Crake saying. "Symbolic thinking of any kind would signal downfall. . . . Next they'd be inventing idols, and funerals, and grave goods, and the afterlife, and sin, and Linear B, and kings, and then slavery and war" (361). The Crakers, even in the short time that Snowman has stood watch over them, have begun to change. Where they were once content with nature, they are now beginning to create art. It is fitting that their first creation is an image of Snowman, who was himself not a scientist but an aesthetician, a lover of arcane words and artistry. Crake created these people, Oryx taught them how to live in harmony with nature, but Snowman has unwittingly fostered in them the symbolic thinking that their maker was so determined to breed out of them. The Crakers' garden on the beach is a paradise, but one from which we suspect they will eventually fall as innocence gives way to experience.

* * *

If there is an overarching moral to *The Handmaid's Tale* and *Oryx and Crake*, therefore, it may be this: Men and women cannot remake the earth as a new paradise. Utopian thinking quickly devolves into systematic oppression and state-licensed mass murder, for the utopian visionaries must destroy the old order before they can usher in their new one. This willingness to destroy in the interests of perfection may be grounded in the logic of Adam. In Eden, God charged Adam with naming the animals and granted him dominion over the earth, saying, "Be fruitful and multiply; fill the earth and subdue it; have dominion over the fish of the sea, over the birds of the air, and over every living thing that moves on the earth" (Genesis 1:28). Later, seeing that Adam was lonely, God made Eve to be his companion: "He took one of his ribs, and closed up the flesh in its place. Then the rib which the Lord God had taken from man He made into a woman" (Genesis 2:21-22). Both the Commanders of Gilead and Crake's biologists subscribe to an Adamic worldview, using social engineering or genetic engineering to assert their dominance over a new paradise of their creation. It is telling, for example, that both Offred and Snowman have been given new names to bear in a new world. But the logic of Adam soon leads to the nihilism of MaddAddam, the collective screen name for the bioterrorists with whom Crake studies. When one goes looking for Eden, one may find oneself instead in Golgotha, the valley of skulls. For if the new Adam is truly to be the steward of the earth, then anything he cannot dominate he must destroy. Both the Gileadeans and Crake accept death and chaos as a necessary clearing of the ground on which they may found their new societies. Utopia becomes dystopia in Atwood's novels precisely because the utopian thinkers are willing to sacrifice the basic human rights of the individual in order to bring about the perceived good of the many.

Does this suggest that Atwood's social and political vision is fundamentally reactive, and that one should come away from her novels believing that the status quo is better than any number of possible futures? If, after all, respect for individual differences and rights ought to outweigh the possible good that a benevolent Adam could bring about through sweeping change, then we should be happy with the messiness and the contradictions of present-day society. Certainly, dystopian literature flirts with this sort of self-iterative moral. If the future an author describes is too terrible, it may serve not to caution readers but to placate them. Indeed, the reveries of characters living in postapocalyptic futures—Offred's memories of domestic life in her shabby apartment, for example, or Snowman's memories of the change of seasons—can be a sort of nostalgia for the present. If a character can think wistfully of a time like ours, how bad can our time really be?

Yet to characterize Atwood's dystopias as affirmations of the status quo would be to miss the point entirely, for the present day that her narrators pine for is an imminently threatened one. Sven Birkerts, writing in *The New York Times*, argues that *Oryx and Crake* is particularly disconcerting in that our present-day situation seems to be catching up rapidly with the future Atwood describes:

> What Atwood could not have intended, and what is no less alarming and exponentially more urgent, is the resonance between her rampaging plague scenario and the recent global outbreak of SARS. Moving from book to newspaper, or newspaper to book, the reader realizes, with a jolt, how the threshold of difference has been lowered in recent months. The force of Atwood's imagining grows in direct proportion to our rising anxiety level.

The novel, Birkerts argues, is meant to "goad us to thought." But perhaps thought is not enough; perhaps we ought to be goaded into action. Like many of us, Atwood and Offred watched as the central values they now pine for, a loving family life or communion with nature, were being eroded by a culture of consumerism, oppression, and violence. Ironically, both the Commanders and Crake are reacting against this same trash culture, using it as their justification for bringing about sweeping social change. But the new orders they usher in leave no room for Offred's domestic life or for Snowman's aesthetic one. Atwood's narrators thought much, but acted little, about the two extremes that threatened their free lives, and both eventually miss the rights for which they never stood up and fought.

Atwood's narrators have survived the fall of their old world precisely because they watched meekly while it fell. In a sense, each is like the impotent men that T. S. Eliot describes in "The Hollow Men." The poem's speaker confesses: "Our dried voices, when/ We whisper together/ Are quiet and meaningless." The same might be said of Offred and Snowman's narratives. Both Offred and Snowman whimpered while the world fell to pieces around them, and in telling their stories they speak in lamentation rather than in protest. Their mothers, on the other hand, were fighters. Offred's mother was a product of the civil rights movement and marched in rallies for women's rights. Although Snowman's mother grew up in the insulated world of the Compounds, she eventually rebels against it. After sinking deeper and deeper into despair over the immoral activities in which her husband's corporation is engaged, she leaves this insular world in order to join a resistance movement. Both Offred and Snowman catch their last glimpses of their mothers not in person, but on videotaped footage of each woman participating in a rally. It is a striking parallel: Both narrators chose to be silent rather than to follow their mothers' path of speaking truth to power, and each therefore survives his or her mother to live in the nightmarish social order that she foresaw and fought against.

The dystopian narrator's backward-looking nostalgia for the freedom of the present day is therefore the mirror image of the dystopian author's forward-looking concern for it. What would be politically reactive in the imagined future is politically engaged in the present moment. As Atwood said of *Oryx and Crake* in a *New York Times* interview: "This book is not a prediction. . . . You're really writing about now, about your concerns in this life." Atwood's concerns, in both *The Handmaid's Tale* and *Oryx and Crake*, lie with the extremes that threaten a democratic way of life: radical religious intolerance on one hand and radical free global markets on the other. In his seminal 1992 article "Jihad vs. McWorld," Benjamin Barber argues that these forces have one thing in common: "neither offers much hope to citizens looking for practical ways to govern themselves democratically." Hope instead may lie in the willingness of the individual to take on him- or herself the prophetic role of speaking truth to power, whatever form that power takes, in order to keep the world from ending with either a bang or a whimper.

Works Cited

Atwood, Margaret. *The Handmaid's Tale*. New York: Anchor, 1998 [1985].
_____. *Oryx and Crake*. New York: Anchor, 2004 [2003].
Barber, Benjamin R. "Jihad vs. McWorld." *The Atlantic Monthly*, March 1992. http://www.theatlantic.com/doc/199203/barber.
Birkerts, Sven. "Present at the Recreation." *The New York Times*, May 18, 2003.
Eliot, T. S. *The Complete Poems and Plays: 1909-1950*. New York: Harcourt, Brace & World, 1962.
Gussow, Mel. "Atwood's Dystopian Warning: Hand-Wringer's Tale of Tomorrow." *The New York Times*, June 24, 2003.

Feminism and *The Handmaid's Tale*

Jennifer E. Dunn

Margaret Atwood's *The Handmaid's Tale* would seem, on the surface, a straightforward feminist text. The narrative is set in a speculative future, exploring gender inequalities in an absolute patriarchy in which women are breeders, housekeepers, mistresses, or housewives—or otherwise exiled to the Colonies. In Atwood's fictional Gilead, all of the work of twentieth-century feminism has been utterly undone, and the text explores the effects of this from a first-person point of view that elicits the reader's sympathy. Offred's tale functions as a critique of women's oppression, as we can see from one of her earlier statements problematizing biological determinism: "I avoid looking down at my body, not so much because it's shameful or immodest but because I don't want to see it. I don't want to look at something that determines me so completely" (72-73). Yet Offred's story is neither wholly triumphant nor wholly straightforward. Offred's narrative is potentially undermined, and certainly deconstructed, by the future historians featured in the text's epilogue. At the same time, Offred herself is an unreliable and elusive narrator. Can we believe her story? And does her unreliable status enhance or detract from the text's feminist messages? In raising these questions, Atwood's *The Handmaid's Tale* engages with the debates of feminist politics, dramatizing a complicated and ongoing ideological history. This is a complex novel, one that is open to more than one interpretation, but there are certain affinities with some of the major developments in feminist thought in the twentieth century, from Virginia Woolf's arguments about women's roles and women's writing to later discourses on the male gaze, the binary division of male and female, and the radical potential of language.

In *A Room of One's Own* (1929), Virginia Woolf posits that "a woman must have money and a room of her own if she is to write fiction" (3). Although Woolf suggests an income of "five hundred a year" would be sufficient for a woman writer, the amount of money is less important than the economic independence it represents. Likewise, the "room of one's own" is both literal and figurative, signifying an actual space for retreat as well as a woman's right to privacy, independent thought, and personal expression. In the Republic of Gilead in *The Handmaid's Tale*, income and a room of one's own—and, most important, the freedoms they represent—are systematically denied to women. In Offred's flashbacks to the time before Gilead, we learn how the new Gilead regime moved quickly to take away women's financial independence. In the space of a single day, Offred is fired from her job at the library and denied access to her bank account. The new legislation banning women from employment and taking away their financial assets immediately demotes Offred and all other women to the status of second-class citizens, making them dependent on the men who now control all household income. Even the dynamic in Offred's own marriage changes:

> Something had shifted, some balance. I felt shrunken, so that when [Luke] put his arms around me, gathering me up, I was small as a doll. I felt love going forward without me.
> He doesn't mind this, I thought. He doesn't mind it at all. Maybe he even likes it. We are not each other's, anymore. Instead, I am his. (191)

This is a major change from the earlier stages of their relationship, when both Offred and her husband had taken equality between the genders for granted. Offred's mother, a feminist activist, had even taken exception to their complacency on this matter:

> You young people don't appreciate things, she'd say. You don't know what we had to go through, just to get where you are. Look at [Luke], slicing up the carrots. Don't you know how many women's lives, how many women's *bodies*, the tanks had to roll over just to get that far? (131)

Under the Gilead regime, Offred enjoys certain privileges denied other women, including her own room in the Commander's household. Soon after her arrival, she makes an effort to claim the space as her own, examining its contents slowly and in detail: "There has to be some space, finally, that I can claim as mine, even in this time" (60). Yet this is not truly a room of her own, just as the Handmaids' very names—all patronymics—are not their own. Offred is not the first Handmaid to sleep in the room, and during her stay she is not allowed to keep personal belongings. The bedroom door cannot be locked, allowing the Commander to peer into the room at will. (It is unusual and meaningful that Cora, one of the Marthas, shows respect by knocking before entering.) Constant surveillance fosters an atmosphere of paranoia, so that Offred must hide the stolen butter she uses to moisturize her face, just as she must monitor her words and actions in public. For the women of Gilead, there is no such thing as private space or ownership, and certainly no room for free personal expression.

The latter is further reinforced by the Handmaids' appearance. Like all of the other women in Gilead, the Handmaids are marked by their uniform. Paradoxically, the uniforms of the Wives, Marthas, Handmaids, and Econowives are meant to be marks of distinction, yet the effect of this mandatory dress is to make all of the women in a given group indistinguishable from one other. This is particularly true of the Handmaids' uniform, which takes the design of a nun's habit but is made with red cloth instead of the conventional black and white. The long gown conceals the Handmaid's body and is accompanied by long gloves and a wimple with large wings that conceal the face: "They are to keep us from seeing, but also from being seen" (18). The habit, particularly the wimple, restricts its wearer's movements, much like Victorian corsetry. Intriguingly, Offred's description of her uniform is followed by a description of the Commander's house as "late Victorian" (18). Like women's clothing, decor has a symbolic function in this novel. Here, the decor links the Handmaids to the Victorian cult of domesticity, the notion of "separate spheres" that relegated women to the home and reserved professional and public spaces for men alone. Dressed as a Handmaid, Offred is a perverse version of the Victorian Angel in the House, the idealized, self-sacrificing wife and mother with whom Woolf does battle in order to express herself as a writer ("Professions for Women"). In Gilead, Offred suffers where Woolf has gained, as the main effect of the Handmaid's uniform is to repress her individuality. One Handmaid looks much like any other, a fact reinforced by the text's recurring image of Handmaids walking two by two around the town or of Offred reflected and thus doubled in mirrors. Indeed, the Commander's interest in Offred has little, or perhaps nothing, to do with who she is as an individual; for him, as for other men in Gilead, she is simply a replacement for the Handmaid that preceded her. Offred's own sense of selfhood is greatly diminished by the rules governing Handmaids' appearance and behavior. She has trouble remembering what she looked like before she became a Handmaid, and during her time in Gilead she is dissociated from her own body and reflection. She does not look down at her body when she takes a bath, and in the mirror she sees only the confusing signifiers of her uniform: "a distorted shadow, a parody of something, some fairytale figure in a red cloak, descending towards a moment of carelessness that is the same as danger. A Sister, dipped in blood" (18).

The Handmaid's uniform is telling in other ways as well, since it operates as a signifier of the Handmaid's contradictory sexual status. The nunlike habit works to desexualize the Handmaid, recalling chaste servants of God and concealing the woman's face and body from men who might find her sexually attractive. Yet the uniform simultaneously marks out its wearer as someone whose sole function in Gilead *is* sexual. The red material is meant to represent the blood of the womb and the sacred rite of reproduction, yet this symbolically resonant color retains historical connotations of both sexual allure and sexual shame (e.g., Hester Prynne's "scarlet letter" in Nathaniel Hawthorne's novel). The Handmaids are officially protected and untouchable, but they remain powerful objects of taboo desire; indeed, their inaccessibility and sham aura of chastity might make them even more desirable. Early on in the narrative, Offred describes the lingering look of two young Guardians: "As we walk away I know they're watching, these two men who aren't yet permitted to touch women. They touch with their eyes instead" (32). The moment conforms to feminist theories of the male gaze, which reduces women to *objects* (often sexualized ones) rather than active, individual *subjects*. Laura Mulvey argues: "In a world ordered by sexual imbalance, pleasure in looking has been split between active/male and passive/female. The determining male gaze projects its fantasy onto the female figure, which is styled accordingly" (442). The gaze makes the woman the "bearer, not maker, of meaning" (Mulvey 439). Offred becomes a passive object, a blank screen onto which the gazer might project any meaning at all—including, but not limited to, objectifying sexual fantasies. In *The Handmaid's Tale*, even Aunt Lydia recognizes the power of the beholder:

> Modesty is invisibility, said Aunt Lydia. Never forget it. To be seen—to be *seen*—is to be—her voice trembled—penetrated. What you must be, girls, is impenetrable. (39)

The Handmaids' habits do little to prevent the penetrating gaze of others. Although only men of higher rank are allowed sexual access to women, the Guardians' leering goes unpunished as long as the young men do not act on their desires. Yet their gaze speaks to the power that accompanies looking in Gilead, especially when it comes to looking at women. Gilead is a society that has outlawed pornography and sexual images of women, yet one of its basic organizing principles is the sexual objectification of the Handmaids.

This objectification occurs via hypocritical but official routes in public, in the way the Handmaids are classified and dressed, and it occurs through unofficial, more familiar means in private. The Commander, for instance, has access to illicit materials such as fashion magazines and pornography, and numerous high-ranking officers secretly frequent the Jezebel's club. Here, male officers consort with women wearing forbidden lingerie and cosmetics. When the Commander takes Offred to the club, he first provides her with a new "uniform" of sequined, feathered lingerie. Moving through the crowd at Jezebel's, Offred is uncomfortable with the unusual sight of exposed female flesh and realizes that she, too, is on display:

> [The Commander] is showing me off, to them, and they understand that, they are decorous enough, they keep their hands to themselves, but they review my breasts, my legs, as if there's no reason why they shouldn't. But also he is showing off to me. He is demonstrating, to me, his mastery of the world. He is breaking the rules, under their noses, thumbing his nose at them, getting away with it. (248)

The Commander, who "retains hold of [Offred's] arm" as he displays her to the crowd, is also showing off his mastery of her. Being the object of the gaze means being in someone's power, especially in a society so highly controlled by surveillance. The mysterious surveillance force known only as the Eyes is perhaps the most powerful authority in all of Gilead; even upper-level members of the regime, including the Commander, fear their transgressions being "seen" by higher authorities—authorities that remain, significantly, unseen themselves. It is telling that Offred occasionally gains some power by manipulating the dynamics of the gaze. When she senses the young Guardians watching her, she realizes she has them in her thrall to some extent:

> I move my hips a little, feeling the full red skirt sway around me. It's like thumbing your nose from behind a fence or teasing a dog with a bone held out of reach. . . . I'm ashamed of myself for doing it. . . .
> Then I find I'm not ashamed after all. I enjoy the power: power of a dog bone, passive but there. (32)

The language used here is similar to Offred's description of the Commander "thumbing his nose" at the crowd at Jezebel's. Offred describes the Commander's behavior as a "juvenile display" of power, but a display she understands (248). Likewise, Offred's teasing of the Guardians is "passive," but it is a form of resistance and subversion nonetheless. Later, in her relationship with the Commander, Offred gains more power through witnessing the Commander's transgressions. Her shopping companion Ofglen recognizes this knowledge as real power and asks Offred to pass on any incriminating information to Mayday, the secret rebel organization.

Gilead's separation of men and women into mutually exclusive roles points to a system of binary divisions coded by gender. Feminist critics and theorists have explored how such binaries form the foundation of patriarchal societies, especially as they tend to promote a hierarchy in which one term, usually that coded as female, is subordinate to the other, usually that coded as male. Hélène Cixous demonstrates how oppositions such as father/mother, head/heart, and activity/passivity are gendered and assigned different status: "Logocentrism subjects thought—all concepts, codes and values—to a binary system, related to 'the' couple, man/woman" (91). Woolf gestures toward this organizational hierarchy in *A Room of One's Own*, when she realizes that "women have served all these centuries as looking-glasses possessing the magic and delicious power of reflecting the figure of man at twice its natural size" (32).

In her illegal relationship with the Commander, Offred's subordinate position serves to flatter the man and reinforce his power, as made evident in the scene at Jezebel's. The Commander's grip on her arm symbolizes his personal control and ownership of her, even as her body is put on public display. As both a "Jezebel" and a Handmaid, Offred is an accessory and object of patriarchal authority rather than a subject in her own right. Similarly, the women who work at Jezebel's find themselves in a subordinate position to the men who visit them. Like the Handmaids who hide butter or quietly tease the staring Guardians, their own subversions operate within a small range. These women are not confined by the blue gowns of the Wives or the red habits of the Handmaids, or by Econowives' and Marthas' lives of drudgery. The Jezebels can be sexually expressive to a point, and even have the opportunity to experience true affection and intimacy in relationships with each other. But, as Moira explains, the women—some former prostitutes, others former professionals and intellectuals—have little choice in being there: "Nobody gets out of here except in a black van" (255). To Offred, Moira's acceptance of this fate suggests an upsetting "lack of volition" (261). Offred wants to think of Moira as retaining her former agency and assertiveness: "I want gallantry from her, swashbuckling, heroism, single-handed combat" (255). But Moira has had to accept the passive role on the other side of this binary opposition: "Give in, go along, save her skin. That is what it comes down to" (261).

If men and women are separated by different levels of freedom and power, Gilead's social classifications work to separate women from each other, as well. The division between Handmaid and Jezebel recreates the classic dichotomy of angel and whore, opposing the sexually pure woman with the sexually promiscuous ("fallen," "ruined") one. The two terms are made absolute and mutually exclusive, denying the Handmaid sexual identity and the Jezebel moral principle. Some women are complicit in this system founded on absolute, gendered difference; even Aunt Lydia, we are told, is "in love with either/or" (18). The Aunts are represented ironically, of course. They are not nurturing maternal or sisterly figures, but rather operate as agents of Gilead's oppressive patriarchal regime, a "crack female control agency" (320).

The Wives, too, are enemies rather than companions. Their blue gowns, an allusion to the Virgin Mary, belie their position as rivals: to the infertile Wife, the Handmaid would seem a competitor for her husband's affection and sexual desire, and, ultimately, for the highly prized role of mother. The Commander's Wife, Serena Joy, is particularly malevolent. Offred tells us: "She doesn't speak to me, unless she can't avoid it. I am a reproach to her; and a necessity" (23). In a society that prizes children so highly, the Handmaid's role as surrogate mother breeds rivalry and tension. When Serena Joy finally discovers that the Commander has been taking Offred to Jezebel's, she accuses Offred of being "vulgar" and a "slut" (299). She must realize that Offred had little choice in the matter, and she unwittingly reveals the real cause of her resentment, telling Offred, "You could have left me something" (299).

Women of lower social rank are also enemies. Econowives resent the Handmaids' privileges and high social status, while Rita, one of the Marthas in the Commander's household, quietly judges the Handmaids. Rita's statement that "she wouldn't debase herself like that" (20) points to the unspoken fact that the sexually "pure" Handmaid is not that different from a mistress or prostitute. The Marthas, like the Wives, can share or withhold valuable information. Offred listens to kitchen gossip when she can, but Rita is tight-lipped about certain matters, including the fate of Offred's predecessor (we later learn she committed suicide). Similarly, Serena Joy uses information about Offred's birth daughter as a means of control. Even other Handmaids cannot fully be trusted. When completing errands in town, Offred and Ofglen test each other, unsure of the other's affiliations and beliefs. When a new Ofglen appears near the end of the novel, Offred soon senses she cannot trust her new companion. This "new, treacherous Ofglen" recognizes Offred's code word, "Mayday," but discourages further discussion, giving one of many sanctioned responses: "Under His Eye" (297). Like Offred, Ofglen's replacement might be too worried about spies to respond to Offred truthfully.

Thus, even women in the same position are divided from one another. Isolation fosters the culture of fear and reinforces the assimilation process initiated at the Red Center. Most important, it prevents solidarity among women. There is little opportunity in Gilead for collective political action; the feminist "sisterhood" of the past, in which Offred's mother played a significant role, is no more. Even when women are allowed to gather in groups—during Birthing, Salvaging, or Particicution ceremonies, for instance—these gatherings are highly ritualized and regulated. They are licensed outlets for emotional expression, what Professor Pieixoto calls "a steam valve for the female elements in Gilead" (320). During the Particicution ceremony near the end of Offred's story, we see how the presiding Aunt Lydia encourages the Handmaids to bond in anger and violence, and work together to attack an accused rapist. As Ofglen reveals, the man in question is not a rapist but a subversive agent working to liberate Gilead's female slaves. Here, the spontaneously formed women's collective becomes a mob controlled by the authorities, upholding the status quo and destroying their would-be savior rather than providing an opportunity for real expression or political action.

Those who oppose Gilead's patriarchal regime must find other ways to rebel against and undermine it. As discussed above, rebellion often works on an individual scale and through small gestures: in Offred's minor thefts of butter or sugar packets, for instance, or the furtive exchanges of information between Handmaids. Any large-scale movement must work secretly, beyond the vision of the Eyes and Commanders. We see this in the hidden "Underground Femaleroad" and in Mayday's careful placement of spies within the regime. But we might also interpret Offred's very narrative as an act of rebellion and protest. By recording her story, Offred reveals suppressed truths, passing on crucial information not only for other refugees of Gilead and the international community of the story but also for posterity, for the future readers and historians represented in the text's concluding "Historical Notes." As an important historical document, and as a tale that articulates forbidden truths and emotions, Offred's narrative gives a voice to the silenced, marginalized, and subjugated women of Gilead. *The Handmaid's Tale* tells their side of the story, becoming what feminist critics might call "herstory." In "Women and Fiction" (1929), Woolf observes that "very little is known of women. The history of England is the history of the male line, not of the female" (141). Information about women's writing and female experience, Woolf suggests, "lies at present locked in old diaries, stuffed away in old drawers . . . in those almost unlit corridors of history where the figures of generations of women are so dimly, so fitfully perceived" (141). Offred's narrative is a modernized version of the old diaries Woolf describes; hers is a disguised story, recorded between songs on cassette tapes and locked away in an old Army surplus box, only to be found and analyzed almost two centuries later. Feminist criticism of the 1970s and 1980s (significantly, the years that precede the Gilead regime in Atwood's novel) sought to uncover hidden stories not unlike Offred's and to establish the women's history Woolf outlines in "Women and Fiction." Studies such as Ellen Moers's *Literary Women* (1976) and Elaine Showalter's *A Literature of Their Own* (1977) examined and celebrated marginalized women writers, establishing a female literary tradition. In 2195 in *The Handmaid's Tale*, the work of Professor Pieixoto and other academics conducts a similar reconstruction of women's experiences and stories, and Offred's tale plays a key role in this.

This Handmaid's tale is what Adrienne Rich calls re-vision: "the act of looking back, of seeing with fresh eyes, of entering an old text from a new critical direction" (18). *The Handmaid's Tale* is a rewriting in many ways, drawing on the tropes of the gothic genre, satire, and the slave narrative to tell a new story about women's experience. As signified by the text's first epigraph, it is also a rewriting of Genesis. If the Gilead regime interprets the Bible to suit its own purposes, Offred's story enacts yet another reinterpretation and retelling, giving a voice to Bilhah, Rachel's handmaid in Genesis. The text has also been compared to George Orwell's *Nineteen Eighty-Four* (1949); both novels imagine a dystopian world controlled by surveillance, although *The Handmaid's Tale* recenters Orwell's story on a woman's experience in such a world rather than a man's. For Rich, the re-vision of familiar stories is "an act of survival" for women writers and women readers (18). This speaks to Offred's experience, which is very much an effort to survive. Telling her story is part of that effort. Indeed, Offred sometimes offers more than one version of events, and she calls attention to the constructed nature of her tale as it goes on. Like daydreaming of liberty or love, and like remembering her daughter and husband, telling stories is a coping strategy. It allows her to preserve a sense of hope but also to distance herself from the horrors of her reality:

> I would like to believe this is a story I'm telling. I need to believe it. I must believe it. Those who can believe that such stories are only stories have a better chance. (49)

The "story" in question is re-visionary in other ways, as well. It offers alternatives to Gilead's problematic definitions of women. In this sense, Offred's tale is what Rachel Blau DuPlessis calls a "displacement," a representation of "the other side of the story" that offers positive images of women (108). Offred's friend Moira, for instance, is often cast as a hero and rebel. Offred's mother, a feminist activist, is also seen in a heroic light as the narrative unfolds and Offred better understands her struggle for women's rights. Scenes of feminists marching in the streets and of Moira's daring escape attempt are beacons of hope, counternarratives to the grainy television image of Offred's mother enslaved in the Colonies, and to the final image of Moira as a resigned Jezebel. The narrative potentially positions Offred herself as a heroine, in that the discovery of her cassette tapes in Bangor, Maine, suggests she has escaped and survived to tell the tale.

As shown in the text's "Historical Notes" section, Offred's account ultimately functions as an alternative to the official history of Gilead. Conventional historical accounts strive for objectivity and factual truth, and typically focus on the macro scale; Offred's story is clearly a subjective, even autobiographical, account, and one that focuses on everyday, domestic reality. She is not the hidden, omniscient narrator of history textbooks, but rather a deeply unreliable storyteller. She admits to a limited knowledge of events, displays a problematic memory, and sometimes changes her story:

> If it's a story I'm telling, then I have control over the ending. Then there will be an ending, to the story, and real life will come after it. I can pick up where I left off.
> It isn't a story I'm telling.
> It's also a story I'm telling, in my head, as I go along. (49)

The text is thus a rewriting of history, a way of "telling it slant," to paraphrase Emily Dickinson. If the text challenges and revises familiar tales and images of women, it also confronts historiography, offering "herstory" instead. As Coral Ann Howells notes, "Offred's tale claims a space, a large autobiographical space, within the novel and so relegates the grand narratives [of the Bible, of history] to the margins as mere framework" (93). Just as Offred's own story offers multiple versions of events and multiple kinds of truth, the text as a whole presents "history" and "herstory" as competing but also equal discourses. This is another kind of re-vision, one DuPlessis calls "delegitimation." Unlike displacement, which gives the reader access to "other side of the story," delegitimation is an "active rupture of a narrative order" that highlights how "stories are ideologies that shape our sense of reality—indeed, that stories themselves can colonize" (112). In other words, delegitimation acknowledges the power that language has over us. In *The Handmaid's Tale*, language is shown to be a source of power, one as effective as the gaze. The Commander's illicit games of Scrabble are a metaphor for control over language and an acknowledgment of its potential. At first, the game seems to offer merely the thrill of the forbidden:

> This was once the game of old women, old men. . . . Now of course it's something different. Now it's forbidden, for us. Now it's dangerous. Now it's indecent. Now it's something he can't do with his Wife. (148-149)

Offred even compares the game to a fetish: Playing with words has become a replacement for the sexual taboos of the past. Yet, in Gilead, playing with words is much more than a game. Like telling one's story, it is a means of subversion and survival. The text is full of puns, codes, and gossip, all of which serve to pass on—or to hide—vital information. Offred's own narrative both passes on and disguises the truth. As Professor Pieixoto discusses, Offred has probably used pseudonyms, and she even disrupts the order of her own story by not labeling the cassette tapes. Nathalie Cooke argues that Offred is ultimately not in control of her own story, since Pieixoto's team creates the final, authoritative version: "In the war of words, Offred has lost" (131). Yet we might see the very elusiveness of Offred's tale as a final gesture of subversion. Her text resists closure and fixed meanings, defying the logical paradigms of historiography and the penetrating gaze of the reader, even some two centuries later. After all, as many critics have noted, even Atwood's post-Gilead society displays sexist tendencies, as seen most clearly in Professor Pieixoto's lewd pun on the Handmaid's "tail." The self-reflexive qualities of Offred's tale, and the way it draws attention to the plurality of meaning and the unreliability of any narrative, forces the reader to consider the effects of language in any context and to think about who is telling and retelling stories.

The Handmaid's Tale is exceptionally open-ended, lending itself to more than one feminist reading. In its explicit critique of gender inequalities and positive images of women, the text answers to the demands of academic feminist criticism. In its elusiveness and playfulness with meanings, it reflects a preoccupation with the instability of language and radical potential of rewriting and retelling, thus conforming to many feminist approaches. Yet the text is sometimes a satire of feminist politics, too, just as it is a satire of patriarchal ideology and authority. As Fiona Tolan observes, the terrifying Aunts "ironically echo the slogans of early utopian feminism": Aunt Lydia's society of "freedom from," though repressive and dystopian, is in some ways a solution to earlier problems of "freedom to" (Tolan 152-53). Atwood's images of women are not all positive, and the text does not always offer happy endings, as we see in the case of Moira. This does not detract from the novel's feminist import. On the contrary, *The Handmaid's Tale* illustrates that both positive and negative endings—like straightforward and elusive narratives—can highlight social injustice, criticize repressive ideologies, and prompt the reader to think about the effects and applications of language, especially as they relate to gender inequality.

Works Cited

Atwood, Margaret. *The Handmaid's Tale*. 1985. London: Virago, 1987.

Cixous, Hélène. "Sorties: Out and Out—Attacks/Ways Out/Forays." *The Feminist Reader*, ed. Catherine Belsey and Jane Moore. 2nd ed. Basingstoke: Macmillan, 1997. Pp. 91-103.

Cooke, Nathalie. *Margaret Atwood: A Critical Companion*. Westport, CT: Greenwood Press, 2004.

DuPlessis, Rachel Blau. *Writing Beyond the Ending: Narrative Strategies of Twentieth-Century Women Writers*. Bloomington: Indiana University Press, 1985.

Howells, Coral Ann. *Margaret Atwood*. 2nd ed. New York: Palgrave Macmillan, 2005.

Mulvey, Laura. "Visual Pleasure and Narrative Cinema." *Feminisms: An Anthology of Literary Theory and Criticism*, ed. Robyn R. Warhol and Diane Price Herndl. Rev. ed. Basingstoke: Macmillan, 1997. Pp. 438-448.

Rich, Adrienne. "When We Dead Awaken: Writing as Re-Vision." *College English* 34.1 (October 1972): 18-30.

Tolan, Fiona. *Margaret Atwood: Feminism and Fiction*. Amsterdam: Rodopi, 2007.

Woolf, Virginia. "Professions for Women." *A Room of One's Own/Three Guineas*. Ed. Michèle Barrett. London: Penguin, 1993, repr. 2000. Pp. 356-361.

_____. *A Room of One's Own/Three Guineas*. Ed. Michèle Barrett. London: Penguin, 1993, repr. 2000.

_____. "Women and Fiction." *Collected Essays*. Vol. 2. London: Hogarth, 1966. Pp. 141-148.

CRITICAL READINGS

The Handmaid's Tale
Coral Ann Howells

> My room, then. There has to be some space, finally, that I claim as mine, even in this time.
> —(Margaret Atwood, *The Handmaid's Tale*, p. 60)[1]

These words, spoken by Atwood's Handmaid, deprived of her own name and citizenship and known simply by the patronymic 'Offred', might be taken as emblematic of a woman's survival narrative told within the confines of a patriarchal system represented by the dystopia known as Gilead. Restricted to private domestic spaces and relegated to the margins of a political structure which denies her existence as an individual, nevertheless Offred asserts her right to tell her story. By doing so she reclaims her own private spaces of memory and desire and manages to rehabilitate the traditionally 'feminine' space assigned to women in Gilead. Atwood's narrative focuses on possibilities for constructing a form of discourse in which to accommodate women's representations of their own gendered identity while still acknowledging 'the power of the (male/'universal') space in which they cannot avoid, to some extent, operating'.[2] Like *Bodily Harm*, this is another eye-witness account by an 'ignorant, peripherally involved woman', this time interpolated within the grand patriarchal narratives of the Bible and of history, just as Offred's tale is enclosed within an elaborate structure of prefatory materials and concluding Historical Notes. However, her treasonable act of speaking out in a society where women are forbidden to read or write or to speak freely effects a significant shift from 'history' to 'herstory'. Offred's tale claims a space, a large autobiographical space, within the novel and so relegates the grand narratives to the margins as mere framework for her story, which is the main focus of interest. Storytelling is this woman's only possible gesture of resistance to imprisonment in silence, just as it becomes the primary means for her psychological survival. In the process of reconstructing herself as an individual, Offred becomes the most important historian of Gilead.

Since its publication in 1985, *The Handmaid's Tale* has become Atwood's most popular novel. It has been translated into more than thirty languages, made into a film by German director Volker Schloendorff and into an opera by Danish composer Poul Ruders. The novel that began as a satirical critique of religious and political trends in early 1980s North American society has slipped away from its historically specific context to become a political fable for our time, as if the present is rushing in to confirm Atwood's dire warnings about birth technologies, environmental pollution, human rights abuses, religious fanaticism, extreme right-wing political movements—and since 11 September 2001, international terrorism followed by the war in Iraq. In 2003, one reviewer of the opera commented on the novel's increasing relevance in today's world with its 'jostling theocracies and diminished civil liberties'.[3] A great deal of attention has been paid to it as dystopian science fiction and as a novel of feminist protest.[4] Certainly Atwood's abiding social and political concerns are evident here in her scrutiny of structures of oppression within public and private life, yet the novel exceeds its definition as feminist dystopia and it is not exactly science fiction,

> if by that you mean Martians, teleportation, or life on Venus. Nor is it a sort of travelogue of the future. It's the story of one woman under this regime, told in a very personal way, and part of the challenge for me was the creation of her voice and viewpoint.[5]

A critical reading which focuses attention on Offred as narrator, on her language and the structural features of her storytelling, might allow us to see how *The Handmaid's Tale* eludes classification, just as Offred's storytelling allows her to escape the prescriptive definitions of Gilead.

Nevertheless, the political dimensions of the dystopian model need to be considered in order to gauge the purpose of the fiction, while bearing in mind Atwood's definition of what 'politics' means: 'What we mean is how people relate to a power structure and vice versa' [in *Margaret Atwood: Conversations*, edited by Earl G. Ingersoll, 1992, p. 185]. Set in a futuristic United States at the beginning of the twenty-first century after a military coup has wiped out the President and the Congress, Gilead is a totalitarian regime run on patriarchal lines derived from the Old Testament and seventeenth-century American Puritanism plus a strong infusion of the American New Right ideology of the 1980s. Individual freedom of choice has been outlawed and everyone has been drafted into the service of the state, classified according to prescribed roles: Commanders, Wives, Aunts, Handmaids, Eyes, down to Guardians and Econowives. There is strict censorship and border control, as Offred reminds us in her recurrent nightmare memory of her failed escape to Canada with her husband and daughter, which has resulted in her being conscripted as a Gileadean Handmaid. The novel is an exposure of power politics at their most basic: 'Who can do what to whom'. Women are worst off because they are valued only as child-breeders in a society threatened with extinction where, because of pollution, AIDS and natural disasters, the national birthrate has fallen to a catastrophically low level. This essentialist definition of women as 'two-legged wombs' works entirely in the interests of a patriarchal elite, denying women any freedom of sexual choice or of lifestyle. Atwood's feminist concerns are plain here but so too are her concerns for basic human rights. Most men are oppressed in this society: there are male bodies hanging every day on the Wall, while homosexuals, Roman Catholic priests and Quakers of both sexes are regularly executed, and male sexual activity is severely restricted as well. A more comprehensive reading of the novel would suggest that it is closer to the new feminist scholarship, which has moved beyond exclusively female concerns to a recognition of the complexities of social gender construction. Offred's tale challenges essentialist definitions, whether patriarchal or feminist, showing not only how state sexual regulation criminalises male violence against women and suppresses women's sexuality but how it also militates against basic human desires for intimacy and love. As Offred reminds her Commander, Gilead's policies of social engineering have left out one crucial factor:

> Love, I said.
> Love? said the Commander. What kind of love?
> Falling in love, I said. (pp. 231-2)

The novel represents Atwood's version of 'What If' in the most powerful democracy in the world. She describes her dystopian project precisely, in an unpublished essay:

> It's set in the near future, in a United States which is in the hands of a power-hungry elite who have used their own brand of 'Bible-based' religion as an excuse for the suppression of the majority of the population. It's about what happens at the intersection of several trends, all of which are with us today: the rise of right-wing fundamentalism as a political force, the decline in the Caucasian birth rate in North America and northern Europe, and the rise in infertility and birth-defect rates, due, some say, to increased chemical-pollutant and radiation levels, as well as to sexually-transmitted diseases.[6]

When describing the origins of her book, Atwood has acknowledged a variety of influences both literary and historical, though always emphasising contemporary social issues and anxieties.[7] When she began thinking about the novel in the early 1980s she kept a clippings file (now in the Atwood Papers, University of Toronto Library) of items from newspapers and magazines which fed directly into her writing. These show her wide-ranging historical and humanitarian interests, where pamphlets from Friends of the Earth and Greenpeace sit beside Amnesty International reports of atrocities in Latin America, Iran and the Philippines, together with items of information on new reproductive technologies, surrogate motherhood, and forms of institutionalised birth control from Nazi Germany to Ceauşescu's Romania. It is to be noted that Gilead has a specifically American location, for Offred lives in the heartland of Gilead in a city that was formerly Cambridge, Massachusetts, and Harvard Campus (where Atwood was herself a student) has become the site for the Rachel and Leah Women's Re-education Centre, the setting for public rituals like Prayvaganzas and Particicutions, and Gilead's Secret Service headquarters. When asked why she had not set her novel in Canada, Atwood replied: 'The States are more extreme in everything.... Canadians don't swing much to the left or the right, they stay safely in the middle.... It's also true that everyone watches the States to see what the country is doing and might be doing ten or fifteen years from now' (*Conversations*, p. 223).

When we consider that the American religious right, or the 'New Right' as it was called in the 1980s, is one of Atwood's prime satiric targets, the location takes on a particular significance. The clippings file contains a lot of material on the New Right with its warnings about the 'Birth Dearth', its anti-feminism, its anti-homosexuality, its racism and its strong religious underpinnings in the Bible Belt.[8] Perhaps by coincidence one of the best known New Right studies (also in the Atwood papers) is a collection of essays, *The New Right at Harvard* (1983), edited by Howard Phillips, which refer to the desirability of building a coalition, 'a small dedicated corps' to 'resist the Liberal democracy' with its 'libertarian positions'. Chillingly the militaristic rhetoric of Gilead could already be heard at Harvard three years before *The Handmaid's Tale*, set in and around that university, was published. It is possible to read the novel as an oblique form of Canada-U.S. dialogue where a Canadian writer warns Americans about their possible future.

The Handmaid's Tale may be set in the future, but Gilead is a society haunted by the past, and there is continual tension between a collective social memory of life in late twentieth-century America, which has to be vilified and erased, and Gilead's new ideological reinterpretation of the nation's history. With its passion for 'traditional values' as a way of legitimating the repressive regime as thoroughly American, Gilead has adopted a peculiarly American version of religious fundamentalism which leans heavily on the country's Puritan inheritance. As Atwood explained, 'The mind-set of Gilead is really close to that of the seventeenth-century Puritans' (*Conversations*, p. 223). Atwood's interest in Puritan New England is signalled from the start in her dedication of the novel to Mary Webster and Perry Miller. Mary Webster was her own favourite ancestor, who was hanged as a witch in New England in 1683 but who survived her hanging and went free.[9] Professor Perry Miller, a great scholar of seventeenth-century Puritan history, was Atwood's Director of American Studies at Harvard. Much of the rhetoric and many of the cultural practices of Gilead are to be found in Miller's histories, such as the Founding Fathers' references to women as 'handmaids of the Lord' or Cotton Mather's description of a dissenting woman as 'an American Jezebel'. Gilead also employs many of the Puritan practices associated with childbirth, like the Birthing Stool, and the provision of refreshments at a birth which were known as 'groaning beer' and 'groaning cakes'.[10] While paying tribute to Miller's scholarship, Atwood shifts the emphasis from the seventeenth century to the twenty-first, showing how Gilead's attempt to reinvent Puritan history results in nothing better than antiquarianism and a grotesque parody of that history, and underlining the fundamentalist ideology of the regime.

Not only does Atwood satirise the New Right and its Puritan inheritance, but she also takes a critical look at North American feminism since the 1960s. As a feminist with a deep distrust of ideological hardlines, she refuses to simplify the gender debate or to swallow slogans whole, for slogans always run the risk of being taken over as instruments of oppression, like the late 1970s feminist phrase 'a women's culture', which Gilead has appropriated for its own purposes. It is significant that Gilead is a society 'in transition' where all the women are survivors of the time before, and their voices represent a range of feminine and feminist positions dating back to the Women's

Liberation Movement of the late 1960s. Offred's mother belongs to that early activist group, with its campaigns for women's sexual freedom, their pro-abortion rallies, and their 'Take Back the Night' marches. Thanks to the feminist movement, in the United States women gained an enormously widened range of life choices when equal rights and legalised abortion were endorsed by Congress in the early 1970s, though in 1982 the Equal Rights Amendment failed to be ratified, owing to the opposition of Pro-Life campaigners and fundamentalist Christians. These voices are represented by the Commanders' Wives and the terrible Aunts. Among the Handmaids (who are women of childbearing age who grew up in the 1980s and early 1990s) positions are equally varied, ranging from the classic female victim figure of Janine (later Ofwarren), to radical feminists like Moira the lesbian separatist, to Offred herself, who highlights the paradoxes and dilemmas of contemporary feminism. Offred, aged 33 at the time she tells her story, must have been born in the early 1970s, a date which would fit with her mother's feminist activities and the film about the Nazi's mistress that she sees at the age of eight; she would have been at university with Moira in the late 1980s.[11] Just as there are many different kinds of women, so there is no simple gender division between masculine and feminine qualities: if men are capable of violence then so are women—even the Handmaids themselves at the Particicution—and Aunt Lydia with her coyly feminine manner is probably the most sadistic character in the novel. *The Handmaid's Tale* may be a critique of feminism but it is a double-edged one which rejects binary oppositions, just as Offred's double vision allows her to evaluate both Gilead and her own, lost, late twentieth-century America. It is she, the witty heterosexual woman who cares about men, about mother-daughter relationships, and about her female friends, whose storytelling voice survives long after Gilead has been relegated to past history.

Offred's narrative forms the bulk of this novel, refiguring the space she can claim as her own within the confines of Gilead. *The Handmaid's Tale* is inner-space fiction or perhaps space-time fiction, for it deals with the continuities of memory and those persistent traces of social history that survive to undermine the authority of even the most repressive regime. Though trapped within a system where there would seem to be no room for individual freedom, Offred claims her own private space by her refusals; she refuses to forget the past, she refuses to believe in the absolute authority of Gilead, just as she refuses to give up hope in her anguished version of the Lord's Prayer: 'Then there's Kingdom, power, and glory. It takes a lot to believe in those right now. But I'll try it anyway. *In Hope*, as they say on the gravestones . . .' (p. 205).

Crucially Offred refuses to be silenced, as she speaks out with the voice of late twentieth-century feminist individualism, resisting the cultural identity imposed on her. She manages to lay claim to a surprising number of things which the system forbids: 'my own time' (p. 47), 'my room' (p. 60), 'my own territory' (p. 83), and even 'my name' (p. 94). She guards her lost name as the secret sign of her own identity and as guarantee of her hopes for a different future:

> I keep the knowledge of this name like something hidden, some treasure I'll come back to dig up, one day. I think of this name as buried . . . the name floats there behind my eyes, not quite within reach, shining in the dark. (p. 94)

Incidentally, this name is one of the secrets Offred keeps from the reader, though she does trust her lover Nick with it, and at the end the name acts as promise of a future beyond Gilead. One Canadian critic argues that Offred's real name is hidden in the text, there to be deduced from one name in the whispered list of Handmaids' names at the end of the first chapter: 'Alma. Janine. Dolores. Moira. June' (p. 14).[12]

Offred's assertion about the 'space I claim as mine' (p. 60) directly addresses questions about the feminine subject's position within a rigidly patriarchal system and a woman's possible strategies of resistance. Appropriating her temporary room in the Commander's house as her own, Offred makes her surprising declaration of freedom as she transforms that prison cell into an escape route out into the spaces of private memory:

> I lie, then, inside the room . . . and step sideways out of my own time. Out of time. Though this is time, nor am I out of it.
>   But the night is my time out. Where should I go? Somewhere good.
> (p. 47)

There is a surprising amount of mobility in this narrative as Offred in imagination moves out and away from Gilead. Her story induces a kind of double vision in the reader as well, for she is always facing both ways as she shifts between her present life and her past, or sometimes looks longingly towards the future.

In the face of state repression and domestic tyranny Offred manages to tell her wittily dissident tale about private lives, not only her own story but the stories of other women as well, all of them willing or unwilling victims of the Gileadean regime and so in some sense her own doubles. Appropriating their remembered turns of phrase, Offred's storytelling voice multiplies to become the voices of 'women' rather than the voice of a single narrator. There is the story of Moira the rebel, who spectacularly defies the power of the Aunts and escapes from the rehabilitation centre, only to reappear in the brothel scene at Jezebel's, where she satirises male sexual fantasies by looking totally ridiculous as a Bunny Girl with a floppy ear and a draggly tail. There is also the story of Ofglen, Offred's shopping partner and member of the secret Mayday resistance, who finally hangs herself, and Offred's unnamed predecessor at the Commander's house, who scratched a secret message in the wardrobe before hanging herself from the light fitting in the room Offred now occupies. The blank space where the fitting has been removed is seen by Offred as a 'wreath' or a 'frozen halo' (p. 17) as she comes to regard that absent woman as her own dark double. She also tells the stories of older women like her mother, the old-fashioned

Women's Libber condemned by the Gileadean regime as an Unwoman and sent to the Colonies to die, but who refuses to stay dead. Instead she reappears to Offred and to Moira, preserved on film at the rehabilitation centre, and haunts her daughter's memory. By contrast, there is the story of the Commander's Wife, whom Offred remembers from the time before as 'Serena Joy', a popular gospel television show personality, now trapped within the New Right ideology that she had helped to promote: 'She stays in her home, but it doesn't seem to agree with her. How furious she must be, now that she's been taken at her word' (p. 56). Sitting in her beautiful enclosed garden in her blue gown, Serena appears to Offred like an ageing parody of the Virgin Mary, childless, arthritic and snipping vengefully at her flowers. All these women are casualties of the system, though perhaps the saddest figure of all is Janine, a female victim in both her lives. Gang-raped in the time before Gilead, she becomes the Handmaid Ofwarren, who produces the required baby only to have it condemned to death as a 'shredder'. When Offred sees Janine for the last time, after the Particicution, she has become a madwoman, a 'woman in free fall' drifting around grasping a clump of the murdered man's bloodstained blond hair.

Combined with fragments of gossip overheard from the Wives and the Marthas, Offred's story presents a mosaic of alternative female worlds which undermine Gilead's patriarchal myth of women's submissiveness and silence, though it must be said that women's chances of survival are slim, and many of the stories remain unfinished so that we never know what happened to most of these women.

Offred describes her narrative as 'this limping and mutilated story', using that metaphor to refer both to its structure and to the violent social conditions out of which it is told:

> I'm sorry there is so much pain in this story. I'm sorry it's in fragments, like a body caught in crossfire or pulled apart by force. But there is nothing I can do to change it. (p. 279)

Composed of isolated scenic units with gaps and blanks in between where the episodes drift free of present time, the fragmented narrative represents the mental processes of someone in Offred's isolated situation as her mind jumps between vividly realised present details and flashbacks to the past. Offred's narrative self-consciousness is also one of the identifiably postmodern features of her narrative, for she is continually drawing our attention to her storytelling process, commenting on the ways this telling shapes and changes real experience, giving reasons why she needs to tell her story at all, and reminding readers that she may not always be a reliable narrator as she recounts what happened in Gilead. At the time, she tells it in her head in order to survive by seeing beyond the present moment where she does not wish to be, and also because she needs to believe there is still someone outside Gilead who is listening to her: 'Because I'm telling you this story, I will your existence. I tell, therefore you are' (p. 279). Storytelling becomes a substitute for dialogue, though Offred also likens her narrative reconstruction to a letter addressed to '*Dear You . . . You* can mean thousands' (p. 50). It takes a couple of hundred years for her letter to be delivered, when it is presented (in a third reconstruction) at a Symposium on Gileadean Studies long after the regime has become ancient history. Through this radical dislocation the reader's own position in time becomes ambiguous, for we are reading in a fictive future that bears an uncomfortable resemblance to our present society.

Offred's story is incomplete and her account of life in Gilead is in danger of being overlaid by a male professor's academic reconstruction at the end, yet it is her voice, coming through the transcribed tapes, which gives the narrative its interest and continuity. This is history in the feminine gender, addressed directly to its listeners:

> I wish this story were different . . . I wish it were about love, or about sudden realizations important to one's life, or even: about sunsets, birds, rainstorms, or snow.

Maybe it is about those things, in a sense; but in the meantime there is so much else getting in the way. (p. 279)

Though Offred may adopt a conventionally feminine tone here of wistful apology and sentimentality, she slips into an entirely different register when speaking about her own body in her challenge to Gilead's doctrines of biological essentialism. Her tale is as profoundly subversive as Hélène Cixous's feminist text of the mid-1970s, 'The Laugh of the Medusa', with which it has much in common as a project to inscribe the complex dimensions of female being.[13] Atwood's novel enacts in practice what Cixous's essay proposes as theory, for Offred is Cixous's woman 'confined to the narrow room' and 'given a deadly brainwashing' but who becomes the 'I-woman, escapee', 'breaking out of the snare of silence' to 'write herself'. (The vocabulary here is entirely taken from 'Medusa'.) Offred's situation might be read as a literal translation of Cixous's highly metaphorical text, except that Atwood is sceptical of any utopian vision of woman's glorious liberation from the shackles of patriarchy. Offred is not a revolutionary; she refuses to join the Mayday resistance movement in Gilead and she does not want to adopt Moira's separatist feminism, though she admires her friend's recklessness and swashbuckling heroism. Her own position is much closer to the traditionally feminine role of woman as social mediator, for though she resists the brutal imposition of male power in Gilead she also remembers the delights of heterosexual love and her story is about love, with a strong traditional female romance component. It is symptomatic of Offred's non-confrontational role that though she finally defeats the Commander's assurance of male superiority, she herself is not in a commanding position at the end (unlike the film version, where she murders the Commander and escapes). Led out of his house as a prisoner and feeling guilty at having let down the household, she has no idea whether she is going to her death or towards a new life of freedom when she steps up into the Black Van. Offred fails to make Cixous's 'shattering entry into history'; on the contrary, she never finishes her story and her voice is almost drowned out by the voice of a male historian.

However, Offred's story is a 'reconstruction' in more senses than one, for not only is it her narrative of memory but it is also the means by which she rehabilitates herself as an individual in Gilead. Though she begins her tale as a nameless woman traumatised by loss and whispering in the dark, Offred refuses to believe that she is nothing but a Handmaid, 'a two-legged womb': 'I am alive, I live, I breathe, I put my hand out, unfolded, into the sunlight' (p. 18). She insists on chronicling her subjective life from within her own skin, offering her own personal history of physical sensation and emotion, together with those imaginative transformations through which body space opens out into fantasy landscape. According to Cixous's prescription, 'By writing herself [or in Offred's case "speaking herself"] woman will return to the body which has been more than confiscated from her, which has been turned into the uncanny stranger on display' ('Medusa', p. 250). This is for Offred the uncanny shape of the red-robed Handmaid. Indeed, it is from within this role that Offred finds her strength to resist, for just as Gilead is obsessed with the female body and its reproductive system so Offred silently talks back to those patriarchal prescriptions in Atwood's version of *écriture féminine*. Cixous asserts that the 'dark continent' of the female body is neither dark nor unexplorable and Offred answers that challenge, using similar images of immense bodily territories, volcanic upheavals and the Medusa's own subversive laughter. On the evening of the monthly Ceremony of sexual intercourse with the Commander (a time when her body would seem least of all to be her own), Offred becomes the explorer of her own dark inner space:

> I sink down into my body as into a swamp, fenland, where only I know the footing. Treacherous ground, my own territory. I become the earth I set my ear against, for rumours of the future. . . . Each month I watch for blood, fearfully, for when it comes it means failure. I have failed once again to fulfil the expectations of others, which have become my own. (p. 83)

With her minute attention to physical details, Offred chronicles her bodily awareness and her shifts of perspective under the influence of cultural doctrines which have effected a change in her imaginative conceptualisation of her self. No longer a 'solid object, one with me', her body has become a 'cloud' surrounding the dark inner space of her womb, whose dimensions expand till it becomes Cixous's 'immense astral space' or Atwood's cosmic wilderness, 'huge as the sky at night and dark and curved like that, though black-red, rather than black'. Her meditation offers a kind of imaginative transcendence though without Cixous's promise of erotic pleasure, for Offred knows that she is nothing more in Gilead than a breeding machine serving the state. What Offred experiences is a sense of dissolution within her body as every month its only issue is menstrual blood: 'To feel that empty again, again. I listen to my heart, wave upon wave, salty and red, continuing on and on, marking time' (p. 84). This is the hidden female space where time is kept by the body: 'I tell time by the moon. Lunar, not solar' (p. 209), though 'marking time' also reminds Offred that time is running out and she will be sent to the Colonies if she does not soon produce a child. Offred's condition is one of compromised resistance, where she regrets not becoming pregnant as the system requires of her ('*Give me children, or else I die*' has more than one meaning for a Handmaid, as she ironically remarks), while at the same time she steadily resists Gilead's imposition of control over her mind.

Yet it would be wrong to forget the comic dimension in this novel, for Offred's simmering humour bubbles up at the most inappropriate times, and she can hardly contain her laughter the first time the Commander invites her to play an illicit game of Scrabble with him. The game provides her with the welcome opportunity to play with words, and her image of the Scrabble counters as candies, which she would like to put into her mouth, makes a beautifully literal equivalent for Cixous's metaphor of women's seizing language 'to make it hers, containing it, taking it into her mouth' ('Medusa', p. 257).[14] As soon as she gets back to her room, we hear the muffled explosion of her own Medusa laughter:

> Then I hear something, inside my body. I've broken, something has cracked, that must be it. Noise is coming up, coming out, of the broken place, in my face. . . . My ribs hurt with holding back, I shake, I heave, seismic, volcanic, I'll burst. Red all over the cupboard, mirth rhymes with birth, oh to die of laughter. (p. 156)

Her language at this point displays a disturbing mixture of merriment and hysteria, tinged with irony. She likens her laughter to an epileptic fit, and the images she uses are not simply about loss of control but also about bodily damage. Standing in the cupboard scrawled with her hanged predecessor's secret message, Offred is aware that she too, like that other Handmaid, is trapped: 'There's no way out of here.' Yet her irrepressible energy impels her towards life rather than death, as she listens to her heartbeat 'opening and closing, opening' (p. 156).

Offred keeps adapting Gilead's patriarchal script as she tells her autobiographical narrative, for like the flowers in the Commander's Wife's garden, her silent discourse of resistance is dynamic, lyrical, and as difficult to stop as a natural process:

> There is something subversive about this garden of Serena's, a sense of buried things bursting upwards, wordlessly, into the light, as if to point, to say: Whatever is silenced will clamour to be heard, though silently. (p. 161)

The summer garden provides a sublimated image of Offred's own repressed desires, but more than that it becomes suddenly and overwhelmingly the space of romantic fantasy, a 'Tennyson garden, heavy with scent, languid; the return of the word *swoon*' (p. 161), where traditional images of femininity breathe through Offred's prose as the garden itself 'breathes, in the warmth, breathing itself in. To walk through it in these days, of peonies, of pinks and carnations, makes my head swim.' In this eroticised feminine space conjured by Offred's imagination, everything signifies romance, temptation and desire. For her it is a pagan garden of delights, presided over by goddesses and not by a faded version of the Virgin Mary like Serena, as she riots verbally in her rhapsody of the flesh. Of course it is characteristic of Offred's ironic self-awareness that she should see round her fantasy even while revelling in it, wryly recognising that such excess is at least in part a sublimation of her sexual frustrations, where longing generates its own scenarios. Yet it is the very intensity of her desire which allows Offred for a moment to transcend her human limits and to enter into the life of the pulsating organic world around her, 'as if I'm a melon on a stem, this liquid ripeness' (p. 162). Offred's language runs in harmony with Cixous's *écriture féminine*, where images of desire deriving from the human body and the natural world constitute a 'feminine' alternative language which resists Gilead's polluted technological nightmare and its compromised 'biblico-capitalist rhetoric' ('Medusa', p. 257).

Offred's text is truly self-seeking as she tries to win back 'her womanly being, her goods and her pleasures' ('Medusa', p. 250), which have been stolen from her. Appropriately enough, it is through her body that Offred finds her way to emotional survival, for in the unpropitious circumstances of Gilead she falls in love—not with the Commander, whose image is irretrievably tainted with patriarchal authority, but with Nick his chauffeur. She turns a situation of coercion into a love story during her secret meetings with Nick, which are arranged by the Commander's Wife solely for the purposes of making her pregnant. In a curious way, Offred's re-visioning of Gilead's dystopian plot looks like a cultural survival of 'the time before' when 'falling in love' was the fashion, for this forbidden love story follows a traditional romance plot, with its strong undercurrent of sexual magnetism leading the heroine into dangerous territory with a dark stranger who turns out to be her rescuing hero at the end. That Offred is aware of such conventionality is evident in the triple versions through which she tells the story of their illicit affair (p. 273), but there is no doubt that falling in love is for her an act of survival. This reawakening of sexual desire releases her into what Cixous has called 'the marvellous text of herself' as she allows Nick to read her body:

> He seems indifferent to most of what I have to say, alive only to the possibilities of my body, though he watches me while I'm speaking. He watches my face. (p. 282)

By a double irony, that love relationship achieves precisely the goals which Gilead intended and that Offred has resisted for so long. She becomes pregnant and she is reconciled to staying where she is: 'The fact is that I no longer want to leave, escape, cross the border to freedom. I want to be here, with Nick, where I can get at him' (p. 283).

Offred may try to refashion the social rules of Gilead into a private utopia (though she knows that 'this is a delusion of course', p. 281) but dystopian conventions dominate the plot, and the love story is cut short through a series of violent events and discoveries which reaffirm Gilead's control over life and death. The romance plot is put to a crucial test when one day Nick bursts into Offred's room accompanied by a party of Eyes (secret police), to take her away in the dreaded Black Van reserved for dissidents. Is this a betrayal or a rescue? Offred does not have the faintest idea and she realises that she knows so little about Nick that 'trust' is, ironically, all that she is left with: 'Trust me, he says, which in itself has never been a talisman, carries no guarantee' (p. 306). Her narrative ends with Offred laying herself open to all risks and all possibilities as she departs from the Commander's house like a criminal under guard and climbs into the van:

> I have given myself over into the hands of strangers, because it can't be helped.
> And so I step up, into the darkness within; or else the light. (p. 307)

Offred's own story ends when she climbs into the Black Van, but the novel does not end here. There is also a supplement in the Historical Notes, told by a different narrator in a different place and at a different time, setting one woman's private autobiographical record in a wider historical context, and incidentally suggesting that she was indeed rescued by Nick. These Notes are a transcript of a lecture given by a Cambridge Professor, Darcy Pieixoto, at an academic symposium on Gileadean Studies held in the year 2195 at the University of Denay, Nunavit, in Arctic Canada, long after the regime has fallen and Offred is dead.[15] It is this professor who is responsible for the transcription of the story we have just finished reading, because it turns out that Offred's story was recorded on cassette tapes, which he has edited and entitled 'The Handmaid's Tale' in 'homage to the great Geoffrey Chaucer' (p. 312). Already the voice of the male historian threatens to drown out Offred's voice, for Pieixoto is not at all concerned with her as an individual but is preoccupied with establishing the authenticity of her tale and its value as objective historical evidence. His reconstruction effects a radical shift from 'herstory' to 'history' as he attempts to discredit Offred's narrative by accusing her of not paying attention to significant events. In response, the reader may feel that it is the professor who is paying attention to the wrong things, for the historical facts that Pieixoto selects as significant effectively erase Offred from the Gileadean narrative: of the twelve pages of his account a mere one and a half pages are devoted to her, and her fate 'remains obscure'. In fact, he does exactly what Offred feared history would do to the Handmaids: 'From the point of view of future history, we'll be invisible' (p. 240).[16]

The abrupt shift from Offred's voice to the historian's voice challenges the reader on questions of interpretation. We have to remember that *The Handmaid's Tale* was Offred's transcribed speech, reassembled and edited by a male historian and not by her. Her tale has been appropriated by an academic, who seems to forget that his reconstruction is open to questions of interpretation too. He is abusing Offred as Gilead abused her, removing her authority over her own life story and renaming it in a gesture that parallels Gilead's patriarchal suppression of a woman's identity in the Handmaid's role. No wonder the professor claims to have lost Offred, as like Eurydice's ghost 'she slips from our grasp and flees' (p. 324), though he is quite wrong to accuse her of not answering him, when he has refused to listen to what she has been saying. The challenge of interpretation is finally directed out to the readers, who have heard the story in its multiple reconstructions. Finally, I would suggest that just as Offred's story has shown up the limits of Gilead's autocratic power to control the subjective lives of at least two of its inhabitants, so it defies Pieixoto's appropriation two centuries later. This may look like a case of the 'disappearing author', though that is a postmodern position that Atwood vigorously resists ('Deny None of It') in the interests of our shared moral responsibility. By telling her story Offred has put herself 'into the world and into history', challenging readers to connect her world with our own in the present, in the hope of averting a nightmare like Gilead for our own future.

From *Margaret Atwood* (New York: Palgrave Macmillan, 2005): 93-109. Copyright © 2005 by Palgrave Macmillan. Reprinted by permission of Palgrave Macmillan.

Notes

1. Margaret Atwood, *The Handmaid's Tale* (London: Vintage, 1996). All further page references will be to this edition and included in the text.

2. Linda Hutcheon, *The Canadian Postmodern* (Toronto: Oxford University Press, 1988), p. 110.

3. *Guardian* Review, 26 April 2003, p. 23.

4. For discussions of dystopian and feminist elements, see Krishan Kumar, *Utopianism* (Milton Keynes: Open University Press, 1991); Lynette Hunter, '"That Will Never Do": Public History and Private Memory in *Nineteen Eighty-Four* and *The Handmaid's Tale*', in Marta Dvorak (ed.), *The Handmaid's Tale: Margaret Atwood* (Paris: Ellipses, 1998), pp. 19-29; C. A. Howells, 'Transgressing Genre: A Generic Approach to Atwood's Novels', in R. M. Nischik (ed.), *Margaret Atwood: Works and Impact* (New York: Camden House, 2000), pp. 139-56.

5. Margaret Atwood Papers, MS Collection 200, University of Toronto, '*The Handmaid's Tale*: Before and After', November 1986, Box 96: Folder 11.

6. Atwood Papers, MS Collection 200.

7. 'Genesis of *The Handmaid's Tale* and Role of the Historical Notes', in J.-M. Lacroix, J. Leclaire and J. Warwick (eds), *The Handmaid's Tale: Roman Protéen* (Rouen: Presses Universitaires de Rouen, 1999), pp. 7-14; Margaret Reynolds, 'Interview with Margaret Atwood', in M. Reynolds and J. Noakes (eds), *Margaret Atwood: The Essential Guide* (London: Vintage, 2002), pp. 11-25. Interview also available on Random House website: www.randomhouse.com.

8. Zillah R. Eisenstein, 'The Sexual Politics of the New Right: Understanding the "Crisis of Liberalism" for the 1980s', in N. O. Keohane, M. Z. Rosaldo and B. C. Gelpi (eds), *Feminist Theory: A Critique of Ideology* (Brighton: Harvester, 1982), pp. 77-98; Priscilla Ollier Morin, '*The Handmaid's Tale* and American Protestant Fundamentalism', in M. Dvorak (ed.), *Lire Margaret Atwood: The Handmaid's Tale* (Rennes: Presses Universitaires de Rennes, 1999), pp. 33-46.

9. Margaret Atwood, 'Witches', in *Second Words: Selected Critical Prose* (Toronto: Anansi, 1982), pp. 329-33.

10. See Mark Evans, 'Versions of History: *The Handmaid's Tale* and Its Dedicatees', in Colin Nicholson (ed.), *Margaret Atwood: Writing and Subjectivity* (Basingstoke: Macmillan; New York: St Martin's Press, 1994), pp. 177-88.

11. Lee Thompson cites Atwood's manuscript notation of Offred's birth date as 1978 though, significantly, Atwood has crossed it out. See Lee Briscoe Thompson, *Scarlet Letters: The Handmaid's Tale* (Toronto: ECW Press, 1997), p. 36.

12. Constance Rooke, 'Interpreting *The Handmaid's Tale*: Offred's Name and "The Arnolfini Marriage"', in *Fear of the Open Heart* (Toronto: Coach House, 1989), pp. 175-96.

13. Hélène Cixous, 'The Laugh of the Medusa' (1976), trans. Keith and Paula Cohen, repr. in *New French Feminisms: An Anthology*, ed. E. Marks and I. de Courtivron (Brighton: Harvester, 1981), pp. 245-54. All further page references to Cixous's essay will be taken from this edition and included in the text.

14. See Marta Dvorak, '"What's in a Name?" Readers as Both Pawns and Partners, or Margaret Atwood's Strategy of Control', in J.-M. Lacroix and J. Leclaire (eds), *Margaret Atwood: The Handmaid's Tale/Le Conte de la servante: The Power Game* (Paris: Presses de la Sorbonne Nouvelle, 1998), pp. 79-97.

15. The name Denay, Nunavit, clearly signals the Canadian location of this second futuristic scenario, for Nunavut is the name of Canada's first aboriginal self-governing territory, which in the 1980s was scheduled to come into existence in 1999. This has now happened.

16. In the context, the choice of Pieixoto's name is significant. At a conference in Rouen, France, in 1998, Atwood revealed that she had found the Portuguese name in a Brazilian novel, referring to a man who keeps being reincarnated in the same form century after century. Pieixoto exemplifies the same sexist values as the Gilead regime, who modelled themselves on the Old Testament patriarchs.

Suggestions for Further Reading

Atwood, Margaret, 'Witches', in *Second Words: Selected Critical Prose* (Toronto: Anansi, 1982; repr. 1996), pp. 329-33.

Cixous, Hélène, "The Laugh of the Medusa," in *New French Feminisms: An Anthology*, ed. E. Marks and I. de Courtivron (Brighton: Harvester, 1981), pp. 245-54.

Dvorak, Marta, 'What's in a Name? Readers as Both Pawns and Partners, or Margaret Atwood's Strategy of Control', in J.-M. Lacroix and J. Leclaire (eds), *Margaret Atwood: The Handmaid's Tale/Le Conte de la servante: The Power Game* (Paris: Presses de la Sorbonne Nouvelle, 1998), pp. 79-97.

Howells, Coral Ann, 'Transgressing Genre: A Generic Approach to Atwood's Novels', in Reingard M. Nischik (ed.), *Margaret Atwood: Works and Impact* (New York: Camden House, 2000), pp. 139-56.

Hunter, Lynette, '"That Will Never Do": Public History and Private Memory in *Nineteen Eighty-Four* and *The Handmaid's Tale*', in Marta Dvorak (ed.), *The Handmaid's Tale: Margaret Atwood* (Paris: Ellipses, 1998), pp. 19-29.

Reynolds, Margaret and J. Noakes (eds), *Margaret Atwood: The Essential Guide* (London: Vintage, 2002).

Thompson, Lee Briscoe, *Scarlet Letters: The Handmaid's Tale* (Toronto: ECW Press, 1997).

"Trust Me":
Reading the Romance Plot in
Margaret Atwood's *The Handmaid's Tale*_____
Madonne Miner

Midway through Margaret Atwood's *Handmaid's Tale*, the Commander sends a message to his wife's handmaid, Offred, that she is to meet him that evening in his study. Imagining that the Commander may ask her to engage in some kind of forbidden sexual activity, Offred is surprised when he expresses his desire: "'I'd like you to play a game of Scrabble with me'" (179). As the Commander takes the Scrabble box from his desk drawer and dumps out the counters, Offred realizes that this game is forbidden sexual activity. Under the Commander's watchful eye, Offred, no longer allowed to read or write, takes up the wooden counters, delicious, "like candies, made of peppermint, cool like that," and shapes them into luxurious words: "*Larynx*, I spell. *Valance. Quince. Zygote*" (180).

On subsequent evenings, Offred and the Commander repeat their game. Initially, she moves slowly: "My tongue felt thick with the effort of spelling. It was like using a language I'd once known but had nearly forgotten, a language having to do with customs that had long before passed out of the world" (199). During early meetings, Offred and the Commander obey the rules of the game, of the language. When Offred, for example, spells "Zilch" ("A convenient one-vowel word with an expensive Z" [238]), the Commander challenges her, and she suggests "'We could look it up. . . . It's archaic'" (238). But as time passes, these two Scrabble players begin to alter the game. After a few drinks, the Commander "becomes silly, and cheats at Scrabble. He encourages me to do it too, and we take extra letters and make words with them that don't exist, words like *smurt* and *crup*, giggling over them" (271).

I suggest that in this sequence, and various others throughout *The Handmaid's Tale*, we readers receive instructions in the reading process, lessons in how to construct meaning out of disparate pieces. Like Offred, we obey a grammar, a set of rules, as we put together episodes, make chains ("words") out of segments of *The Handmaid's Tale*. First, Offred's words must belong to that club of words adjudged legitimate by a dictionary; our readings are similarly legitimized by signs of their membership in acceptable schools/traditions of reading. Second, when composing words, Offred must restrict herself to letters she draws from those spread out on the desktop; similarly, we are to compose our readings of *The Handmaid's Tale* relying upon what is "in" the text. But finally, just as Offred and the Commander "bend the rules" to allow for a more freewheeling creativity, so too we may find that "taking up extra letters" and playing with seemingly bizarre connections actually may lead us to some new understandings of the text.

The Handmaid's Tale worries over the plight of women in a society governed by religious fundamentalists committed to bolstering a seriously low birthrate (the result of toxic wastes, acid rain, and other environmental disasters which lead to sterility). In this "Republic of Gilead," fertile women are trained to serve as handmaids to infertile ones; each month, upon ovulation, the handmaid copulates with her mistress's husband (a Commander) and prays "let there be fruit." If conception occurs, the handmaid receives assistance in her labor and delivery from other handmaids, and then surrenders the child to her mistress. Having given birth successfully, the handmaid can rest assured that she will not be sent to the Colonies, where "unwomen" clean up toxic dumps and radiation spills.

Most readings of *The Handmaid's Tale* approach the text, quite rightly, as a dystopic novel, a cautionary vision of what might happen if certain attitudes are carried to extremes. Reactions to the *Tale* focus on its horrific presentation of "theocratic ambitions of the religious right," on its understanding of the sinister implications of an exaggerated cultural feminism (Ehrenreich 156), and on its critique of our own gender arrangements (Gileadean "solutions" highlight the problematic nature of sexual/social interactions in the 1980s). Many of these reactions also posit love as a force subverting Gilead's power. Coral Ann Howells, for example, argues that "heterosexual love is the excess term which the system can neither accommodate nor suppress. Its stubborn survival continually subverts the regime's claims to absolute authority, creating imaginative spaces within the system and finally the very means of Offred's escape from Gilead" (69). In like fashion, Barbara Ehrenreich maintains that in *The Handmaid's Tale*, "as in *1984*, the only truly subversive force appears to be love" (34). And Amin Malak suggests that as the novel "upholds and cherishes a man-woman axis" (15), it enables its heroine to progress from "helpless victim" to "sly, subversive survivor." These reactions to the text make sense; but I argue that if we pay attention to the *Tale*'s own statements about signifying systems and the construction of meaning, we may put together other readings, readings that further complicate the political signification of love in the novel. In the pages that follow, I "play Scrabble" with three "counters" from *The Handmaid's Tale*: Offred's relationship with Luke, with the Commander, and with Nick. Moving these counters, occasionally superimposing them, I suggest that the novel expresses real ambivalence about its characters' enactment of "the love story." As much as we readers may want to posit love as a revolutionary force, we must attend to the novel's statements about love's tendency to follow decidedly conservative narrative forms.

In *The Handmaid's Tale*'s first few sentences, Offred describes her situation at the Rachel and Leah Center:

> We slept in what had once been the gymnasium. The floor was of varnished wood, with stripes and circles painted on it, for the games that were formerly played there. . . . I thought I could smell, faintly like an afterimage, the pungent scent of sweat, shot through with the sweet taint of chewing gum and perfume from the watching girls. . . . Dances would have been held there; the music lingered, a palimpsest of unheard sound, style upon style. (3)

This suggestive mixing of past and present typifies speculative fiction, which most often generates other worlds as comment upon our own.[1] Such fiction raises questions not only about what might happen, but also about what is happening. Certainly, *The Handmaid's Tale* belongs to this genre; but to a greater extent than many other speculative novels, *The Handmaid's Tale* also asks questions about how we put together future, present, and past, how we construct meaningful connections across time and place. Offred's description above, for example, insinuates connections between past basketball games and the "games" to which Offred and her fellow handmaids are subjected, between past "dances" (sexual interactions) and those performed by the handmaids. As the novel proceeds, however, it insists upon probing the nature of these connections. In what ways are they arbitrary, and if arbitrary, how meaningful can they be? If such connections resemble those between layers of writing on a palimpsest, can we claim significance for readings moving both forward and backward between layers? What about those readings that move across a layer, picking up resemblances between discrete units (in the above quote, for example, between the smells of sweat, chewing gum, and perfume)? Attempting to "compose" herself and her world, Offred cannot escape these questions. Nor can we, who attempt to "compose" some kind of reading of *The Handmaid's Tale*.

Offred confronts such questions several times in the novel, but I want to look closely at just two such moments as introduction to my larger claims about how we might read the novel. The first moment occurs early on, as Offred describes a typical walk she takes with her "double," Ofglen. The two women do their shopping, then pause before "the wall" where bodies of traitors are hung on display, the heads covered with white bags. Blood stains one of these bags, blood that seeps from the dead man's mouth and takes the shape of "another mouth, a small red one, like the mouth painted with thick brushes by kindergarten children" (43). Offred finds herself drawn to the red mark, and she meditates on its connection with other red marks:

I look at the one red smile. The red of the smile is the same as the red of the tulips in Serena Joy's garden, towards the base of the flowers where they are beginning to head. The red is the same but there is no connection. The tulips are not tulips of blood, the red smiles are not flowers, neither thing makes a comment on the other. The tulip is not a reason for disbelief in the hanged man, or vice versa. Each thing is valid and really there. It is through a field of such valid objects that I must pick my way, every day and in every way. I put a lot of effort into making such distinctions. I need to make them. I need to be very clear, in my own mind. (44-45)

Although we might accept Offred's assertion that "each thing is valid and really there," I think we must question her claim that "there is no connection" between the red of the blood and the red of Serena's tulips.[2] Obviously, Offred herself sees a connection; she yokes the two together metaphorically: the red is the same. Thinking about the red of a smile and that of tulips, we might argue that at least superficially, both items suggest a type of sensual pleasure; both convey positive connotations. But we can sustain this positive reading only as long as we repress the source of the red; the smile of the hanged man is a smile of blood. This fact must then push us to ask about the source of the tulips' redness; metaphorically, it is the blood of other women that allows Serena the time to cultivate her colors. In other words, for some women to enjoy the freedom of playing with red flowers, other women must wear the red of handmaids.

Although Offred herself enjoys the flowers, they, like the bloody smile of the hanged man, signify her own dismal state; as beautiful as they may be, they finally are only "fruiting bod[ies]," subject to the breeding policy of their gardener. Later in the novel when Offred comes upon Serena, shears in hand, snipping at the seedpods of the tulips, Offred wonders: "Was it . . . some blitzkrieg, some kamikaze, committed on the swelling genitalia of the flowers? The fruiting body" (195). This elaboration on the flowers as fruiting bodies points us once more to connections between the flowers and Offred.

Thus, once having suggested a connection between flowers and the bloody smile of a dead man, Offred cannot stop a flowering of associations unless, like Serena, she takes a kitchen shears and insists upon dissection—which is precisely what she does. Why does she retreat from relationships of similarity? As if anticipating such a question, Offred insists that she *needs* to make distinctions, needs to be very clear. But such insistence provides no real answer and so again we ask why, and ask what kind of clarity Offred achieves by cutting off these connections at the bud. If allowed to come to fruition, the connection cited above (between the red smile and the red tulips) pulls in Offred herself; in her red outfit, an outfit signifying both her fertility and her oppression, she is like a blood-red smile, like a flowering plant. She, and they, may provide a moment's pleasure, but at tremendous cost. Such metaphorical representations of her dismal situation can make Offred only more dismal. She represses them. Again, although I accept Offred's claim that distinctions are important, that objects exist separately, I read her denial of connection as reflecting a desire to protect herself from the hardest truths in her life.

A second moment of reflection on connection (and denial thereof) occurs somewhat later in the text, as Offred sits in a chair and prepares for breakfast: "I sit in the chair and think about the word *chair*. It can also mean the leader of a meeting. It can also mean a mode of execution. It is the first syllable in *charity*. It is the French word for flesh. None of these facts has any connection with the others" (140). Once more, as Offred allows her mind to play with the signifier chair, she spins out a series of signifieds, connected only in sound. But the fact of this connection forces us to consider other connections: do these signs comment upon each other in some way? Does their juxtaposition force new meanings, new readings? Again, Offred says no.[3] But her denial is suspect, especially in light of two subsequent narrative facts. First, in the sentence following those quoted above, Offred observes: "These are the kinds of litanies I use, to compose myself" (140). That is, to keep from falling into emotional disarray, Offred chants ritual sequences of words. But to keep herself from the other extreme—a kind of emotional overload, a composition that has no boundaries—Offred denies connections between the words. The second fact that should prompt our suspicions with regard to Offred's denial is that in the "Historical Notes on *The Handmaid's Tale*" pompous Professor Pieixoto opens his commentary on the *Tale* by referring to the same string of signifiers Offred has played upon in the *Tale*: "I am sure we all enjoyed our charming Arctic Char last night at dinner, and now we are enjoying an equally charming Arctic Chair. I use the word 'enjoy' in two distinct senses, precluding, of course, the obsolete third" (381). Here Pieixoto highlights the connection between "char" and "chair" which Offred does not want to acknowledge: in a sexist society, women and flesh are interchangeable. It is precisely this interchangeability that characterizes Gileadean culture, and that Offred would prefer to keep out of the "composition" which she calls herself.

These two moments—Offred contemplating a blood-red smile and tulips; Offred spinning out a chain of "chairs"—suggest that the signifying system cannot be arrested, cannot be contained. Containment attempts may tell us something about the desires and fears of a person who declares "there is no connection," but should not constrain us to some limited reading; repeatedly, the novel declares that there *is* a connection, numerous connections (hence, I would argue, Pieixoto's play on "chair" in "The Historical Note" is connected to Offred's earlier play on this same word; the later reference forces us to make comparisons, to look for similarities and differences in the two chains of signifiers).

Having laid out these operating premises, I now turn to the novel's representation of Offred's relationships with three men: Luke, Commander Fred, and Nick. Not surprisingly, Offred wants to imagine these men as unique: Luke as her "real love," husband, and father to her child; the Commander as her Gileadean "sugar-daddy"—powerful, distant, in control of her future; Nick as her illicit love, companion in crime. For example, before Offred begins her affair with Nick she gazes hungrily out at him from her window (just as she looks hungrily at the Scrabble counters). She tells herself: "They [Luke and Nick] cannot be exchanged, one for the other. They cannot replace each other. Nick for Luke or Luke for Nick. *Should* does not apply" (248). And Offred most certainly would not imagine the Commander replacing either of them; as far as she is concerned, the Commander exists in a different realm altogether (a realm of duty, obligation; a realm in which love does not exist). But the text makes a very different argument. All three men merge, and this merging requires us to reassess supposed distinctions among husbands, lovers, and commanders. Other readers have noticed some of the similarities among these men; Mary McCarthy, for example, observes: "Characterization in general is weak in *The Handmaid's Tale*. . . . I cannot tell Luke, the husband, from Nick, the chauffeur-lover who may be an Eye (government spy) and/or belong to the 'mayday' underground. Nor is the Commander strongly drawn" (35).[4] But no one has pursued implications of this blurring.

In looking first at Luke and the Commander, I attend to two categories of character definition: personal characteristics, and what we might call situational characteristics (relational dynamics). In the former category, I locate Luke's familiarity with various languages, his interest in "old things," and his insistence upon certain "old values." The latter includes his position of relative power in a culture that requires women to depend on men, his enactment of this power relationship within marriages or affairs, and his history of past involvements with women.

Several times throughout *The Handmaid's Tale*, Offred comments upon her husband Luke's knowledge of and interest in foreign languages. He frequently provides her with etymologies and translations. For example, when Ofglen remarks "'It's a beautiful May day'" (58), Offred finds herself thinking about the word "Mayday," a word whose derivation Luke explained to her in her pre-Gileadean life. "*Mayday, mayday*, for pilots whose planes had been hit, and ships—was it ships

Reading the Romance Plot

too?—at sea" (58). He asks if she knows what the word comes from, and then tells her, "It's French, he said. From *m'aidez*" (58). He is the "word authority" in this marriage, as we see in yet another example. Wishing she might sit and talk with the servant Rita, gossip and exchange secrets, Offred muses upon the word "fraternize":

> *Fraternize* means to behave like a brother. Luke told me that. He said there was no corresponding word that meant to *behave like a sister. Sororize*, it would have to be, he said. From the Latin. He liked knowing about such details. The derivations of words, curious usages. I used to tease him about being pedantic. (15)

"From the Latin": Luke, obviously, has had a somewhat different education than the narrator. Like so many men of privilege throughout history, he knows the language of the classical curriculum and he uses this knowledge in a subtle reaffirmation of classical gender roles and inequalities (men can be brothers, one to the other; women cannot).

Two other male characters employ their knowledge of Latin in similar fashion: the Commander and Professor Pieixoto. Pieixoto is beyond my consideration here; I limit myself to consideration of fraternal language bonds between Luke and the Commander. Like Luke, the Commander both knows Latin and likes to play with "curious usages." We get some insight into the Commander's learning on the evening that Offred asks him to translate *"Nolite te bastardes carborundum"* for her (she has found this phrase carved into the floor of her closet). Unable to pronounce the phrase so as to make it intelligible, Offred writes it out on a pad; as soon as the Commander reads it he begins to laugh: "'That's not real Latin,' he says. 'That's just a joke'" (241). Offred does not want to believe that the phrase that means so much to her might be a joke (presumably the previous "Offred," the handmaid who occupied the room before our Offred, carved out the phrase for those who were to come later); and she gratefully accepts a dog-eared textbook that the Commander pulls down from the shelf:

> What I see first is a picture: The Venus de Milo, in a black-and-white photo, with a mustache and a black brassiere and armpit hair drawn clumsily on her. . . . 'It's sort of hard to explain why it's funny unless you know Latin,' he says. 'We used to write all kinds of things like that. I don't know where we got them, from older boys perhaps.' Forgetful of me and of himself, he's turning the pages. 'Look at this,' he says. The picture is called *The Sabine Women*, and in the margin is scrawled: *pim pis pit, pimus pistis pants.* 'There was another one,' he says. '*Cim, cis, cit* . . .' he stops, returning to the present, embarrassed. (241-42)

The Commander stops, because the next word in the series is "cunt"; this little joke exemplifies typical schoolboy play, play that exploits the female body. Certainly, the Commander's Latin games are cruder and more childish than those of Luke, but both men wield their language prowess so as to keep women in the position of the unempowered.

Further reinforcing this positioning is the interest taken by both Luke and the Commander in "old things" and the ways of the past. When the Commander gives Offred a popular women's magazine from the 1970s and she asks why he has such forbidden material in his study, he responds, "Some of us . . . retain an appreciation for the old things" (202). Other "old things" appreciated by the Commander are on display at Jezebel's, a Felliniesque whorehouse with women dressed in an amazing mélange of costumes from the past:

> Some of these have on outfits like mine, feathers and glister, cut high up the thighs, low over the breasts. Some are in olden-day lingerie, shortie nightgowns, baby-doll pajamas, the occasional see-through negligee. Some are in bathing suits, one piece or bikini; one, I see, is wearing a crocheted affair, with big scallop shells covering the tits. (305)

As the Commander escorts Offred through this display of flesh, he observes, "'it's like walking into the past'" (306), and Offred senses that "his voice sounds pleased, delighted even" (306). She tries to remember "if the past was exactly like this," and concludes that although it contained these things, "the mix is different" (306). The "past" called up by the Commander, the past that brings delight into his voice, is one in which women are on display for men, and are dependent upon men.

Luke too enjoys "old things." When married to him, the narrator works translating books onto computer disks; occasionally she takes books home, pleased with "the feel of them, and the look" (223). Luke tells her she has the "mind of an antiquarian." She comments, "He liked that, he liked old things himself" (224). We might discuss the narrator's antiquarian pleasures, but more important here, I think, is the association of Luke with items from the past; he likes old books, and, as we learn more about Luke we realize that he likes old ideas as well. Perhaps one of his favorite old ideas involves differences between the sexes. Twice in the novel we hear about Luke's position with regard to difference. First, when the narrator and Luke are shopping, he attends to the meat purchases:

> He liked to choose what kind of meat we were going to eat during the week. He said men needed more meat than women did, and that it wasn't a superstition and he wasn't being a jerk, studies had been done. There are some differences, he said. He was fond of saying that, as if I was trying to prove there weren't. (83)

Although we might accept Luke's comments as simple, good-humored teasing, there is more at stake here; Luke is the one who introduces the topic of difference, as if intent upon sustaining it (we have no evidence of the narrator denying difference).

Luke's comments on this topic become more exaggerated when he is in the company of the narrator's mother, who pushes on such questions much more seriously than does the narrator. Thus, we hear for a second time about Luke's chauvinism when the narrator tells us that in answer to her mother's claims that there is something missing in men, Luke teases her, "pretending to be macho, he'd tell her women were incapable of abstract thought" (156). Again, we might dismiss Luke's comment as teasing and good fun, were it not for the fact that the specific charge he levels against women is repeated, in slightly more specific form, by the Commander, when he tells Offred that women cannot add: "For [women] one and one and one and one don't make four" (240). In both cases, the men hang on to their belief that abstract thought is beyond women, who seemingly cannot put concepts together.

The personal characteristics of Luke and the Commander examined above contribute to an overall pattern of relational dynamics between these two men and women in the text. If, for example, women are incapable of abstract thought, then women will have to accept such thought from men; once this dynamic is established, others follow as a matter of course: women depend on men intellectually, economically, physically, emotionally. We see the evolution of this dependence in scenes depicting the narrator and Luke immediately after she learns that all women have lost their jobs and that their credit accounts have been transferred to their nearest male relatives. Devastated, terrified, the narrator turns to Luke for consolation:

> Did they say why? I said.
> He didn't answer that. We'll get through it, he said, hugging me.
> You don't know what it's like, I said. I feel as if somebody cut off my feet. I wasn't crying. Also, I couldn't put my arms around him.
> It's only a job, he said, trying to soothe me. (232)

Notice that although Luke is sympathetic during this exchange, he does *not* respond to the narrator's question: "Did they say why?" Her question suggests that Luke may have access to an answer; his sidestepping implicates him in some way. But more damning is the text's juxtaposition of the narrator's thought, "I couldn't put my arms around him," with Luke's "soothing" statement: "It's only a job." Reading these lines one after another, reading them in light of what we know about women's jobs in Gilead, we cannot avoid the insinuation that even before Gilead, it was women's job to put their arms around men. Although reluctant to address such an insinuation (look what it does to one's belief in "love"!) the narrator does express certain doubts about what happens between her and Luke:

> He doesn't mind this, I thought. He doesn't mind it at all. Maybe he even likes it.
> We are not each other's, anymore. Instead, I am his. (236)

Although she chastens herself for such thoughts ("unworthy, unjust, untrue" [236]) the narrator also notes that she never discusses her doubts with Luke: "I was afraid to. I couldn't afford to lose [him]" (236). Newly subordinated, the narrator relies upon and so must retain the good will of her superior. Honesty in such a relationship becomes impossible.

Similarly impossible is any kind of equal interaction (and therefore, any kind of honesty) between Offred and the Commander. Like Luke, the Commander has control over Offred's life; she knows as much, and knows she must remain in his good graces. When she receives the first call to his study, for example, she enters the room determined to engage in a good bargaining session; she envisions their interaction, quite rightly, as an exchange: "I'm not giving anything away: selling only" (178). She goes yet further on later reflection, thinking about the Commander's desire as something that "could be important, it could be a passport" (186). She might say the same about the importance of maintaining Luke's desire in the scene above; it may provide her with a way out.

And, as a matter of fact, an extremely significant moment in her relationship with Luke involves their use of passports. As the narrator tells the story of their attempt to cross the border into Canada, she suggests that Luke undertakes this journey out of love for her and their child, but the actual text of her account turns this suggestion on its head. She explains that the three of them drive the car to the border, where they hand their false passports to a border guard who takes the forms inside the immigration building:

> Then Luke got back into the car, too fast, and turned the key and reversed. He was picking up the phone, he said. And then he began to drive very quickly, and after that there was the dirt road and the woods and we jumped out of the car and began to run. A cottage, to hide in, a boat, I don't know what we thought. He said the passports were foolproof, and we had so little time to plan. Maybe he had a plan, a map of some kind in his head. As for me, I was only running: away, away. I don't want to be telling this story. (291)

Failing to specify antecedents for the various "he's" above, the narrator incriminates Luke. Who said the passports were foolproof? Who had a plan? And what kind of plan? Encompassing whom? It may very well be that Luke's "plan" is larger than the narrator realizes. We can read her final comment, "I don't want to be telling this story" as suggesting that "the story" she does not want to tell (and does tell only through mistakes and gaps) is the story of Luke's betrayal of her.

If the term "betrayal" sounds too harsh, perhaps we need to think about Luke's treatment of his wife—that is, of his first wife. We do not meet this wife in the text; the narrator never has seen her, only has seen pictures and heard her "voice on the phone, late at night, when she was calling us, before the divorce" (96). The narrator also has heard Moira express disapproval of the narrator's affair with a married man: "She said I was poaching, on another woman's ground. I said Luke wasn't a fish or a piece of dirt either, he was a human being and could make his own decisions" (221). But the decision he makes is to betray his wife. We do not know whether he is tired of her, bored with her, angry with her; whatever the reason, Luke begins an affair, spending afternoons in hotel rooms with the narrator.

Quite appropriately, when Offred begins her "affair" with the Commander (another man married to another woman), he takes her to the very hotel in which she has spent time with Luke: "I know where I am. I've been here before: with Luke, in the afternoons, a long time ago" (304). As if to underline the overlap between these two affairs, Offred comments on "sameness" when she enters the hotel room with the Commander:

> Everything is the same, the very same as it was, once upon a time. The drapes are the same, the heavy flowered ones that match the bedspread, orange poppies on royal blue, and the thin white ones to draw against the sun. . . . All is the same. (326)

The setting is the same, because the interaction is the same: unmarried woman with married man.

Although the narrator protests against Moira's disapproval of her affair with Luke, she is not immune to the force of Moira's arguments. The narrator tells us, for example, about a dream in which she stands in the apartment she shares with Luke. The apartment is bare, empty, except for clothes hanging in the cupboard:

> they're my clothes, but they don't look like mine, I've never seen them before. Maybe they're clothes belonging to Luke's wife. . . . I pull out dresses, black, blue, purple, jackets, skirts; none of them will do, none of them even fits, they're too big or too small.
>
> Luke is behind me, I turn to see him. He won't look at me, he looks down at the floor. . . .
>
> *Luke*, I say. He doesn't answer. (96)

The narrator has this dream after she and Luke are married; but notice that in her account she refers to Luke's ex-wife as his wife. Yet further suggestive of the narrator's difficulties as "the second woman" is the fact that the clothes do not fit; although they are hers, they also are not hers. And finally, in the dream Luke will not look at her or answer her.

One imagines that his response to his first wife is precisely the same; that is, he undoubtedly looks away from her, refusing to answer her questions. We can easily make the argument that this dream expresses the narrator's otherwise unexpressed reservations about her relationship with Luke, and about Luke himself, a man who betrays women.

Offred's understanding of male betrayal is sharper with regard to the Commander. Because her own feelings are not entangled with his, she recognizes the banality of his statement that he seeks Offred's company because he and his wife "don't seem to have much in common, these days" (203). Offred observes: "So there it was, out in the open: his wife didn't understand him. That's what I was there for, then. The same old thing" (203). In other words, in this instance, Offred has read the story, knows the plot line, and she is not impressed. As a matter of fact, she feels some guilt with regard to Serena Joy, and expresses this guilt in terms similar to those used by Moira earlier:

> I felt I was an intruder, in a territory that ought to have been hers. . . . I was taking something away from her, although she didn't know it. I was filching. Never mind that it was something she apparently didn't want or had no use for, had rejected even, still, it was hers, and if I took it away, this mysterious 'it' I couldn't quite define . . . what would be left for her? (208)

While Offred may be awakening to the costs of extramarital affairs (costs borne most heavily by the wife who is betrayed), the men with whom she enacts these betrayals give no signs of a similar awakening. Luke expresses no repentance for his affair, and the Commander, rather than repent, multiplies his sins (Offred is not the first woman to spend time with him in his study and at Jezebel's; the handmaid preceding Offred did so, and ended up hanging herself).

What am I arguing here? Looking at both personal characteristics and relational dynamics, we see that *The Handmaid's Tale* provides us with two male characters who mirror one another; structurally, these two are twins. Offred does not draw attention to parallels between the two men, and might protest against such connections ("None of these facts has any connection with the other" [140]) but the text insists upon them. *The Handmaid's Tale* encourages us to read the future in light of the past, and the past in light of the future; doing so, we cannot exclude male figures from our consideration—no matter how disquieting the results of such consideration. Here, recognition of similarity between Luke and the Commander is disquieting; it casts doubt not only upon the narrator's story of Luke's love, but also upon love stories generally.

"But wait," the romantic reader may object, "there's a third male in this story, and he does credit to the love plot." Lucy M. Freibert, for example, argues that "Offred's real breakthrough to her courageous sexual self comes not with the Commander, who soon bores her, but with Nick. . . . Her joyous reaction to her desire embodies precisely the French *jouissance*" (288). Certainly, we may argue that it is through Nick's intervention that Offred seemingly "comes to life," escapes from Gilead, tapes her account, and thereby provides us with the story of her past. Nick, unlike Luke and the Commander, does not exhibit any penchant for "old ways," any knowledge of patriarchal languages of power, or any inclination to implicate Offred in triangulated desire (there is apparently no wife in Nick's life). Also unlike Luke and the Commander, Nick risks his own life to save that of Offred; he instructs her to go with the two Eyes who have come to take her away: "'It's all right. It's Mayday. Go with them'" (376). Although we may suspect Nick, just as Offred does ("My suspicion hovers in the air above him, a dark angel warning me away" [376]), the fact that we have a text at all suggests that Nick tells the truth, that he has arranged for Offred's escape. In other words, he functions as a fairy-tale prince, setting the princess free with a kiss. Early in the novel, Offred expresses her faith that Luke will perform as her fairy-tale savior—"sooner or later he will get me out, we will find her [their daughter], wherever they've put her. She'll remember us and we will be all three of us together" (135)—but Luke never makes a showing. So Offred makes do with what is available, and falls in love with Nick.[5]

In paragraphs above, I suggested that parallels between the Commander and Luke should prompt us to read the narrator's "love story" (that is, the story in which she and Luke are stars) with real skepticism. When the cast of this story changes, with Nick standing in for Luke, can we forgo the skepticism? Despite differences between the two men, the text pushes us to answer in the negative; it continues to represent the love plot as something potentially dangerous to women who entangle themselves therein. Let me pinpoint three narrative components that qualify the positive representation of Nick's and Offred's affair.

First is Offred's seemingly casual reference to mushroom-colored carpeting on the stairs to Nick's room: "I feel my way up, stair by stair: carpet here, I think of it as mushroom-colored" (336). The only other mushroom-colored carpeting in this novel is that at Jezebel's, the whorehouse to which the Commander takes Offred earlier on that same evening she climbs Nick's stairs, the former-hotel whorehouse in which the narrator met Luke for afternoons of illicit sex. Although it is too dark for Offred actually to see the color of the staircase carpeting, she imagines it to be the same color as carpeting on which she treads in moving toward other bedrooms. Thus, Offred herself suggests connections between this affair and those, suggests similarities at work.

If the sole similarity between this affair and those were carpet dye, we might dismiss the suggestion of parallels, but two more features of the narrative militate against this dismissal: the effect on Offred of "being in love" and the grammar according to which she articulates being in love. When in love with Luke, the narrator tends to give in to him, to accept his direction of her toward passivity. For example, when a woman kidnaps Luke's and the narrator's child in a supermarket, Luke dismisses the incident as an individual woman's craziness, encouraging the narrator to see such kidnappings as isolated events rather than as structural phenomena demanding a response. Later, when the narrator considers joining marches to protest women's loss of their jobs, Luke again intervenes: "Luke said it would be futile and I had to think about them, my family, him and her" (233). And finally, when several weeks pass without a word from the narrator's mother, the narrator searches her mother's apartment, and determines to call the police:

> Don't, said Luke.
> Why not? I said. I was glaring at him, I was angry now. He stood there in the wreck of the living room, just looking at me. He put his hands into his pockets, one of those aimless gestures people make when they don't know what else to do.
> Just don't is what he said. (329)

And so the narrator doesn't.

Similarly, after Offred begins her affair with Nick, she loses all interest in Mayday and in the possibility of escape. She comments, "The fact is that I no longer want to leave, escape the border to freedom. I want to be here, with Nick, where I can get at him" (348). She barely listens to Ofglen, who "whispers less, talks more about the weather" (349). Whatever political commitment Offred might be capable of making vanishes in light of her commitment to romance. This evanescence is particularly frightening in light of Offred's childhood memory of a televised interview with the mistress of a man who supervised a death camp during World War II. This woman "said she didn't notice much that she found unusual. She denied knowing about the oven. . . . He was not a monster, she said" (188). While the accommodation of this Nazi mistress may be extreme ("She was thinking about how not to think" [188]), it is not different in nature from Offred's accommodation:

> I said, I have made a life for myself, here, of a sort. That must have been what the settlers' wives thought, and women who survived wars, if they had a man. Humanity is so adaptable, my mother would say. Truly amazing, what people can get used to, as long as there are a few compensations. (349)

So, Offred "makes a life for herself," a life involving no community or political commitment, but only commitment to "having man."

Perhaps equally worrisome is Offred's reliance upon traditional grammars with which to structure her relationship with this man. For example, in Offred's first account of her visit to Luke's room, she relies heavily on the language of Harlequin romances. She and Luke do not talk:

> Outside, like punctuation, there's a flash of lightning; almost no pause and then the thunder. He's undoing my dress, a man made of darkness, I can't see his face, and I can hardly breathe, hardly stand, and I'm not standing. His mouth is on me, his hands, I can't wait and he's moving, already, love, it's been so long, I'm alive in my skin, again, arms around him, falling and water softly everywhere, never-ending. (337-38)

"A man made of darkness"? "Falling and water softly, everywhere, never-ending"? Offred's account comes right out of mass-market bodice rippers (a dangerous source of role models for women who want to maintain any sense of integrity). As if aware of the silliness of this version of her encounter with Nick, Offred revises: "I made that up. It didn't happen that way. Here is what happened" (338). And then we get a second version, in which the new lovers have trouble talking to one another, until they fall into the language of old movies. They toss "lines" at one another, "quoting from late movies, from the time before" (339). This act of quotation is bizarre because, as Offred realizes, the movies themselves do not quote from "real life": "Not even my mother talked like that, not when I knew her. Possibly nobody ever talked like that in real life, it was all a fabrication from the beginning" (339). These two lovers enact the fabrication, hoping to conjure forth something real with these magic words. Offred cannot sustain the illusion for very long. She senses the talk is "faded music, faded paper flowers, worn satin, an echo of an echo" (339); that is, she senses that the words actually keep the two of them apart, referring, as they do, to "echoes of echoes." After concluding this account, Offred again admits: "It didn't happen that way either. I'm not sure how it happened; not exactly. All I can hope for is a reconstruction" (340).[6]

Sadly, both of the reconstructions she offers us, as well as the fairy-tale construction she employs when she thinks about this affair, limit the range of activities and options available to male and female characters. Operating within this traditional grammar (men are princes or made of darkness; women are princesses or damsels in distress), Offred can individuate neither herself nor Nick; both fall into roles assigned to them by fairy tales and romances. Is the novel's reliance upon fairy tale/romance paradigms so destructive as to counteract its positive representation of Nick as "the prince"—the daring young man who saves the maiden? "Counteract" may be too strong a claim, but I argue that every representation of romance in *The Handmaid's Tale*, including that most positive representation, Nick with Offred, is highly qualified, highly ambivalent. The novel seems to want to believe in its own novelistic representations of love (and, by implication, in "real-life" love) at the same time it expresses extreme reservations about how we (authors, characters, readers, real-life lovers) typically realize this emotion. In one of the most perceptive reviews of Atwood's novel, Gayle Greene argues precisely this point. Greene observes that when Offred answers the Commander's question about Gilead's possible lacks—"What did we overlook?"—with the response, "Love, falling in love," it is tempting to hear Atwood's voice in Offred's. But, according to Greene, we also must hear her voice in the Commander's: "oh yes . . . I've read the magazines, that's what they were pushing, wasn't it?" (Greene 14). That is, while there may be something importantly human about falling in love, narratives enact this emotion according to a limited number of scripts (those provided in magazines, romance novels, fairy tales) and we readers all too easily buy the line these scripts are pushing. Sadly, at the moment such scripts promise us individual love ("you, yes you, can love and be loved") they undermine the very possibility of individuality (and love) as they restrict experience to a small number of decidedly limited plot lines.

Thus, I must take exception to Barbara Ehrenreich's claim that in *The Handmaid's Tale*, "the only truly subversive force appears to be love" (Ehrenreich 34) and to Victoria Glendinning's assertion that "what has been overlooked by the regime is the subversive force of love. On this the plot turns, as in all romantic narratives since the world began" (Glendinning 147). I also must question Amin Malak's optimistic assessment that while *The Handmaid's Tale* condemns a "male misogynous mentality, [it] upholds and cherishes a man-woman axis" (Malak 15). Instead, I argue that the novel subverts the subversive force of love, and that it raises serious questions about a man-woman axis, when this axis models itself upon patterns that restrict rather than liberate. In its representation of such patterns in relationships between Offred and Luke, Offred and the Commander, Offred and Nick, the novel insists upon love's limitations, rather than upon its latitudes.

I began this essay by suggesting that my way of reading *The Handmaid's Tale* parallels the way Offred and the Commander play Scrabble: like them, I draw letters from the text, rearrange them, and thereby compose new words, new texts. I like that parallel, and enjoy the element of playfulness in both versions of Scrabble (Offred and the Commander take extra letters and make words that do not exist; I juxtapose characters and push on connections that, at least according to the narrator, do not exist). Here, at the end of this essay, I return to the Scrabble episode, again employing it as parallel—this time, not to the act of reading *The Handmaid's Tale*, but to the act of "falling in love" as represented in *The Handmaid's Tale*. Unlike my first analogy, however, this one leaves me feeling uneasy, uncomfortable, as it points to the closed nature of the games in question. Playing Scrabble, the Commander and Offred generally operate within certain rules; the two of them occasionally bend these rules, coming up with words like *smurt* and *crup*. In my first parallel, I suggest that such breaches are examples of creative play; here, in contrast, I argue that they actually are part of the game. That is, they do not change underlying grammars, do not question essential rules (note, for example, that the "made-up" words follow conventions within English with regard to consonant blends and the presence of vowels). Similarly, the romances enacted in *The Handmaid's Tale* operate within the rules, within the conventions of "falling in love." In case we have forgotten our fairy-tale education in this process, Offred reminds us of its elements in a lengthy meditation thereon:

> Falling in love.... Falling into it, we all did then, one way or another.... It was the central thing; it was the way you understood yourself....
>
> *Falling in love*, we said; *I fell for him*. We were falling women. We believed in it, this downward motion: so lovely, like flying, and yet at the same time so dire, so extreme, so unlikely....
>
> And sometimes it happened, for a time. That kind of love comes and goes and is hard to remember afterwards, like pain. (292)

The narrator "falls" for Luke; later she "falls" for Nick. In both instances she becomes a "fallen woman"—a woman who surrenders herself to a plot already written, a story already told. Following the rules, the narrator enjoys love's loveliness and its pains—and never does she stop to ask if this game is the only way love can be played. Although some readers might see the narrator's premarital affair with Luke as stepping outside the game, I have to read this affair, finally, as akin to made-up words like "smurt" and "crup"; the affair, like the words, may not be accepted in polite company, but it, like them, is an integral part of the game. Similarly, Offred's affair with Nick (an apparent violation of her love-marriage to Luke) does nothing to challenge the general rules of romance; the affair simply provides readers with yet another example of "*J.H. loves B.P. 1954. O.R. loves L.T.*" (145), "short stories" carved into the wooden desktops at the Rachel and Leah Center. Rather than engaging in a radical revision of such stories (which remind Offred of "inscriptions I used to read about, carved on the stone walls of caves, or drawn with a mixture of soot and animal fat" [145]), Offred accepts these archaic plot lines as model for her own.

But is *The Handmaid's Tale* structured according to "the story" or "the plot"? Although the novel does not provide an alternative vision of love's enactment, its portrait of love's typical realization is highly qualified. Yes, Offred's love for Nick leads to her escape from Gilead, but as that love is associated with her love for Luke (a love that colludes in the very foundation of Gilead) it must be interrogated.[7] Such interrogation does not lead to a rejection of the importance of love,[8] but it must lead to a critical assessment of how we have shaped love's plot, and how it has shaped us. The structural power of this plot is apparent in a seemingly casual description, from Offred, of the handmaids preparing for a Prayvaganza:

> We line up to get processed through the checkpoint, standing in our twos and twos and twos, like a private girls' school that went for a walk and stayed out too long. Years and years too long, so that everything has become overgrown, legs, bodies, dresses all together. As if enchanted. A fairy tale, I'd like to believe. (276)

If this is a fairy tale, a prince will arrive and make life better with a kiss. Because Offred so much wants to believe in the fairy tale, she closes off other plot options: what would happen if she were to work with Ofglen, to spy on the Commander and communicate his secrets to Mayday? The novel does not give us these stories; but it does encourage us to break out of the old plots, to shape a future different from those offered us in the *Tale* and its *Historical Note*.

From *Twentieth Century Literature* 37, no. 2 (Summer 1991):148-169. Copyright © 1991 by Twentieth Century Literature. Reprinted by permission of Twentieth Century Literature.

Notes

1. Lacombe begins her article by quoting this passage and observing the ways in which it "multiplies layers of signification" (4). Later she makes reference to other passages that I too find to be important (the "smiling snowman" and "tulips" passages, for example, as well as the passage in which Offred meditates on the word "chair"). Despite our common interest in Atwood's play with text as palimpsest, we pursue different effects of this play. She is particularly interested in Offred's sexual relationship with the Commander and textual relationship with her readers; I am more intrigued by ways in which the palimpsest sheds light on heterosexual romance in general.

2. Howells quotes this passage as evidence of Offred's humanism: "In entirely unpropitious circumstances, Offred insists on believing that individuals are significant" (66). Certainly, individuals are significant, but what Offred really wants to argue here is that they are significant and discrete. Atwood's text deconstructs the latter claim.

3. Ehrenreich seemingly says no as well. Before quoting this passage on the word *chair*, Ehrenreich comments that "Offred spends a lot of time on aimless mental word games" (34). Obviously, in my reading of the text, these games are far from aimless; instead, they provide readers of the text with reading lessons.

4. Also "the same" is the fact that in neither situation do we know Offred's/the narrator's "real" name. Although we, along with McCarthy, may play detective and come up with the narrator's name through a process of elimination ("my textual detective work says it is June" [35]), the text never supplies us with the name by which the narrator thinks of herself, that is, the name with which she identifies herself. This lack is significant as it affects not only our reading of Offred's relationship with the Commander but also of her relationship with Luke.

5. Freibert wants to see Offred's interaction with Nick as an example of positive risk-taking (risk-taking that allows women like Offred "to transcend their conditioning, establish their identity, joyfully reclaim their bodies, find their voices, and reconstruct the social order" [285]). In my reading, Offred's affair with Nick represents precisely the conditioning that Freibert imagines the affair as overcoming; that is, Offred has been trained/socialized to follow a romance plot, and Nick happens to be around to play one of the necessary roles. Rather than reconstructing the social order, their affair repeats it.

6. Again, I have to disagree with Freibert, who reads Offred's revisionist accounts as exemplifying Offred's increasing perfectionism: "The risk-filled spirit of adventure permeates Offred's actions and choices, turning her into a perfectionist. She creates and recreates accounts of her meetings with Nick, each time making them more intense, more precise" (288-89).

7. Freibert says, "when Offred listens to Nick's 'trust me'—the traditional patriarchal ploy for co-opting women—Offred hears with an experience and knowledge that enable her to speak out, tell her tale, and perhaps precipitate the action that will bring Gilead to an end" (289). But we have heard "trust me" all too often out of the mouths of deceivers; and, what we see of post-Gileadean culture (in the form of the *Historical Note*) does not suggest that this deception has come to an end (see Davidson's essay).

8. If it did, we could read Aunt Lydia as its spokesperson: "*Love*, said Aunt Lydia with distaste. Don't let me catch you at it. No mooning and June-ing around here, girls. Wagging her finger at us. *Love* is not the point" (285).

Works Cited

Atwood, Margaret. *The Handmaid's Tale*. New York: Crest, 1986.

Davidson, Arnold E. "Future Tense: Making History in *The Handmaid's Tale*." *Margaret Atwood: Vision and Forms*. Ed. Kathryn VanSpanckeren and Jan Gordon Castro. Carbondale, IL: Southern Illinois UP, 1988. 113-21.

Ehrenreich, Barbara. "Feminism's Phantoms." *New Republic* 17 Mar. 1986: 33-35.

Freibert, Lucy M. "Control and Creativity: The Politics of Risk in Margaret Atwood's *The Handmaid's Tale*." *Critical Essays on Margaret Atwood*. Ed. Judith McCombs. Boston: Hall, 1988. 280-91.

Glendinning, Victoria. "*Lady Oracle*." *Saturday Night* Jan. 1986: 39-41.

Greene, Gayle. "Choice of Evils." *Women's Review of Books* July 1986: 14-15.

Howells, Coral Ann. *Private and Fictional Worlds: Canadian Women Novelists of the 1970s and 1980s*. London: Methuen, 1987.

Lacombe, Michele. "The Writing on the Wall: Amputated Speech in Margaret Atwood's *The Handmaid's Tale*." *Wascana Review* 21.2 (1986): 3-20.

Malak, Amin. "Margaret Atwood's *The Handmaid's Tale* and the Dystopian Tradition." *Canadian Literature* 112 (1987): 9-16.

McCarthy, Mary. "Breeders, Wives and Unwomen." *New York Times Book Review* 9 Feb. 1986: 1, 35.

"Just a Backlash":
Margaret Atwood, Feminism, and *The Handmaid's Tale*

Shirley Neuman

Margaret Atwood conceived the Republic of Gilead in *The Handmaid's Tale* as one logical outcome of what she termed the 'strict theocracy' of the 'fundamentalist government' of the United States' Puritan founding fathers.[1] Her Gileadean government maintains its power by means of surveillance, suppression of information, 're-education' centres, and totalitarian violence. Its major national issue, sterility consequent on nuclear and chemical pollution, it addresses through sexual surrogacy, turning its few fertile women into 'Handmaids' to its highest-level Commanders and their wives, using as justification the biblical story in which the barren Rachel directs her husband Jacob to 'go in unto' her servant Bilhah: 'and she shall bear upon my knees, that I also may have children by her' (epigraph).

We learn about Gilead through one of its (self-described) 'two-legged wombs' or 'ambulatory chalices' (128), the Handmaid Offred, who records her story after she has escaped the regime. Caught up in a dystopian state that the novel hypothesizes as the logical extension not only of Puritan government but also of the agenda articulated during the 1980s by America's fundamentalist Christian Right, what Offred knows is that power pervades every aspect of Gileadean life. Power: 'who can do what to whom and get away with it, even as far as death,' 'who can do what to whom and be forgiven for it' (126-27). What Offred also knows is that the temptations of power offer a feminine inflection: 'if you happen to be a man,' she addresses her future reader, 'and you've made it this far, please remember: you will never be subjected to the temptation of feeling you must forgive, a man, as a woman' (126). The novel's outwardly conformist and once independent Offred has seen her social value reduced to reproduction, and her personal freedom completely curtailed. But the retrospective monologue in which she tells her story reveals her as observant of the gendered configurations of power in both the personal and the political realms, in both 'the time before' and the present of the novel. It also shows her as analytic and ironic about those relations and as capable of using them to her own advantage. Offred, in short, is a fictional product of 1970s feminism, and she finds herself in a situation that is a fictional realization of the backlash against women's rights that gathered force during the early 1980s.

Between 1965, when Atwood wrote her first published novel, *The Edible Woman*, and 1985, when she published *The Handmaid's Tale*, women—especially middle-class women like Atwood's heroines—had seen major improvements in their access to higher education and the professions, in employment equity, in access to legal abortion, and in divorce law. Atwood herself had been embraced as a feminist novelist by a panoply of writers and critics representing a wide variety of feminist positions.[2] She had responded initially by resisting the label *feminist* (a label that she noted was sometimes used by reviewers to dismiss her early work), then by carefully defining the kind of feminist she was. By 1976, she described herself as 'probably . . . a feminist, in the broad sense of the term' (Sandler, 56), but in a 1979 interview she also found the term insufficiently 'inclusive' of her interests (Gerald and Crabbe, 139). When *The Handmaid's Tale* was about to appear, Atwood gave an interview to feminist theorist Elizabeth Meese, in which she iterated her definition of feminism as a 'belief in the rights of women . . . [as] equal human beings' but in which she also firmly distanced herself from feminist or doctrinaire separatism: she would have no truck with attempts—feminist or otherwise—to control what people write or say, and 'if practical, hardline, anti-male feminists took over and became the government, I would resist them' (Meese, 183). She had put the matter more positively two years earlier, just before she turned to the writing of *The Handmaid's Tale*: 'Am I a propagandist? No! Am I an observer of society? Yes! And no one who observes society can fail to make observations that are feminist. That is just . . . commonsense' (Jamkhandi, 5).[3]

Such a commonsense observer, alert in the years between 1965 and 1985, could not have helped but see a world that, if still far from perfect, looked to be getting better and better for women. Nor could an alert observer have helped but notice that, for some, the world seemed to be getting a little too free for women. Atwood, like many feminists of the period, was keenly aware of the fragility of the newly acquired rights and equalities of women: of the opposition to these rights and equalities in many quarters, of the many places and ways in which these gains were threatened or actively eroded, and of the intersection of women's issues, feminist issues, and broader human rights issues.

By 1984, the year in which pundits looked back on George Orwell's dystopia to assess how much of his vision we had escaped and also the year in which Margaret Atwood sat down to write *The Handmaid's Tale*, both totalitarianism and those who hoped to retrench some of the gains of feminism had made significant inroads on the successes of the 1970s. Atwood kept a file of these inroads on human rights and women's freedom, which she took with her on book tours as evidence for her insistence that she had 'invented nothing' in Gilead.[4] If Gilead is, in the logic of the novel, one possible extension of the real world of 1984, we can understand something of the impulse to its creation and of the character of Offred by briefly recollecting early 1980s reactions to the successes of the women's movement as well as the intersections of these reactions with some of the totalitarian excesses of the period.

By 1984, Ayatollah Khomeini had forced women out of Iranian universities, out of their jobs, and back into their *burqas* and their homes. Iranian prison refugees reported torture including the use of electric prods and frayed steel cables in beatings, and such a report by one woman found its way into Atwood's file. In Afghanistan, as Atwood herself observed, 'Thinking that it's O.K. for women to read and write would be a radically feminist position' (Brans, 140). And, as Professor Pieixoto reminds us in the novel's epilogue, the Philippines, under the rubric of 'salvaging,' engaged in state-sanctioned murder of dissidents, while Ceauşescu's government in Romania monitored women monthly for pregnancy, outlawed birth contro, and abortion, and linked women's wages to childbearing. The professor appears to have read Atwood's file: both these precedents for the actions of Gilead had found their way into her clippings documenting her assertion that she had invented nothing in Gilead.

By 1984, in the United States, the gains women had achieved during the previous decade had come under attack from several directions. During Ronald Reagan's presidency, women made up an increasing percentage of those in the lowest-paid occupations, and they made no gains or lost ground in the better-paid trades and professions.[5] The number of elected and politically appointed women declined. One-third of all federal budget cuts under Reagan's presidency came from programs that served mainly women, even though these programs represented only 10 per cent of the federal budget. The average amount a divorced man paid in child support fell 25 per cent. Murders related to sexual assault and domestic violence increased by 160 per cent while the overall murder rate declined; meanwhile the federal government defeated bills to fund shelters for battered women, stalled already approved funding, and in 1981 closed down the Office of Domestic Violence it had opened only two years earlier. Pro-natalists bombed and set fire to abortion clinics and harassed their staff and patients; Medicaid ceased to fund legal abortions, effectively eliminating freedom of choice for most teenage girls and poor women; several states passed laws restricting not only legal abortion but even the provision of information about abortion. The debate about freedom of choice for women flipped over into court rulings about the rights and freedom of the fetus. The Equal Rights Amendment died.[6]

By 1984, the American New Right had metamorphosed into Jerry Falwell's Moral Majority. Televangelists, some of them at home in the White House, told their congregations that 'feminists encourage women to leave their husbands, kill their children, practice witchcraft, destroy capitalism and become lesbians' (letter of Pat Robertson to his congregation, quoted in Lapham, 37) and that AIDS was divine retribution for the 'sin' of homosexuality. Right-wing wives such as bestselling Phyllis Schlafly made a handsome income telling other women to return home, to let their husbands provide, and to use their femininity and feminine wiles as the core of their success and fulfilment as women. Schlafly put forward Katharine Hepburn as a role model—not Hepburn the successful actress to be sure, but Hepburn at the feet of Spencer Tracy, 'submissive and more abnegating than any wife this side of the Orient' (Schlafly, 55).[7] Several readers identify Schlafly as the prototype of Aunt Lydia at the 'Red,' or re-education, Centre of *The Handmaid's Tale* and of her 'implicit' (136) advice to the Handmaids: 'Men are sex machines . . . and not much more. . . . You must learn to manipulate them, for your own good. . . . It's nature's way. It's God's device. It's the way things are' (135). Others find in her the prototype for the Commander's wife, Serena Joy, of whom Offred ironically observes, 'She stays in her home, but it doesn't seem to agree with her. How furious she must be, now that she's been taken at her word' (44).

In 1984, the 'most popular talk show' in the United States was hosted by Rush Limbaugh, who used it as a platform from which to attack what he called '"femi-Nazi[s]"' (Faludi, xxi). The media began to announce that the world had moved into a 'post-feminist' era, while at the same time it gave wide circulation to a number of badly designed, badly analysed, badly misrepresented, or dishonestly co-opted studies claiming to prove that single career women had high rates of neuroses and unhappiness, that women's incomes declined an average of 70 per cent post-divorce, that the United States was in the grip of an 'infertility epidemic,' that a professional woman over thirty was about as likely to win a lottery jackpot as to find a man (see both Faludi and Bouson). Across North America, young women in universities, in the confidence born of their mothers' success, in the desire for self-differentiation that ever characterizes the young, overly credulous of the media and perhaps anxious to find a man, asserted that they didn't need feminism.

Offred, in 'the time before' of *The Handmaid's Tale*, is one such young woman, sceptical of and embarrassed by her mother's feminist activism, which includes 'Take Back the Night' marches, bonfires of pornography, and planned single motherhood. 'As for you,' her mother tells her, 'you're just a backlash.... You young people don't appreciate things.... You don't know what we had to go through, just to get you where you are. Look at him,' pointing to her son-in-law, 'slicing up the carrots. Don't you know how many women's lives, how many women's *bodies*, the tanks had to roll over just to get that far?' (115). The scene finds its way into the opera, where the oddly non-idiomatic use of the term *backlash* is replaced by Offred's mother's emphatic 'God knows where *you* came from' (Ruders and Bentley, 139). The substitution effectively contributes to the opera's erasure of a historical 'backlash' against feminism as one of the strongest motivations in the novel for the establishment of Gilead.

Reading the novel, we spend a great deal of time inside Offred's head. And Offred spends a great deal of time not only remembering 'the time before' and observing the circumstances of her present, but also commenting on both. Her commentary is often ironic, often analytic, often critical of herself and of her peers in 'the time before.' It also shows her as having gained political awareness and as reassessing her earlier more individualist positions. In her thoughts, for example, she engages in a rich dialogue with her mother, recollecting her earlier negative reactions to her mother's feminist activism but also learning to acknowledge some of the ways in which her mother was right. Like the novel's historically based premise of a backlash against women, this recognition gets lost in the opera.

Opera, of course, is a particularly difficult medium in which to represent a character's book-long interior monologue. The brute physical reality of the time it takes to sing means that such monologues get reduced to emblematic moments of particularly intense feeling, such as Offred's aria in the doctor's office, 'Every moon I watch for blood.' In opera, such moments of sung introspection focus on emotion and do not dwell analytically on the political or social circumstances in which the characters find themselves.

Typically, too, a novel's interior monologue is dramatized in opera as stage action around recitative, duets, and ensemble singing. This dramatization can, and often does, shift the balance away from the introspection of a character's interior monologue. We see this happening, for example, in this opera's depiction of Offred's life with her husband Luke and her daughter, and in its 'flashbacks' to the moment when she and her family are intercepted in their escape, Luke shot, her daughter taken away, and she imprisoned to be 're-educated' as a Handmaid. Necessarily relying on action and sung dialogue, the libretto offers us a harrowing scene of capture but it cannot recapture the level of analysis and expanded, if bitter, knowledge recorded in the novel's interior monologue. The opera's effect is to increase the emphasis on the personal trauma suffered by Offred and her family, but to diminish the novel's emphasis on its social and political roots.

Remembering this past, the novel's Offred concludes that 'I took too much for granted; I trusted fate, back then' (27). As her story unfolds she becomes tougher on her earlier life: 'We lived,' she says, 'by ignoring. Ignoring isn't the same as ignorance, you have to work at it. . . . There were stories in the newspapers, of course, corpses in ditches or the woods, bludgeoned to death or mutilated, interfered with as they used to say, but they were about other women, and the men who did such things were other men. . . . We lived in the gaps between the stories' (53). Her willed ignorance anaesthetizes any impulse to resist the increasingly repressive actions leading to the coup that establishes Gilead. When a strange woman attempts to abduct her child, Offred works at ignoring: 'I thought it was an isolated incident, at the time' (59). When the Pornomarts and the mobile brothels on Harvard Square suddenly disappear, she fails to challenge a sales clerk's apathetic comment: 'Who knows, who cares' what happened to them (163). And when all women are told they no longer have a job, she asks, 'What was it about this that made us feel we deserved it?' (166). Willed ignorance, Offred learns, is sister to victimization and to passive acceptance of blame for what is done to one.

In Gilead, Offred decides against being a victim: 'I intend to last' (7), she declares. To last, she must pay attention. Especially early on in the novel, she is alert to every detail around her. Some of her observation is undertaken to fill the time, as when she minutely inspects every corner of her room. Some of it is a device to distance herself from the horror of her situation: 'One detaches oneself. One describes,' she remarks as the Commander does his 'duty' on the lower half of her body (89) in the 'Rachel' ceremony, or as she lays her hand on the rope about to hang two women. Most of her attention is in aid of survival. Entering the Commander's household, meeting her shopping companion Ofglen for the first time, she pays the closest heed to the smallest gestures of everyone around her, 'reading' them constantly. 'Watch out, Commander, I tell him in my head. I've got my eye on you. One false move and I'm dead' (83).

The measure of the distance Offred has travelled, by means of attentiveness, from her willed ignorance in 'the time before' comes when she gains some small power over the Commander as a consequence of having read the signs of what happened to the Handmaid before her. When she once would have worked to ignore those signs, she now seeks knowledge. Asked what she would like, she responds, 'I would like to know. . . . Whatever there is to know. What's going on' (176).

We must be wary, however, of the impulse to make an unmitigated heroine of the novel's Offred. Her desire to survive and to know comes with a necessary degree of complicity and a tendency to relapse. In her new self-awareness, Offred specifically accepts the element of complicitous choice in her situation. Lying on her back, she reasons: 'Nor does rape cover it: nothing is going on here that I haven't signed up for. There wasn't a lot of choice but there was some, and this is what I chose' (88). She also recognizes and acknowledges her enjoyment of her own small exercises of power, however ignoble: her sexual teasing of the Guardians at the checkpoint, her slight power not only over the Commander, because he wants something from her, but over his wife, whom they are deceiving. She comes to understand that the Commander craves some unspoken forgiveness for the conditions of her life and that to bestow or to withhold forgiveness is 'a power, perhaps the greatest' (126), as well as a temptation. 'How easy it is to invent a humanity, for anyone at all,' she reflects, thinking of the Commander's request that she play Scrabble in the same breath as she recollects an interview with the mistress of one of the supervisors of a concentration camp (137).

It is in this matter of humanizing the Commander that the opera makes its largest gesture towards domesticating Atwood's plot, especially in the brothel scene when Offred's refusal of sex—'I'm sorry. I don't think I can'—is met by the Commander's 'Don't worry about it. I understand' and a kindly pat (Ruders and Bentley, 239). Emotionally, that scene runs directly counter to its prototype in the novel, where no such 'out' for Offred is on the bed: 'Fake it, I scream at myself inside my head. You must remember how. . . . Move your flesh around, breathe audibly. It's the least you can do' (239).

The personal is political, this scene tells us, just as feminism had already told us in the wake of Virginia Woolf's eloquent demonstration in *Three Guineas* of the relationship between domestic and fascist despotism. Nowhere is the personal more political than in Gilead, where the very choice of becoming a Handmaid or a Jezebel over going to the Colonies to sweep up radioactive waste signals a degree of complicity with the regime and where playing a game of Scrabble with the Commander renders him both human and comic. Nowhere more so than in Gilead, where each Handmaid must pull the rope to tighten its noose around the necks of state-murdered women. Nowhere more so than in Gilead, where the Handmaids accept the party line that the men given them to kill in 'particicutions' are rapists and where Offred acknowledges her own 'bloodlust; I want to tear, gouge, rend' (262).

If Offred's survival depends on attention and on astute choices about complicity, her affair with Nick marks a relapse into willed ignorance. Readers have tended to identify strongly with the sense of connection and renewed sexuality Offred discovers in her relationship with Nick and to understand this couple in light of the conventions of the romance plot, in which the male lover rescues the hapless heroine.[8] Atwood is, I would argue, telling us something else. There is no evidence in the novel that Nick's 'rescue' of Offred is motivated by anything other than self-preservation. In the world of sexual relationships, after all, his final words, 'Trust me' (275), are as clichéd and unreliable as the Commander's explanation that his wife doesn't understand him or as Serena Joy's final reproach as Offred is hustled out the door: 'After all he did for you' (276). Most importantly, when Offred falls under the spell of her rendezvous with Nick, she no longer wishes to escape and she no longer wants to know from Ofglen what is going on. Her relapse into willed ignorance partly motivates the shame that so strongly marks her narrative at this point. She has ceased, she realizes as she sees the dreaded black van arrive for her at the end of the novel, 'to pay attention' (275).

In dystopias, the present is co-opted to evil ends, driven to one logical (though not inevitable) conclusion, its understandings and language perverted. In dystopias, Handmaids greet each other with words from the Catholic litany to the Virgin, 'Blessed be the fruit,' while the state hangs priests. In dystopias clichés from 'the time before' signal both normalcy and extreme differences of power. In dystopias, the call of some radical feminists for a 'woman's culture' becomes the birthing scene of *The Handmaid's Tale* or the brothel called Jezebel's. In dystopias, the doxology of the Christian fundamentalist Right that would return women to their homes to fulfil their putative biological destiny is realized by a Handmaid lying between a wife's legs in a parody of the biblical story of Rachel and her servant Bilhah.[9]

But also implicit in every dystopia is a utopia. As Atwood herself observed, 'we the readers are to deduce what a good society is by seeing what it isn't' ('Justice'). And here some readers of *The Handmaid's Tale*, and, to a considerable degree, the opera libretto, have misread the novel by conflating Offred's desire to have 'everything back, the way it was' (116) with Atwood's implicit utopia. I quote John Updike in his egregiously nostalgic *New Yorker* review: 'among [the novel's] cautionary and indignant messages, Miss Atwood has threaded a curious poem to the female condition. Offred's life of daily waiting and shopping, of timorous strategizing and sudden bursts of daring, forms an intensified and darkened version of a woman's customary existence, a kind of begrimed window through which glimpses of Offred's old, pre-Gilead life—its work and laughter and minor dissipations, its female friends and husband and child, its costumes and options—flicker with the light of paradise' (121). The novel, he concludes, 'is suffused . . . by the author's lovely subversive hymn to our ordinary life, as lived, amid perils and pollution, now' (126). Updike is working hard at willed ignorance.

For what does *The Handmaid's Tale*—the novel, not the opera libretto—tell us about 'the time before' by means of Offred's memories, Aunt Lydia's lectures, and the Commander's rationalizations? It tells us that one's husband could slice the carrots for dinner, that one could live with him and one's daughter and cat and argue and banter with one's mother and friends in an easy, loving intimacy, yes.

But it also tells us that it was not safe for a woman to go for a run or into a laundromat at night, to open the door to a stranger, to help a stranded motorist; that women didn't walk in certain places, locked doors and windows, drew curtains, left lights on as precautions or perhaps 'prayers' (212); that women needed to 'take back the night' and to replace kitchen-table abortions with legal freedom of choice; that date rape was common enough to be an accepted subject for a term paper; that pornography, including snuff movies, was a fact of life (112); that women were 'found—often women but sometimes they would be men, or children, that was the worst—in ditches or forests or refrigerators in abandoned rented rooms, with their clothes on or off, sexually abused or not; at any rate killed' (212); that one did not allow one's children to walk alone to school because too many disappeared; that less terminally lethal circumstances included singles bars, blind dates, 'the terrible gap between the ones who could get a man easily and the ones who couldn't' as well as a dedication to anorexia, silicone implants, and cosmetic surgery (205) as means to realize the 'possibilities' proffered by fashion magazines (146); that fathers left without paying child support, mothers wound up on welfare, and the 'wretched little paycheques' of women would have to stretch to unsubsidized daycare (206).

The implicit women's utopia of *The Handmaid's Tale* is not in 'the time before.' It exists outside the 'either/or' thinking so beloved of Aunt Lydia, and outside the novel: outside of the dangers, humiliations, inequities, and backlash that women experience in its 'time before,' but also outside totalitarian Gilead's claims to have improved their lot. A first step to utopia, Atwood's novel tells us, requires that we 'pay attention' and bear witness, as does Offred when she uses her uncertain freedom to tell her story.

From *University of Toronto Quarterly* 75, no. 3 (2006): 857-868. Copyright © 2006 by University of Toronto Press. Reprinted by permission of University of Toronto Press Incorporated.

Notes

1. 'The first government of the United States was a fundamentalist government... a very strict theocracy especially with respect to sex. Countries continue the way they began; they rearrange the symbols and structures but something remains of their origins. And the Presidents of the United States have continued to quote the first theocrats, who referred to their colony as a "city upon a hill" and "a light to all nations." Reagan, for instance, repeated these early Puritan references to the Bible' (Atwood, *Two Solicitudes*, 72). See Evans for a discussion of the allusions in the novel to events in the early history of the United States.

2. Feminist readings of Margaret Atwood's *The Handmaid's Tale* include, among others: Bouson, Davidson, Ehrenreich, Freibert, Hengen, Hollinger, Howells, Mahoney, Provencal, Rigney, Rubinstein, Staels, Stein, and Stimpson.

3. See Bouson, 2-4, for a summary of Atwood's remarks on her writing in relation to feminism.

4. The file of clippings, or some version of it, is deposited in the Margaret Atwood Papers in the Fisher Rare Book Library at the University of Toronto (MS Coll 200, box 96). See the interview with John Godard for one of many assertions by Atwood that she 'invented nothing' in describing Gilead: 'There is nothing in the book that hasn't al-

ready happened. . . . All the things described in the book, people have already done to one another' (8).

5. This was due to a combination of factors: that women made less headway in terms of education and professional and trade employment than could have been wished and that a large number of blue-collar jobs, held disproportionately by men, disappeared during the recession of the early 1980s while the new jobs were in the service industries, long the lowest-paying sector hiring the largest numbers of women.

6. See Susan Faludi, *Backlash*, for much of the data and the documentation of the 'backlash' against feminism cited in this and the next two paragraphs and for careful documentation of the false premises, weak methodologies, and unreliable conclusions of many of the studies by government, media, and academia in support of 'backlash' arguments. Bouson also frames her discussion of oppositional strategies in *The Handmaid's Tale* with reference to the 1980s backlash against 'women's independence and autonomy' (135); Pawlowski, 144-46, briefly discusses *The Handmaid's Tale* in terms of the resurgence of the Right in Iran, Britain, and the United States.

7. Schlafly also quotes Lauren Bacall as putting husband and home well ahead of any career satisfactions, noting that Bacall gets 'Bogie' for her reward. Atwood has some fun with this in *The Handmaid's Tale* by having Offred remark on the very different image these actresses projected on screen in her recollection of the annual 'Humphrey Bogart festival, with Lauren Bacall or Katharine Hepburn, women on their own, making up their minds. They wore blouses with buttons down the front that suggested the possibilities of the word *undone*. These women could be undone; or not. They seemed to be able to choose. We seemed to be able to choose, then' (24).

8. The movie *The Handmaid's Tale* (screenplay by Harold Pinter, direction by Volker Schloendorff) succumbs even more than most 'readers' to the seductions of the romance tale while ignoring the numerous markers in Atwood's text telling us to be wary of those same seductions: in its final scene we see Offred, pregnant at last, living in an isolated area in a mid-twentieth-century Airstream trailer receiving via the underground the occasional love letter from Nick.

9. Not all of Atwood's initial reviewers or later critics found her dystopia plausible. Updike's paean to the 'paradise' of 'the time before' is contextualized in terms of what he regards as the failure of Atwood's dystopian premises to convince. Dean Flower described Atwood's premises in *The Handmaid's Tale* as 'so lacking plausibility or inevitability as to be embarrassing' (318). Tom O'Brien acknowledged the parallels between Gilead and 'contemporary events' but, failing to acknowledge the fictional premise that Offred has no access to information, found it hard to take Atwood's dystopia 'too seriously' because of its lack of reference to industry, business, the economy, and the international context; 'business culture can include coercion, and of course it has been complicit in so many right wing authoritarian dictatorships around the world. But it also includes vast numbers of people in this country [i.e., the United States] whom it would be difficult to tame into cooperative roles in any planned economy' (252)—it couldn't happen here, in short. Mary McCarthy found that the 'essential element of a cautionary tale,' the 'surprised recognition' which warns us by letting us see 'ourselves in a distorting mirror,' is completely absent from the novel: 'The book just does not tell me what there is in our present mores that I ought to watch out for unless I

want the United States of America to become a slave state something like the Republic of Gilead' (1). Chinmoy Banerjee mounts the most sustained critique of Atwood's dystopia, seeing it as grounded in 'a media-generated awareness of the threat of Christian fundamentalism and a somewhat retrospective sense of women's oppression in North America' and concluding that 'Atwood is concerned with the aesthetic enjoyment of a particular kind of victimization, and not with a critical examination of its determinant relations' (80).

Works Cited

Recording
Ruders, Poul. *The Handmaid's Tale* [*Tjenerindens fortælling*]. Libretto by Paul Bentley. Sung in Danish. Recorded live at the world premiere performance, 6 March 2000, Royal Danish Theatre, Copenhagen. Conductor Michael Schønwandt, Royal Danish Opera Chorus and Orchestra. Dacapo 8.224165-66.

Printed Sources
Atwood, Margaret. *The Handmaid's Tale*. 1985; Toronto: Seal 1986.
_____. 'Justice.' Unpublished MS. Margaret Atwood Papers, Thomas Fisher Rare Book Library, University of Toronto.
Atwood, Margaret, and Victor Lévy-Beaulieu. *Two Solicitudes: Conversations*. 1996. Trans Phyllis Aronoff and Howard Scott. Toronto: McClelland and Stewart 1998.
Banerjee, Chinmoy. 'Alice in Disneyland: Criticism as Commodity in *The Handmaid's Tale*.' *Essays on Canadian Writing* 41 (Summer 1990), 74-92.
Bouson, J. Brooks. *Brutal Choreographies: Oppositional Strategies and Narrative Design in the Novels of Margaret Atwood*. Amherst: University of Massachusetts Press 1993.
Brans, Jo. 'Using What You're Given.' 1988. Repr Ingersoll, 140-51.
Davidson, Arnold E. 'Making History in *The Handmaid's Tale*.' *Margaret Atwood: Vision and Forms*. Ed Kathryn VanSpanckeren and Jan Garden Castro. Carbondale: Southern Illinois University Press 1988, 113-21.
Ehrenreich, Barbara. 'Feminism's Phantoms.' *New Republic* 194 (17 March 1986), 33-35.
Evans, Mark. 'Versions of History: *The Handmaid's Tale* and Its Dedicatees.' *Margaret Atwood: Writing and Subjectivity: New Critical Essays*. Ed Colin Nicholson. New York: St Martin's 1994, 77-88.
Faludi, Susan. *Backlash: The Undeclared War Against American Women*. 1991. Repr New York: Doubleday Anchor 1992.
Flower, Dean. 'Fables of Identity.' *Hudson Review* 39 (Summer 1986), 309-21.
Freibert, Lucy M. 'Control and Creativity: The Politics of Risk in Margaret Atwood's *The Handmaid's Tale*.' *Critical Essays on Margaret Atwood*. Ed Judith McCombs. Boston: G. K. Hall 1988, 280-91.

Gerald, Gregory Fitz, and Kathryn Crabbe. 'Evading the Pigeonholers.' 1987. Repr Ingersoll, 131-39.

Godard, John. 'Lady Oracle.' *Books in Canada* 14:8 (November 1985), 6-10.

Hengen, Shannon. *Margaret Atwood's Power: Mirrors, Reflections and Images in Select Fiction and Poetry.* Toronto: Second Story 1993.

Hollinger, Veronica. 'Putting on the Feminine: Gender and Negativity in *Frankenstein* and *The Handmaid's Tale.*' *Negation, Critical Theory, and Postmodern Textuality.* Ed Daniel Fischlin. Dordrecht: Kluwer Academic Publishers 1994, 203-24.

Howells, Coral Ann. *Margaret Atwood.* London: Macmillan 1996.

Ingersoll, Earl G., ed. *Margaret Atwood: Conversations.* Princeton: Ontario Review 1990.

Jamkhandi, Sudhakar. 'An Interview with Margaret Atwood.' *Commonwealth Novel in English* 2:1 (January 1983), 1-6.

Lapham, Lewis L. 'Tentacles of Rage: The Republican Propaganda Mill, a Brief History.' *Harper's Magazine* 302:1852 (September 2004), 31-40.

Mahoney, Elizabeth. 'Writing So to Speak: The Feminist Dystopia.' *Image and Power: Women in Fiction in the Twentieth Century.* Ed Sara Sceats and Gail Cunningham. London and New York: Longman 1996, 28-40.

McCarthy, Mary. 'Breeders, Wives and Unwomen.' *New York Times Book Review* 91:6 (9 February 1986), 1, 35.

Meese, Elizabeth. 'The Empress Has No Clothes.' 1985. Repr Ingersoll, 177-90.

O'Brien, Tom. 'Siren's Wail.' *Commonweal* 113 (25 April 1986), 251-53.

Pawlowski, Merry M. *Virginia Woolf and Fascism: Revisiting the Dictators' Seduction.* London: Palgrave 2001.

Provencal, Vernon. '"Byzantine in the Extreme": Plato's *Republic* in *The Handmaid's Tale.*' *Classical and Modern Literature* 19:1 (Fall 1988), 53-76.

Rigney, Barbara Hill. *Margaret Atwood.* London: Macmillan 1987.

Rubinstein, Roberta. 'Nature and Nurture in Dystopia: *The Handmaid's Tale.*' *Margaret Atwood: Vision and Forms.* Ed Kathryn VanSpanckeren and Jan Garden Castro. Carbondale: Southern Illinois University Press 1988, 101-12.

Ruders, Poul (composer) and Paul Bentley (librettist). *The Handmaid's Tale: An Opera in a Prologue, a Prelude, Two Acts and an Epilogue.* Copenhagen: Edition Wilhelm Hansen 2000 [libretto included in recording of *The Handmaid's Tale*; see under 'Recording' above].

Sandler, Linda. 'A Question of Metamorphosis' 1977. Repr Ingersoll, 40-57.

Schlafly, Phyllis. *The Power of the Positive Woman.* New Rochelle, NY: Arlington House 1977.

Staels, Hilde. *Margaret Atwood's Novels: A Study of Narrative Discourse.* Tübingen: A. Francke Verlag 1995.

Stein, Karen F. *Margaret Atwood Revisited.* New York: Twayne 1999.

Stimpson, Catharine R. 'Atwood Woman.' *Nation* 242:21 (31 May 1986), 764-67.

Updike, John. 'Expeditions to Gilead and Seegard.' *The New Yorker* 62 (12 May 1986), 118-26.

Alice in Disneyland:
Criticism as Commodity in
The Handmaid's Tale

Chinmoy Banerjee

Margaret Atwood has an Arnoldian sense of the function of art in society: "I believe that poetry is the heart of the language, the activity through which language is renewed and kept alive. I believe that fiction writing is the guardian of the moral and ethical sense of the community" ("An End" 346). It is not, therefore, surprising that she is profoundly concerned with the impact of mass marketing on culture.[1] Her novels construct themes of the reduction of life and language to cliché under the domination of mass culture and, at their best, subvert this through parody. Her explicit statement of this concern in "An End to Audience?," quoted above, points to the growth of monopolies in publishing and book distribution as contributing to the fragmentation of audience and the decay of the practice of reading. She sees the "literary equivalent of Muzak" taking over the reading public, while serious literary artists are reduced to being isolated formalists, addressing only each other. "This is already happening to poetry, though in Canada, which as we all know is a cultural backwater, it hasn't happened quite as thoroughly yet" ("An End" 355).

In the light of this concern, Atwood's nonproblematic view of her own popular success and her belief in the possibility of serious art and an audience of demanding readers, seem conspicuously optimistic ("An End" 345-46). This problem of art in relation to mass culture has been studied most systematically by the Frankfurt School, within which Theodor Adorno's radical pessimism is notorious. But although Adorno's utter pessimism about the possibility of art outside the avant-garde has to be rejected because of its basis in extreme elitism and its inability to recognize the possibilities of resistance within mass media, the problem of art within mass culture cannot be ignored. Existing within mass culture, the work of art can resist becoming a commodity only by struggling against the ideological character of mass culture, so that far from being an index of worth, success makes it necessary that a work's claims to artistic and critical status be tested with some care.

The remarkable success Atwood's bestselling novel *The Handmaid's Tale* has had (it was nominated as book of the year for 1986 by *Time* magazine), and the almost universal, and often extravagant, praise it has received from reviewers, makes such a test of artistic and critical status necessary. Given the nature of the mass market (and it is naive to think that the book trade is somehow separate from it), how does one account for the popular and critical success of a book whose author is being compared to Swift and Orwell and that is praised for its moral seriousness and its quality as a disturbing cautionary tale? What is the popular appeal of dystopia?

It seems obvious that dystopia and utopia are critical genres that point to the negativity of the existing social world in antithetical ways, utopia by creating a fictional world that is marked by its difference from the existing one, and dystopia by creating a fictional world that is marked as an extension of the existing one. But it is equally clear that the two critical genres don't necessarily function critically. Criticism and critical forms are routinely absorbed into mass culture and become the basis of entertainment, as a look at television and movies will confirm. Dystopia as such, however grim, is by no means necessarily disturbing: it is a very popular form of entertainment in which a bleak vision of the future, whether it be a world after nuclear holocaust or a world ecologically destroyed and dehumanized through technology, provides the context for exciting adventure, zany comedy, and hilarious mayhem. It would seem that when critical issues become urgent, and awareness of them widespread, they also become eminently marketable. In other words, the passive reception of information through mass media is the base on which entertainment, and particularly critical entertainment, is constructed. Such entertainment, needless to say, doesn't challenge, transform, or advance consciousness since it bases itself in what is already accepted. Its function is ideological in that it denatures criticism by making it consumable and comfortable, and does so especially when disturbing and urgent questions are involved.

Although J. L. Austin kept literature out of his consideration of speech acts, I would suggest, though necessarily tentatively, that certain forms of literary utterance are modes of doing, and as such are defined by their illocutionary force. A satire, for instance, is not a satire if it is directed at a nonexistent target, or if it doesn't reduce its target. Its force depends on at least these three conditions: that it have a target that we recognize as existent, that it reduce this target, and that it attempt to effect in us a change of attitude correlative to the reduction. In other words, such an utterance has an "illocutionary force" and a "perlocutionary" effect. It seems to me that literary forms whose end is to persuade us about a state of affairs must necessarily display this structure. If we do a structuralist analysis of Swift's "A Modest Proposal," we no longer see it as satire but as a text. I would maintain that dystopia, as a critical form, is also characterized by a force that makes urgent for us the negativity it discovers in our world. The difference between a dystopia that retains its critical force and one that has lost it in becoming a commodity, is that the former presents its negative vision as a question on the horizon of our present experience, while the latter simply accepts the vision as its starting point, as the mere condition of its narrative. To put it another way, while in the first the narrative is instrumental in opening its fictional assumptions to urgent examination, in the second the fictional ground is a given that is accepted for the sake of the particular kind of enjoyment the narrative offers. My contention is that Atwood's novel belongs to the latter category.

The Handmaid's Tale is, of course, a dystopia in its form, set sometime in the near future in Gilead, a sexist, fascistic theocracy that has been established in what used to be the United States. A regime that combines Christian fundamentalism, sexism, and racism has taken power after shooting the president and the congress. All civil liberties have been abolished; a fascist state with an all-pervasive police force that practices surveillance, torture, deportation, and public and secret executions has been established; and women, deprived of all power except that of punishing other women, are subjected to oppression along Old Testament lines. Life in Gilead also bears the imprint of ecological disaster: there is a demographic crisis caused by widespread sterility and birth defects. This is explained in the postscript as the result of environmental pollution, syphilis R, and AIDS, which have combined with contraception and abortion to lower the birthrate in the West.

The narrator, Offred, is one of the Handmaids who fill a pivotal role in this society in that they mark the utmost in female abjection according to biblical ideology, and, at the same time, perform the most important function of reproduction in a sterile world. The Handmaids are women who were unmarried or whose marriage was considered void at the time of the coup. They are assigned as breeders to male officials whose wives have failed to bear children, on the assumption that it is always the woman who is barren. If they succeed in bearing a healthy child within three assignments, they are saved; if they fail, they are sent to the Colonies to die gruesomely, handling toxic wastes. Their names, Offred or Ofglen (Offred's partner), for example, indicate that they have no identity other than that of breeders assigned to males whose names they bear with the possessive prefix.

While men have all the power in Gilead, women are nevertheless socially stratified. Wives constitute the social elite, being married to the officials; they are idle, mostly sterile, usually nasty, and spend their time visiting each other. Their breeding function has been given to Handmaids, toward whom they feel intense hostility. Their housework is done by servants called Marthas. The wives of the working class are called Econowives, and have to do all the work of breeding and housekeeping themselves. All these women feel the utmost contempt for the Handmaids, whom they view as whores. There is also a class of Aunts, whose job is the indoctrination of Handmaids and the conducting of public executions for the edification of women. All these women are colour coded: wives wear blue, Marthas green, Econowives blue and green stripes, Aunts brown, and Handmaids red.

Although Handmaids are fed well and not subjected to any physical abuse, their life is not very pleasant. Not being allowed to read (books are banned in Gilead), talk, or work, Handmaids are subjected to excruciating boredom. The basic activity of their life is the daily shopping trip for food. The major excitements are births, mass weddings, and public executions called "Salvaging," which sometimes include "Particicutions" as a special treat. There is, of course, the regular medical checkup, the monthly ritual fucking, and the constant anxiety about pregnancy since most of the men are, in fact, sterile.

While it follows rather to the letter biblical utterances about sex and women, Gilead has locked up the Bible as potentially subversive. With writing disallowed, food shops with names such as "Milk and Honey" and "All Flesh" now identify themselves with pictures of their wares on their signs. Religious feeling, too, has been eliminated and substituted with automated "Soul Scrolls"—numbered prayers that are typed and read out by unattended computers on receipt of telephone orders, and instantly recycled.

Much of this is undoubtedly quite amusing. But while it makes the fiction enjoyable as a parody of televangelism and Christian fundamentalism, it puts the more sinister aspects of the dystopia into some doubt. The participatory execution is stripped of its horror and distanced as a game when it is called "Particicution" (with its reference to the Canadian government's ParticipACTION program); our ability to imagine the terror is undercut by our awareness of verbal play. Atwood's dystopia places side by side two possible modes of imagining the negative: the extension into horror and the reduction into absurdity. The horror, on the one hand, seems both excessive and unmotivated, and the play, on the other hand, seems comfortable and clever.

The critical force of Atwood's dystopia is, first of all, put into doubt by the historical superficiality of the fiction. While we may imagine all kinds of negative worlds, what is needed as a precondition of any critical force is that the imagined world be conceived as an extension of the historically existent world. Huxley's and Orwell's worlds have such force because they embody the technological and totalitarian shadow that their times cast, and that our world continues to cast, on the horizon. Atwood's world, on the other hand, is grounded on a media-generated awareness of the threat of Christian fundamentalism and a somewhat retrospective sense of women's oppression in North America, the fundamental motivation of this dystopia being the reduction of women to mere possessions of men, to decorations, workers, breeders, and whores. But although those involved in the struggle for women's rights continue to deal with basic and urgent issues and to counter any complacency, Atwood's premise requires us to forget the immense gains made in the last 20 years by the women's movement. Despite the fact that Offred's retrospective meditations show a guilty awareness that the complacency of her generation caused it to lose what her mother's had gained, Atwood's fantasy is unlikely to scare a new generation of women into following in their mothers' footsteps, precisely because its premises ignore history and, in so doing, communicate an absence of hope. But that is to assume that the book has any such intention.

Jerry Falwell and Pat Robertson notwithstanding, the premise that Christian fundamentalism may lead to a theocracy in the United States is also flimsy as a foundation for a dystopia. Televangelism and the various scandals surrounding it have been much in the news, and there is indeed no dearth of sexist and racist behaviour on the part of individuals, groups, and governments, usually to the accompaniment of Bible thumping. But to see in these phenomena, rather than in economic, ecological, technological, or military sources, the basis of future horror in an advanced capitalist society is historically frivolous. Also, any nightmare about the political future of American society that does not take into account the interests of Wall Street may be easily dismissed as just a bad dream. This is certainly not to deny that the theocracy premise has as much plausibility as is necessary for our enjoyment of the novel. The point is that the premise is made plausible only by its resemblance to certain current, mass media-generated events, rather than by a close analysis of history, and that the premise is something interesting to imagine rather than something that demands serious concern.

Another important premise of Atwood's dystopia has a different status: the issue of ecological disaster that forms the background to Gilead (though it is not a necessary part of it in that it is neither the cause, nor the effect of Gilead). It is obviously an issue of extraordinary historical urgency, but, significantly, it is only a background. It provides the condition for the interesting breeding arrangement in Gilead, and for the Gulags where Gilead's dissidents and rejects must live. On the contrary, fascist repression in Gilead is all pervasive and brings together images of dictatorship from all over the world. And yet this is not a central issue in the book, whose concern is not so much the question of political liberty as the condition of the Handmaids, or, rather, the question of politics only to the extent that it affects the condition of the Handmaids. We never know why the state needs to maintain this level of terror. The whole society is already set up as an armed camp; spies are everywhere; the police always get their wo/man; and there is spectacular punishment for offenders.

As several reviewers have pointed out, Gilead doesn't seem to have an economy. In fact, we know very little about Gilead except its organization of sexual power. Any sense of a political and administrative structure, or of an educational system for the perpetuation of this society is conspicuously absent. Also absent is any sense of a theology or ideology beyond some sexist clichés, though this is a theocratic, fascistic state. These absences raise many questions for which there are no available answers. Why, for instance, does this society rely so much on force and so little on propaganda, and, given its use of technology and automation, why is there so little use of mass media? Why are Handmaids, on whose reproductive power this society depends, kept in such oppressive boredom that some are driven to suicide? Why has this society kept some superficial aspects of marketing from our time, while totally abandoning what we have learned about the power of marketing and technology in the achievement of hegemony? And why has it opted for the more primitive means of terror? The silence that answers such questions makes us aware of the world of Gilead as a thin surface of arbitrary decisions.

Professor Pieixoto's "academically proper" explanation in the postscript that the limitations of the document reflect the limitations of the narrator seems to be quite persuasive for many readers. Yet the trick involved is clear enough: we do not have a real historical document limited by the limitations of the witness, but a fictional universe embodying, and limited by, the choices made by the author. The fictional universe is necessarily a measure of the fictional narrator, but the choice of a particular point of view with the potentialities and limitations of revelation implicit in it is the responsibility and measure of the author. To ascribe the limitations of the fiction to Offred is only to shift the question, which then becomes one of why a perspective limited in this particular manner is the necessary perspective for this fiction. And the answer is surely that Atwood is concerned with the aesthetic enjoyment of a particular kind of victimization, and not with a critical examination of its determinant relations. Pieixoto's explanation is obviously an attempt by Atwood to preempt expected criticism. It indicates awareness that the fiction is arbitrary in relation to its historical ground and is afforded insufficient internal motivation by the coherence of its imagination.

This sense we have that we are dealing with a surface that conceals no depths also manifests itself when we consider the formal level of the novel. Though related in the continuous present by a narrator who claims to be telling this story in her head as she goes along (37), the narrative is arranged as a series of set spectacles and sequences. After a brief, initial chapter that situates the story in an indefinite past, the narrative continues in the present, suggesting a synchronous relationship between story and discourse with ellipses between the segments of the narrative.[2] In other words, we are encouraged to believe that the story is moving forward from its beginning (which occurs sometime during the sixth week of the narrator's third assignment) to its conclusion (which coincides with her entrance into the Angels' van) at the actual pace at which it is narrated, though much time passes between narrative segments. The story is woven, from time to time, with the narrator's discontinuous memories, ranging from her childhood, to her arrest, to her stay at the Rachel and Leah Centre. This remembered past constitutes a pre-story whose function is to explain the narrator's present situation, to provide the context for the story unfolding within the discourse.

But there is something unusual about the relation between the story and the discourse. The present-tense narration not only offers the narrated experience with immediacy, it also offers it as unique, in the "singulative" mode, to borrow a term from Genette. (This is the basic mode of all narrative, unless the narrative points out that what is reported has happened several times.) Yet, a slightly closer look reveals this to be an illusion: the proper mode of being of what is presented as singulative is actually iterative. That is to say, what appears to be immediate and unique is something that has happened several times, the illusion being created by suppressing or subduing the indicators of the iterative. The opening of the second chapter provides a clear example of this:

> A chair, a table, a lamp. Above, on the white ceiling, a relief ornament in the shape of a wreath, and in the centre of it a blank space, plastered over, like the place in a face where the eye has been taken out. There must have been a chandelier, once. They've removed anything you could tie a rope to. (7)

The order of perception suggests that a room is being seen for the first time; the sequence of atomistic notation using the indefinite article to name the furniture indicates emptiness and distance (using *the* would situate the objects within the realm of familiarity). The eye then moves to the ceiling, where it lingers over details that become increasingly more significant: the plaster in the centre of the wreath suggests torture; it indicates the removal of a chandelier, the attempt to prevent suicide, and therefore, by entailment, the desirability of suicide.

However, the paragraphs immediately following this one establish that this order of perceptions and interpretation is a repetition, and ought to be presented as iterative. The sentence, "When the window is partly open—it only opens partly—the air can come in and make the curtains move," offers a subdued sense of iteration as does a later remark: "Nothing takes place in the bed but sleep; or no sleep" (7). The narrator's ability to interpret the origins and purpose of the braided rug displays her knowledge of the culture that apparently exists in a hostile relationship to her, and yet her question, "Government issue?" reveals her isolation and her newness to the situation. That she observes, interprets, or fails to interpret the objects in her room, indicates either that she is doing it for the first time, or that there is some special significance to this occasion. Yet it turns out that she lives in this room, and this passage just describes a moment before her daily outing to get the groceries. The point of all this is no doubt to communicate that despite spending five weeks on her new assignment, Offred continues to feel a stranger in her room. This feeling is suggested, however, by the author's creation of an illusion of immediacy through the suppression of the iterative mood.

Most of the narration in the novel is in what I will call a pseudo-singulative mode, which I described earlier. This means that things that have happened several times are presented once as if for the first time, and no indication of any particular significance is attached to this rather than any other time. For instance, in chapter 10, Offred looks out of the window and watches the Commander get into the car, noticing his grey hair and comparing him favourably with her previous commander, who was bald. This is not the first time she has seen him—he is silhouetted against the open door of her room at the end of chapter 8. Yet it suggests that this is the first time she has noticed the colour of his hair, though this is at least the sixth week of her assignment, during which she should have already performed one "Ceremony" with him. It has indeed been mentioned that Offred came to this house five weeks ago, but we are given the feeling that her stay is just beginning. In a way, one might say the entire discourse is in this mode, since it presents Offred's third assignment as if it were the first, except for some passing references to the previous commander's undesirability. In other words, there is a story, which we have every reason to believe is much like the one we are now receiving that has been suppressed so that the one we are being told may be presented as a series of unique events. But even within the frame of Offred's last assignment, the pseudo-singulative mode creates immediacy by suppressing temporal depth. The narrator's trip to the store with Ofglen is presented as fraught with anxiety, though it is one of many such trips. Most of the episodes in the novel are constructed in this way—the iterative being suppressed or subdued in the interest of effect, to provide spectacle and generate anxiety. About most of them one may ask why the narrator has chosen this particular occasion rather than another, similar one; why, in other words, the episode lacks temporal density.

Undoubtedly the theatricality that results from this technique has a certain power over readers who find the novel gripping, chilling, disturbing, and so on. This reaction is particularly interesting because it attests to the fact that rather than focusing on the intellectual and political concerns that provide the motive of genuinely critical dystopia, *The Handmaid's Tale* so overwhelmingly concentrates on the creation of effect. In fact, the rather arbitrary character of the fiction that we noted earlier becomes explicable if we consider spectacle and anxiety as the founding motives of the fiction. Seen in this light, the spectacularly costumed Handmaid with her very interesting function and curious ritual is the "concept" (in the Hollywood sense) around which the fiction is organized. The dystopia has as much substance as is needed to display the Handmaid in various situations, and to generate anxiety on her behalf. And given Atwood's long fascination with the Gothic, it is perhaps not an overstatement to say that the novel is a costume Gothic projected against a dystopian setting.

The Gothic element of the novel becomes quite clear under scrutiny. The basic situation is familiar: a woman, totally helpless in a strange environment, continuously finds herself in a variety of situations where a menacing alien power is spectacularly displayed. And, of course, she is almost lost when her partner is apparently arrested, saved when she learns of her suicide, disastrously exposed at the very height of her relief, and miraculously saved by her lover, who happens to be linked both to the ruling power and the underground resistance. This is revealing enough, but Atwood does more. Not only is there the armed camp of Gilead outside, but the Commander's house itself is a castle in which Offred glides through corridors and down the staircase:

> The carpet bends and goes down the front staircase and I go with it, one hand on the banister, once a tree, turned in another century, rubbed to a warm gloss. . . . There's a grandfather clock in the hallway. . . .
>
> There remains a mirror, on the hall wall. If I turn my head so that the white wings framing my face direct my vision towards it, I can see it as I go down the stairs, round, convex, a pier-glass, like the eye of a fish, and myself in it like a distorted shadow, a parody of something, some fairytale figure in a red cloak, descending towards a moment of carelessness that is the same as danger. A Sister, dipped in blood. (8-9)

Surely, the narrator, aware of herself as a parody of Red Riding Hood out for a walk in the forest, is further encased in a parody of her own narration—the self-articulation of a Gothic heroine. It is within this frame that we watch the narrator seek and discover the secret message from her predecessor in her room/dungeon, a message she earnestly repeats to herself, oblivious of what the reader may guess and what she discovers later, that it is a joke in schoolboys' dog Latin.

The Ceremony itself, covered in chapters 15 through 17, typifies the Gothic structure of the narrative. It is the dreadful moment toward which the narrative has been moving, preceded by numerous hints that have led us to expect it to be a moment of horror and mystery. The scene opens with a repetition of the image of the narrator in the mirror, an image that seems to operate like a Gothic key:

> When the bell has finished I descend the stairs, a brief waif in the eye of glass that hangs on the downstairs wall. The clock ticks with its pendulum, keeping time; my feet in their neat red shoes count the way down. (75)

What follows is the equivalent of the description of a hall in a Gothic castle, complete with the portraits of grim ancestors:

> two paintings, both of women. . . . there they hang, their backs and mouths stiff, their breasts constricted, their faces pinched, their caps starched, their skin grayish-white, guarding the room with their narrowed eyes. (75-76)

The episode is constructed for suspense: first, Offred enters and observes the room, and communicates its menace and oppressiveness; after a certain interval, the household staff come in, position themselves, and wait for Serena Joy; then they all wait for the Commander, who arrives and is watched apprehensively by all. The Ceremony as such, both the Bible reading and the fucking, turns out to be not so much dreadful as boring, and this pattern of Gothic deflation is repeated as farce when the Commander's mysterious call turns out to be an invitation to a game of Scrabble.

What I am saying is that *The Handmaid's Tale* is a particularly tricky example of the duplicitous aspect of Atwood's art, an aspect that has often been studied.[3] The novel lacks depth and force as a dystopia because it is not really what it seems; it has the power of suspense that derives from its Gothic character, but it is not, in fact, Gothic. If we look carefully enough, we see that it is a parody of the Gothic.

Most people writing on Atwood notice that doubleness and mirrors are one of her obsessions (Mandel 166), and that her art faces simultaneously in the two opposing directions of seriousness and parody. The Gothic aspect of this doubling through mirrors has already been noted, but there is another telling example in the novel that is worth quoting:

> . . . I walk, one foot set carefully down, then the other, without creaking, along the runner, as if on a forest floor. . . .
>
> Down past the fisheye on the hall wall, I can see my white shape, of tented body, hair down my back like a mane, my eyes gleaming. (91-92)

This is certainly as fine a self-portrait of the narrator as Gothic heroine as one can get.[4] Offred and Ofglen are, of course, doubles, and the narrator points to their mirroring several times; we note also that they begin to communicate only after they look at each other's reflections in the window of a shop. Offred, the narrator, has another double in her predecessor who hanged herself, and who beckons Offred to suicide, and yet another, contrary one in Moira, whose voice of resistance Offred adopts.

This last doubling has a very interesting aspect. The narrator speaks in two distinct voices: that of a passive and suffering victim who remembers the life she has lost, mourns the loss of love and sensuousness, longs for these, and feels oppressed and suicidal; and that of a defiant survivor who refuses assent through a continuous sarcastic reduction and hatred of her oppressors. In other words, there is something of a dialogue between the two voices of the narrator, a dialogue that ends rather ambiguously with the narrator's discovery of orgasm and love in the arms of the silent and sultry chauffeur, Nick. While the defiant, role-model voice of lesbian Moira fades away after the narrator meets her in Jezebel's, where she has accepted the life of a prostitute, the earth moves under the narrator, and her voice becomes contented ("I want to be here, with Nick, where I can get at him" [255]), abject ("I resign my body freely, to the uses of others" [268]), and benign to the extent of feeling sorry for the Commander as she is being taken away.

But this dialogue within the narrator could perhaps be seen as the double of another dialogue: that between Atwood and the critics who have charged her with not providing positive role models, and for being pessimistic. Moira is clearly presented as a role model: a radical feminist heroine who inspires the narrator. This response of Atwood's to her critics is, however, subtly undercut by narrational signs. Not only does Moira's two-part story appear in the form of an inserted tale, a device derived from, and alluding to, romance literature and its parodic forms, but also Moira's adventure has the ring of a cliché, of stories read in childhood. Similarly, in response to the charge of pessimism, Atwood seems to offer the romantic reader a happy ending: Offred, starved for feeling, touch, and sex through the novel, finds happiness with Nick and is rescued. A feminist reader could also interpret this as an affirmation of sensuousness and female sexuality against puritanical and patriarchal denials of both. Yet this reading is surely a trap signposted by the conspicuous banality with which it is prefaced: "I'm sorry there is so much pain in this story. . . . I've tried to put some of the good things in as well. Flowers, for instance, because where would we be without them?" (251). The corniness of this introduction reinforces the doubt we have about the feminist message when we recognize that the pattern of the sensorially deprived female oppressed by a sterile ruling class and saved by the sexual power of a working-class male has its paradigm in *Lady Chatterley's Lover*. It is difficult to decide whether Atwood is seriously offering her heterosexual romance with the emphatically patriarchal twist of D. H. Lawrence as a feminist response to the situation of women. But what is clear is that her text is a duplicitous dialogue in which the surface utterance seems to offer a conciliatory response to her critics, while this message is subverted by the formal signifiers of language and genre.

Pieixoto characterizes the narrator as an "educated woman" (his description qualified by a professorial banality about standards that elicits the usual laughter and groans from his audience [287]), but she seems to have yet another voice: her very sophisticated, ironic, and poetic voice is paired with a somewhat naive, marginally informed, and apologetic one. We hear both voices in the beginning of chapter 2. The first one notes that a piece of plaster in the ceiling seems like "the place in a face where the eye has been taken out," and infers, "There must have been a chandelier, once. They've removed anything you could tie a rope to" (7). This voice understands the culture of the new regime and can interpret the significance of the rug on the floor. The second voice is more innocent, needing to ask whether the furnishings are government issue, and is almost self-congratulatory about being able to figure out what seems perfectly obvious:

> I know why there is no glass, in front of the watercolour picture of blue irises, and why the window only opens partly and why the glass in it is shatterproof. It isn't running away they're afraid of. We wouldn't get far. It's those other escapes, the ones you can open in yourself, given a cutting edge. (7-8)

Another way of recognizing the two voices is that one is allusive, elliptical, and dense, while the other is garrulous, cliché-ridden, and filled with redundancy. The first voice can describe Offred descending as "a Sister, dipped in blood" (9); and the second can say, "I never looked good in red, it's not my colour" (8). The first voice speaks through Marlowe, Shakespeare, and Tennyson without apology. It says, "Though this is time, nor am I out of it" (35), "Context is all; or is it ripeness? One or the other" (180), and "Whatever is silenced will clamour to be heard, though silently. A Tennyson garden, heavy with scent, languid; the return of the word *swoon*" (143). The second voice says: "*Fraternize* means to behave like a brother. Luke told me that. He said there was no corresponding word that meant to behave like a sister. Sororize, it would have to be, he said. From the Latin" (11), or,

> *Mayday* used to be a distress signal, a long time ago, in one of those wars we studied in high school. I kept getting them mixed up, but you could tell them apart by the airplanes if you paid attention. It was Luke who told me about Mayday though. (41)

Having told a story about "pig balls" used in the eighties to entertain bored pigs, this voice has to add, "I read about that in Introduction to Psychology; that, and the chapter on caged rats who'd give themselves electric shocks for something to do. And the one on the pigeons. . . ." (65). Referring to the flowers Serena decks herself in, the voice says, ". . . you can't use them any more, you're withered. They're the genital organs of plants," and then has to add, "I read that somewhere, once" (77).

Both these voices meditate on words, but the first reflects on *lie* and *lay* (35), feels like the word *shatter* (97), and ruminates:

> I sit in the chair and think about the word *chair*. It can also mean the leader of a meeting. It can also mean a mode of execution. It is the first syllable in charity. It is the French word for flesh. None of these facts has any connection with the others. (104)

The second voice, on the other hand, remembers words and phrases once used, such as "humongous," "organic," "I know what you mean," or "I know where you are coming from" (26, 91, 10). It is this second voice that refers to what "Some people call . . . habits" as an appropriate word for what Handmaids wear because habits are hard to break (24), appears innocent of Aunt Lydia's motto, "Pen Is Envy" (174), and seems incapable of recognizing the parodic inversion of Eric Fromm in Aunt Lydia's sermon on freedom:

> There is more than one kind of freedom, said Aunt Lydia. Freedom to and freedom from. In the days of anarchy, it was freedom to. Now you are being given freedom from. Don't underrate it. (24)

These two voices, one of a poet and the other of a normal heroine of a comedy of manners in a Gothic-dystopian land, don't speak to each other, though they inhabit the same "I."[5] They exist as two narrators addressing two narratees (Prince 7-25), who are defined by the codes each requires for communication and what one might call two levels of cultural competence. The competence of the second narratee is obviously limited to an ideological standard that is formed by the normal experience of growing up through school and college; the resentment of mother's activism; the expectation that women shouldn't be too smart, that they shouldn't know too much, and should rely on men; the usual knowledge of the interiors of homes, hotel rooms, supermarkets, media images, phrases in common use; and the expected incomprehension of political reality. This competence excludes the knowledge of Milton, Freud, and Fromm, but includes ballet classes and vodka ads. It excludes the ability to make too many connections, and requires that things be stated very clearly: "What's going on [the ceremony] in this room, under Serena Joy's silvery canopy, is not exciting. It has nothing to do with passion or love or romance . . ." (89). While the code by which the second voice and its narratee are related is the sociocultural code of feminine experience, the first voice and its narratee relate through a literary code that requires a certain literary and semantic awareness, as well as an ability to respond to a parodic, allusive, metaphorical, and ironic use of language. Obviously, these voices and their narratees exist not in a communicative, but a hierarchical relation, since the literary competence subsumes the feminine, while the latter remains blind to the former.

   This particular doubleness becomes quite clear in the concluding "Historical Notes," whose own doubleness—it is both a parody of academic communication and a straightforward section of explanatory notes—links the narrator-narratee relationship to the relationship between author and reader. The main function of the notes is apparently to ground and explain the tale. Pieixoto's speech attributes the initiation of the Handmaids' role to the falling birthrate in the West, the phenomenon of surrogate mothers, and the practice of polygamy among Mormons; it explains the source of various practices in Gilead; and it explains the naming of the Handmaids, and words such as "Particicution" and "Salvaging." Some readers feel offended that the author has found it necessary to explain what is fairly obvious (Carrington 131), but this indicates that they have failed to see the two different readers being addressed, readers who are extratextual versions of the two narratees. The information and explanation, and the continuation of the story through Pieixoto's speculation, are there for the reader who needs them. And this reader, accepting the position of one of Pieixoto's addressees, must remain blind to the parodic nature of this framing discourse. But the other reader, who does not need the content of the notes section, will receive the form, and recognize it as a parody of academic conferences and framing fictions: the former in the play with names, the turning upside down of the discipline of anthropology ("Caucasian Anthropology" [281]), the persistence of sexist jokes, and the piety of a value-free social science, and the latter in the play with reflexivity and the possibilities of illusion.

In regard to the parody of framing fictions, we notice that the novel becomes progressively insistent on its reflexivity. Beginning with a brief reflection on its telling that suggests that it is a story in the narrator's head, told as she goes along (37), the narrative refers to itself as "this story . . . about where I am," before proceeding to tell a naive story about Moira (121). A little later, however, the narrator becomes insistent about the reconstructed nature of her narrative, openly harangues the reader, and offers a teaser before going on with the story of the Scrabble game (126-27). She insists again, at the end of the chapter, that "this is a reconstruction" (132). In chapter 40, she has difficulty choosing between various versions of her visit to Nick, and in chapter 41, she becomes just a storyteller who wants to tell a "more civilized" story for the benefit of the reader (251). Pieixoto's speech puts the final touches to this reflexivity by not only suggesting that ". . . there is a certain reflective quality about the narrative that would to my mind rule out synchronicity," but also that the entire order of the narrative is an editorial decision (285, 284). The pointed denial of synchronicity, of course, highlights the fact that the novel is presented as synchronous, and that the synchronous quality is precisely what Atwood is so conspicuously concealing. One needs to ask why Atwood has to cover her tracks and why the novel becomes progressively reflexive, rather than being so from the beginning.

The point of this game seems to me to be for Atwood to have her cake and eat it. She manages to create an illusion of immediacy that involves the reader in the experience of her dystopian-Gothic world, while framing it in a reflexivity that closes it in on itself. The reflexivity stays as a frame outside the illusion without disturbing it. It doesn't penetrate the narrative to distance it from its audience in its act of narration; it stays outside, and, even if pointed to with increasing insistence, is unable—and of course unwilling—to break the illusion and identification. The content of illusion is securely enclosed within the reflexivity of form.

Though reflexivity is commonly treated as a value in itself, it is necessary to note that it has the antithetical possibilities of being either agonistic or aesthetic. It can be a form of self-demystification that, by breaking illusion, compels the reader to construct his or her meaning, a way of refusing closure that transfers the site of meaning from the text to the decision-making reader, or it can be a form of self-referentiality that closes art in on itself to become a self-sustaining construct, and places the reader in a position of contemplative enjoyment.

I hope my argument has shown that Atwood's blindness to the problematic nature of her popular success within a culture increasingly dominated by the mass market and culture-industrial production is somewhat less than innocent. Her theoretical statements affirm the need for an art that is critical, and *The Handmaid's Tale* promises criticism by virtue of both its form and its content as a feminist dystopia. Yet, as we have seen, the novel is a pseudo-dystopia whose structure generates two levels of response: one of naive consumption through illusion and identification, and the other of sophisticated enjoyment of parodic exercise and play with illusion. At the first, or popular level, criticism is only a lure for consumption; at the second, or aesthetic level, it is dissolved through parodic frames and is ultimately irrelevant. Criticism, I have argued, is not only a form but a force, and *The Handmaid's Tale* uses only the form for consumption and enjoyment.

From *Essays on Canadian Writing* 41 (1990): 74-93. Copyright © 1990 by ECW Press Ltd. Reprinted by permission of ECW Press Ltd.

Notes

1. The next sentence is even more revealing:

> Especially now that organized religion is scattered and in disarray, and politicians have, Lord knows, lost their credibility, fiction is one of the few forms left through which we may examine our society not in its particular but in its typical aspects; through which we can see ourselves and the ways in which we behave towards each other, through which we can see others and judge them and ourselves. ("An End" 346)

2. The distinction between story and discourse is now common, though definitions vary. I mean by discourse the textual dimension of the narrative, what is actually given to us, and by story the virtual dimension we project from the discourse: discourse is a "telling" of story. I am using some concepts from Genette.

3. The two most important studies of this are by Grace and Lecker.

4. The double tradition of the Gothic heroine as the passive victim of male fantasy and the bold adventuress of female fantasy has been pointed out by Moers.

5. Jane Rule has noted the pursuit of normalcy as a theme in Atwood's novels.

Works Cited

Adorno, Theodor W. "On the Fetish Character in Music and the Regression of Listening." Trans. Maurice Goldbloom. *The Essential Frankfurt School Reader*. Ed. Andrew Arato and Eike Gebhardt. 1982. New York: Continuum, 1985. 270-99.

Atwood, Margaret. "An End to Audience?" *Second Words: Selected Critical Prose*. By Margaret Atwood. Toronto: Anansi, 1982. 334-57.

──────. *The Handmaid's Tale*. 1985. Toronto: McClelland-Bantam-Seal, 1986.

Austin, J. L. *How To Do Things with Words*. New York: Oxford UP, 1962.

Carrington, Ildikó de Papp. "A Swiftean Sermon." Rev. of *The Handmaid's Tale*, by Margaret Atwood. *Essays on Canadian Writing* 34 (1987): 127-32.

Davidson, Arnold E., and Cathy N. Davidson, eds. *The Art of Margaret Atwood: Essays in Criticism*. Toronto: Anansi, 1981.

Genette, Gérard. *Narrative Discourse: An Essay in Method.* Trans. Jane E. Lewin. Ithaca: Cornell UP, 1972.

Grace, Sherrill E. "Margaret Atwood and the Politics of Duplicity." Davidson and Davidson 55-68.

Lecker, Robert. "Janus through the Looking Glass: Atwood's First Three Novels." Davidson and Davidson 177-203.

Mandel, Eli. "Atwood Gothic." *Malahat Review* 41 (1977): 165-74.

Moers, Ellen. *Literary Women.* Garden City, NY: Doubleday, 1976.

Prince, Gerald. "Introduction to the Study of the Narratee." *Reader Response Criticism: From Formalism to Post-Structuralism.* Ed. Jane P. Tompkins. Baltimore: Johns Hopkins UP, 1980. 7-25.

Rule, Jane. "Life, Liberty and the Pursuit of Normalcy—The Novels of Margaret Atwood." *Malahat Review* 41 (1977): 42-49.

Selves, Survival, and Resistance in *The Handmaid's Tale*

Elisabeth Hansot

Dystopias are notable for the obsessiveness, if not the finesse, with which their elites attempt to eliminate dissent. The sheer exigencies of survival might be thought to preclude resistance. But the opposite claim is equally compelling. Without some resistance in the name of a humanity the dystopia is fast bent on eliminating, survival lacks meaning.

In his recent work *Domination and the Arts of Resistance*, James Scott provides a framework for discussing resistance. By defining relations between dominant and subordinate groups as socially constructed public and hidden transcripts, Scott recasts post-Marxist debates over hegemony and false consciousness. He uses the term "public transcript" to describe the official or formal relations between the powerful and the weak and the term "hidden transcript" to describe talk and behavior that occurs "offstage," beyond the direct observation of the other group (4; 13-14). Hidden transcripts are a commentary on the public transcript; they may variously confirm, contradict or inflect what appears in the public transcripts or dominant discourses both groups construct (4-5).

> Every subordinate group creates, out of its ordeal, a "hidden transcript" that represents a critique of power spoken behind the back of the dominant. The powerful, for their part, also develop a hidden transcript representing the practices and claims of their rule that cannot be openly avowed. A comparison of the hidden transcript of the weak with that of the powerful and of *both* hidden transcripts to the public transcripts of power relations offers a substantially new way of understanding resistance to domination. (xii)

Scott portrays both hidden and public transcripts as *socially* constructed spaces that are both separate and interlocking. Hidden transcripts exist only to the extent they are articulated and enacted within offstage social sites (119ff.).[1] Scott does not deal with the isolated thoughts of individuals, in part because subordinate people infrequently leave such records.

It may be the province of dystopian narratives (among others) to make salient these even more hidden dimensions of resistance. The genius of Margaret Atwood's *The Handmaid's Tale* (1986) is in the mundane and ordinary quality of the dystopian lives it depicts. Under cover of the familiar routines of shopping, cleaning and cooking, handmaids develop hidden transcripts, short fragments of speech, small deviations in posture and glance. The protagonist, Offred, does much more. In the long stretches of her isolation she elaborates selves for her own sanity—selves that reestablish some continuity with her discredited past and give some amplitude to her impoverished present.

The weakness of Atwood's regime (and a classic dystopian problem) is its failure to elaborate, within the very public transcript which it is in the process of constructing, an even minimally complex persona for its handmaids to inhabit.[2] Such failures encourage restiveness, and beneath her controlled demeanor Offred is very restive indeed. Offred's re-visitings of a past now labeled as retrograde and her probings of a present much of which is off-limits offer an opportunity to explore how she is able to salvage selves amid a coercive regime.

It is clear from the outset that Offred intends to be a survivor. "I try not to think too much. Like other things now, thought must be rationed. There's a lot that doesn't bear thinking about. Thinking can hurt your chances, and I intend to survive" (10).

Offred is a Caucasian woman in her mid-thirties. Middle class, married with an eight year old daughter, she had a prosperous and rather unexceptional existence until the political troubles that culminated in the creation of Gilead. In Gilead, a society devoted to the elimination of sexuality beyond what is required for procreation, Offred is separated from her husband and daughter. Despite widespread ecological and nuclear contamination, her age and child indicate that she may still be fertile. She and similarly chosen handmaids are assigned to the homes of party dignitaries with whom they engage (in the presence of the latter's infertile wives) in emotionless sexual intercourse once a month in the consuming effort to procreate. The handmaids' status and privilege are entirely dependent on the party officials whose first names they assume. Three failed assignments result in the likely slow death that follows being sent to nuclear clean-up sites.

Survival is serious business. Offred's isolated life in the Commander's house revolves entirely around prescribed health and exercise routines designed to nurture her reproductive capacities. Shunned by the lower status Marthas who do the housework, and by the Commander's wife for whom she is an irksome necessity, Offred's isolation is barely broken by the truncated, ritual greetings ("Blessed be the fruit"; "May the Lord open") she exchanges with another handmaid, Ofglen, on their mandatory daily walk. They each are assigned the responsibility to monitor that the other does not "slip through the net" on these daily excursions (26). Ofglen has been Offred's partner for only two weeks since her predecessor disappeared without explanation.

The males in Gilead serve mostly paramilitary functions: lower echelon guards called Angels and an elite corps called Guardians who frequently double as spies or Eyes. Surveillance in this theocracy is honorable; "Under His Eye" is the prescribed farewell. The plethora of guards, the meticulously elaborated routines, the nun-like habit that hides the face and restricts the vision of a handmaid do not prevent licenses from being taken. From their first indoctrination, the future handmaids learn to lip-read and to find out each others' names by soundless whispering.

What do these infractions mean? Are they a method of survival, a rudimentary form of resistance, or merely temporary comforts not possible in the riskier environment of the Commanders' houses? Scott notes that the frontier between public and hidden transcripts is not a solid wall but a zone of struggle between elite and subordinate groups (14). In *Weapons of the Weak* he elaborates the historical dimension of this struggle: "the ideological struggle to define the present is a struggle to define the past as well. . . . [Poor villagers] have collectively created a *remembered village* and a *remembered economy* that serve as an effective ideological backdrop against which to deplore the present" (178). His description of relations between dominants and subordinates (slaves, serfs, peasants, untouchables) stresses that the capacity of dominant groups to define what constitutes the public transcript is an important component of their power; "offstage" behaviors undermine it (4).

Both elites and subordinates produce "off-stage" hidden transcripts, made up of behavior and speech at variance with and potentially subversive of public transcripts. Subordinates generate such transcripts as indirect forms of resistance; their production by elites signals the frustrations of compliance with the comparatively constricted public transcript. Consequently each group, in its own manner and for its own reasons, polices the sequestered social sites where their hidden transcripts are produced (15ff., 114ff).

The night-time communications at the indoctrination center, including the knowledge of "real" names from the now censured (and censored) pre-Gileadean past, constitute just such a hidden transcript. Another hidden transcript, the whorehouse cum nightclub called Jezebel's, is the backstage site where high party officials flout the regime's puritanical sexual norms. That the commander risks taking Offred there, costumed in the gaudy finery of the officially despised past, is a measure both of the elite's belief that they control the public transcript and their confidence that small preferments will buy the silence of their subordinates.

Although Offred is drawn to the subversive potential of such backstage activities, her isolation as well as her fear (of the Eyes of spies among the handmaids, and of the never fully specified punishments if found out) severely limits her involvement.[3] She chooses, instead, another form of discipline: in the blank spaces of her highly routinized existence, when enforced passivity frees her from performing the handmaid's role, she undertakes a sustained and silent interrogation of her former and present personae.

Summoning Selves

The public persona of handmaid is always precarious: a new recruit must adhere to the part minutely and trust to luck that she is fertile and assigned to a fertile male. "Each month I watch for blood, fearfully, for when it comes it means failure. I have failed once again to fulfill the expectations of others, which have become my own" (95).

Offred's response to the demanding work of impersonation is not one readily available to subordinate groups. It springs from her experience of a sharply different past and from the enforced passivity of her existence in the present.[4] It leads her to revisit the selves she summons from disjointed fragments of the past, establishing in the process the points of continuity and discontinuity with the rudely reduced self she is allowed in the present.

These historical probes are complex: in Offred's remembering they still retain some of the solidity of socially produced and shared experience. At the same time they are now the narrative of an isolate aware that "... a movie about the past is not the same as the past" (306). Like a movie, the past is now the stories Offred tells herself to stave off the inevitabilities and evoke the possibilities of the present.

This reworking of the concretely re-imaged past merges with an equally isolated interrogation of the present. The focus and fixity of Offred's gaze at her surroundings (abetted by the prescribed nun-like coif which prevents any side glances) is an exercise in paying attention, a discipline in trying to interpret accurately behaviors that the earlier Offred ignored. She learns fast, repeating almost as a litany the crucial lesson that the red of the tulips that line the walk to the Commander's house is *not* the same red that seeps through the white cloth of a newly hanged man's head bag (44).

Both activities—the narratives of self drawn from a past now seen as land mined and the meticulous attention to the specificity of events in the present—are transgressive. What makes them so is their exactness and their sensuality. The exactness of these probes is created from, and in turn harshly contains, a sensibility rife with longing for remembered touch and feel, suffused with a desire for the odors of forbidden tobacco and perfume (196-97). Their containment is a necessity; they are orthogonal to Gilead's public puritanical celebration of piety and asceticism.

In both their making and their maintenance, the selves that Offred laboriously constructs are potential acts of hidden resistance (39, 173). Her efforts to see exactly and to feel intensely are the opposite of nostalgia. They are attempts to weld together thought and feeling with such exactitude that the selves so crafted acquire stability and are not subject to erasure or dimming. But if resistance (as Scott understands it) requires shared understandings and collective behaviors, Offred's solitary rememberings fall short, at best a necessary preparation for this more public behavior.

It is the case that the selves Offred so laboriously constitutes do not in the long run prove stable. It is not, however, the one dimensional publicly scripted persona of handmaid that is their undoing, but rather their fragility in contact with other more publicly scripted offstage sites of resistance.

Offred's re-viewing of her past and present is a moral and intellectual exercise, as well as an exercise in survival. Why the selves that she summons from these meditations are not more resilient when brought into public purview remains, finally, enigmatic. Are the requirements of survival and resistance so different that the solitary character of the former (as Offred undertakes it) breaks down in the presence of the more collective, less individuated character of the latter? To make a self by oneself, a self not affirmed by action nor confirmed by others, may be too difficult an enterprise to sustain itself over time.

Offred's story is one of groping resistance, of the essentially daily domestic labor of crafting selves capable of surviving her new and impoverished reality. And for all their fragility, these provisional and precarious selves do survive to tell Offred's story. To tell it, finally, in a context in which the telling point is made that there is, of course, never just one story to tell about *any* situation.

The Work of the Past

If personal identity and significance attach to the stories we tell about ourselves (and the stories that others tell about us), the conditions under which Offred undertakes these retellings are cramped and uninviting. Writing and reading are forbidden; the only printed word Offred encounters is a faded cushion in her room with "faith" embroidered on it (75).[5] Physically isolated from other handmaids, she has no reliable collective support for her enterprise. The present from which she must distance herself is officially celebrated for its very *disjuncture* with that past she must rethink (151).

Enveloped in a one dimensional public persona constructed around female reproductive capacity, Offred is patient.[6] What she has in abundance is time; indeed the amount of unfilled time—of white sound, as she calls it—was one of the things for which she was not prepared (89-91). "I wait. I compose myself. My self is a thing I must now compose, as one composes a speech. What I must present is a made thing, not something born" (86).

"Something born" is the earlier Offred who took for granted such luxuries as small soaps and fresh towels in hotel rooms or the option of owning a home. This past appears now to have a fictive character, so easily did that earlier self take its choices and luxuries as givens (68). To Offred's quizzical, almost puzzled gaze, this older self verges on the incomprehensible: the earlier freedom now seems almost weightless; the belief that one's environment is given, not made, naive (32; cf. 67, 294).

The stories Offred composes from these vivid, disjointed images of the past constitute provisional selves, selves that notably lack the composed demeanor and posture of the model handmaid. The images of herself as mother, daughter, friend, wife are counterparts to Offred's now hobbled and increasingly frustrated sensuality:

> I walk around to the back door, open it.... The table has been scrubbed off, cleared of flour; today's bread, freshly baked, is cooling on its rack. The

kitchen smells of yeast. . . . It reminds me of other kitchens, kitchens that were mine. It smells of mothers. . . . It smells of me, in former times, when I was a mother. (62; cf. 82ff.; 103ff.)

The vividness of Offred's recall blurs the distinction between memory and dream. She describes these experiences as "attacks of the past," a faintness, a wave sweeping over her (68). In memory events and their surroundings are sharply re-imaged. A particularly "vivid attack" is promoted by stains discovered on a mattress, sign of some former love. It plunges Offred into acute physical desire for Luke.

But this almost Proustian reimmersion in the past is always in the service of the present. From her new angle of vision, the past Offred reviews was notably fragmented, its coherence and stability illusions. Unimagined events reshaped not only Offred's surround, but also the people in it, until even her husband Luke appears a stranger to her in his relatively more comfortable pre-Gileadean status (232ff.).

Some of these past selves were childlike in their self-absorption. These selves so ignored repeated and insistent harbingers of the impending troubles, Offred concludes, that only a deliberate act of the will could explain such avoidance (74). She contrasts the luxuriant sensuality of these earlier selves with her new need for hardness and coldness (195-97). "We were the people who were not in the papers. We lived in the blank white spaces at the edge of the print. It gave us more freedom. We lived in the gaps between the stories" (74). There is a disturbing continuity between these child-like adults of the past and the child-like postures which the handmaids are taught in the present. The past, at its most reassuring for Offred in its remembered difference from the present, is in too many respects uncomfortably continuous with it.

Offred's probes into her past are, then, both a bulwark and a danger to her stability in the present. She tells herself three stories of Luke's possible fate, all of them meticulously imagined, all of them contradictory (132ff.). This "contradictory way of believing" seems to Offred the only way she can believe in anything now. It arms her with different selves for different possible futures (135).

Offred is quite aware that her experiences, past and present, are reconstructions. "It is impossible to say a thing exactly the way it was ... there are too many shapes which can never be fully described, too many flavors, in the air or on the tongue, half-colors, too many" (173-74). The danger comes from the temptations of a too needy belief: to believe in the story and control the ending; to believe that it is a story and that real life will come after it (52). But the stories are also necessary; they are enlargements of the present. "Otherwise you live in the moment. Which is not where I want to be" (185). Offred's stories, composed as they are out of present necessities, give her perspective, the illusion of depth, multidimensional possibilities in a present denuded of them. And, to the extent that *all* versions of her story are at variance with officially sanctioned Gileadean history, they are a potential seed bed of resistance.

The Work of the Present

The present, too, is a construction, and Offred forces herself to repeat this as she leaves the Commander's study. The invitation to be there, illegal and dangerous, begins with scrabble and a kiss. It is at the same time an invitation to countenance the Commander's backstage behavior, a nostalgic scene in which companionability and mild sex co-mingle. This seduction for Offred is not sexual. The temptation is to invent a humanity for the Commander: of candor, or boyishness, or sadness (189; 181). Such humanity, once constructed, brings with it the further temptation (and perhaps necessity) to forgive (174; 188-89).

It is not generosity of this sort, but a certain exactness that holds Offred in place in the present: the discipline of trying to see each thing as valid and clearly there: "Each thing is valid and really there. It is through a field of such valid objects that I must pick my way, every day and in every way. I put a lot of effort into making such distinctions. I need to make them. I need to be very clear, in my own mind" (44-45).

This discipline is Janus-faced in its effects. On the one hand, to see clearly is not to confound the red face bag of a hanged man with red tulips; it too is an effort at perspective, at keeping things in their place. But to see a *human being* too clearly, denuded of context, as Offred views the Commander at the family prayer meeting that is prelude to their obligatory sex, is not exact either, for the surround is real and must be reckoned with: it is part of the power of the man (111-14). "To be a man, watched by women. It must be entirely strange. To have them watching him all the time.... To have them flinch when he moves.... To have them sizing him up . . . as if he were a garment, out of style or shoddy, which must nevertheless be put on because there is nothing else available" (113).

The continuous task of Offred's present is to know how to enact just such an impoverished self as she fantasizes for the Commander without being captured by it (38). The process of performing it is exhausting (160). Offred learns to be a meticulous student of the body postures, the gestures, the speech forms that the public persona requires, learning at the same time the minute infractions that "are possibilities, tiny peepholes" (28-9; cf. 101ff.). But the effort drains her and the risk is that she becomes this mask, that the energy involved in this by-and-large solitary performance drains into lethargy and acquiescence (91; cf. 258, 291).

How does Offred keep a distance from her performance, preventing the mask of handmaid from obliterating her other selves? Her present sufficiently routinized, as we have seen, she is able to escape her performance into the often treacherous terrain of the past. Another escape is through language. Language, she ironically observes, is a litany she uses to compose herself. "I sit in the chair and think about the word *chair*. It can also mean the leader of a meeting. It can also mean a mode of execution. It is the first syllable in *charity*. It is the French word for flesh. None of these facts has any connection with the others" (140).[7]

Offred is good at such exercises, but they are not foolproof. Unconstrained sensualities threaten to erupt even from within the precisely fashioned surfaces from which Offred constructs her present.

> The first egg is white. . . . The shell of the egg is smooth but also grained; small pebbles of calcium are defined by the sunlight, like craters on the moon. It's a barren landscape, yet perfect; it's the sort of desert the saints went into, so their minds would not be distracted by profusion. . . . The egg is glowing now, as if it had an energy of its own. To look at the egg gives me intense pleasure. (140-41)

In this minimalist life, in which pleasure is a glowing egg, traps abound. A dishtowel, white with blue stripes, seen out of its mundane context, is a "flash of normality" that comes at Offred "from the side, like ambushes. The ordinary, the usual, a reminder, like a kick" (64). The surface of the egg is neither so barren nor so perfect as Offred wills it to be. But it is in such exactnesses that Offred attempts to distance herself from her crudely scripted public persona. And it is also by such exactnesses that Offred distances herself from those past selves who lived carelessly, ignoring their surroundings (74; cf. 68).

An early incident, Ofglen's and Offred's encounter with Western dressed Japanese tourists, neatly captures the hungry sensuality that informs Offred's scrutiny of the details of their now exotic apparel.

> I'm looking down, at the sidewalk, mesmerized by the women's feet. One of them is wearing open-toed sandals, the toenails painted pink. I remember the smell of nail polish . . . the satiny brushing of sheer pantyhose against the skin, the way the toes felt, pushed toward the opening in the shoe by the whole weight of the body. . . . I can feel her shoes, on my own feet. The smell of nail polish has made me hungry. (39)

In a violent doubled image Offred sees herself through their eyes: secret, forbidden, exotic—a creature who would feel violated by the mere lens of a camera. "Modesty is invisibility," her former instructress taught. "To be seen—to be *seen*—is to be—her voice trembled—penetrated. What you must be, girls, is impenetrable" (38). The necessity of correctly inhabiting the public persona (there is particular danger in this encounter; the interpreter is almost certainly an Eye) merges with the risk of inhabiting it too fully (at first sight the Japanese women appear undressed and repellent to Offred). What is alien and exotic shifts rudely from the Japanese to her own persona of handmaid, as Offred tries to thread her way through these multiple identities. The mask of dutiful handmaid, glimpsed through the eyes of now exotic tourists, fits both too well and not at all. But without masks there is no long-term survival.

From Silence to Talk

Offred does much of the work of the past and the present in solitude. But no solitude is ever just that, and Offred knows this too.

> But if it's a story, even in my head, I must be telling it to someone. You don't tell a story only to yourself. There's always someone else.
> Even when there is no one.
> A story is like a letter... without a name. Attaching a name attaches you to the world of fact, which is riskier, more hazardous: who knows what the chances are out there, of survival, yours? (52-53)

> But I keep on going with this sad and hungry and sordid, this limping and mutilated story, because after all I want you to hear it, as I will hear yours too if I ever get the chance, if I meet you or if you escape, in the future or in heaven or in prison or underground, some other place. What they have in common is that they're not here. By telling you anything at all I'm at least believing in you, I believe you're there, I believe you into being. Because I'm telling you this story I will your existence. I tell, therefore you are. (344)

Using a name from the past is treason in Gilead, for it risks bringing in its train an unprescribed humanity. And names are known, from the outset, in the almost silent whispering that the newly inducted handmaids learn in the indoctrination center (4-5).[8] Through such whisperings abbreviated biographies are attached to names, and through such whisperings the handmaids create temporary sites of non-compliance. "There is something powerful in the whispering of obscenities, about those in power. . . . It deflates them, reduces them to the common denominator where they can be dealt with" (287-88).

Gilead is, in fact, shot through with illicit communication. The Marthas have their networks (295). The wives conspire to get handmaids pregnant and gone from their homes (263-67). And the handmaids become expert at the strategic use of public occasions (birthday days, prayvaganzas, salvagings) to track each other as well as those missing from the past. These hidden sites of resistance are furtive and opportunistic; interlaced with the required enactment of the public transcript, they are a barely audible counter to it (159, 278).

Offred's stories, told to a nameless audience of one or thousands, do not easily become a part of the handmaids' backstage transactions. Three episodes suggest how the very speech that creates these collective, hidden sites of resistance breaches the security of Offred's fragile and solitary resistance.

College roommate and lesbian feminist, Moira carries her friendship with Offred over into Gilead. Trust based on a shared past secures their initial speech, attempted through a small hole between two water stalls at the indoctrination center. By her subsequent escape (by locking an instructress in a toilet stall), Moira becomes larger than life for Offred. "The thought of what she would do expanded until it filled the room. At any moment there might be a shattering explosion . . . the doors would swing open . . . Moira had power now . . . she'd set herself loose. She was now a loose woman . . ." (172). As a result of Moira's defiance, authority was "less fearsome and more absurd. . . . The audacity was what we liked" (172).

Moira is next encountered at Jezebel's, the brothel to which the Commander takes Offred. Like Nick who chauffeurs them there, Offred's pass is her non-personhood: no one would believe her if she told; what she thinks has long ago ceased to matter (273, 301). This offstage site, where the elite gather to enjoy women decked out in the glitter and tawdry finery of the past, is a carnival, a masquerade. It is also the work place for Gilead's unsuccessful rebels. For three or four years, until they wear out, they entertain the regime's elite with the help of drink and drugs (325).

What frightens Offred is the indifference, the lack of volition of the new Moira she finds at Jezebel's. This mask, the mask of a tart, appears to have become Moira's face, obliterating the larger-than-life rebel. "I don't want her to be like me. Give in, go along, save her skin. . . . I want gallantry from her, swashbuckling, heroism, single-handed combat" (324).

Offred lets go the story, now turned nightmare, of Moira the rebel. In this backstage site all disguises wear thin, are seen through. The Commander's self-important posturing, his breaking of brothel rules by bringing Offred in the first place, is "a juvenile display, the whole act, and pathetic . . ." (307). Moira's story, shorn of its heroic dimensions, is left blurred: Offred never sees her again. There are two hidden transcripts here: the women's nestled in the masters'. Neither survive the evening.

The stories Offred would have liked to tell herself about Moira do not survive the brief backstage conversation with her. Most damaging of all, perhaps, is the knowledge that this transcript (Moira's and Offred's) may not even be hidden. Conversations among women in the brothel have all been heard before, they don't matter. The bond between the two women is a casualty, not only of Offred's larger-than-life fantasy of Moira the savior, but of the raw factuality of this offstage site. Camaraderie here does not really matter; with nowhere to go, nobody leaves voluntarily (345-46).

Offred's engagement with Ofglen's resistance is both more and less consequential. The Ofglens (there are a series of three, at least two of which are conspirators) are part of a network, whose code word is Mayday. Their backstage transcripts, and presumably similar ones among other handmaids and their allies among the Guardians, are hidden in the interstices of the public transcript. The women do not exchange their real names, personal history counts for less here than the information that can be garnered about their masters (363). The threat of betrayal is always in the background (218; cf. 364ff.).

The speech Offred encounters in these transactions is coded and minimalist: an inflection here, a pause there. "After this ritual viewing we continue on our way, heading as usual for some open space we can cross so we can talk. If you can call it talking, these clipped whispers, projected through the funnels of our white wings. It's more like a telegram, a verbal semaphore. Amputated speech" (260). Offred finds it difficult to believe in these truncated transcripts. The initial elation of finding an ally, a friend in the crowd, gives way to the tedious work of gleaning scraps of information for others to piece together in a picture. The encounters pale beside the remembered conspiracies of children's literature. "Passwords, things that cannot be told, people with secret identities, dark linkages: this does not seem as if it ought to be the true shape of the world" (261). In fact Offred knows that these transactions are the true shape of her world, but this composer of litanies, this lover of speech cannot give enough form, cannot create enough sustenance to sustain herself in this story.

Nor is this a story Offred wants to tell (351). The heroism in it is brutal, not larger than life. (Ofglen kicks a discovered conspirator into insensibility; discovered in turn, she hangs herself.) Even before these happenings this is a failed transcript for Offred. The sensuality and exactness that undergirded her reworkings of the past do not help her construct a persona solid enough to hold her in this spare net (347-49).

The Nick story is the one Offred wants most desperately to believe in. For it, she lets the transcript so laboriously begun with Ofglen slide away. This last story is the one in which her longing for Luke is transposed into love making with Nick. But her infatuation becomes so absorbing that it risks anchoring her too fully in the present. "The fact is that I no longer want to leave, escape, cross the border to freedom. I want to be here, with Nick, where I can get at him" (348).

The offstage site is ambiguous: the liaison is initiated, not by Ofglen or Nick but by the Commander's wife, desperate for a child from Offred. Offred agrees, a matter for her of survival. By continuing the illicit visits beyond what is required for pregnancy, Offred reconfigures the site into one yet more hidden, inhabited by Nick and her alone. But this narrative is Offred's undoing: she cannot get it straight. The story wobbles between what Offred's passions incline her to (an ample present in which sensuality can be expressed) and other needs (guarded love making where the core is "out of reach, enclosed, protected" and where no heroics obtain) (339-40).

Moira's backstage was a setting that made speech meaningless. Ofglen's backstage etiolated speech. But backstage with Nick, speech risks disappearing entirely under the weight of Offred's frantic retellings. "I made that up. It didn't happen that way. Here is what happened" (338). The second approximation appears more real: "There wasn't any thunder though, I added that in. To cover up the sounds, which I am ashamed of making" (340). And finally: "It didn't happen that way either. I'm not sure how it happened: not exactly. All I can hope for is a reconstruction: the way love feels is always only approximate" (340).

What does happen in the end is considerably more straightforward. The Commander's wife discovers the visit to Jezebel's. A black van, of the sort used by the Eyes, comes to pick Offred up. Nick (Guardian as well as chauffeur) assures Offred, whom he here calls by her real name, that the van is part of the escape network. Offred, doubtful but with no choice, enters.

The ambiguity with which the narration ends (whether Offred is saved; whether Nick is a traitor; who is resisting what) is further complicated by the final chapter where survival and resistance are reviewed once again, this time from the secure vantage point of the twelfth symposium on Gileadean Studies, at the University of Denay, Nunavit on June 25, 2195. The attendees at this event appear to be the final audience for the incomplete tapes that now constitute Offred's "limping and mutilated story" (344).[9]

Flattened Identities

Offred's tale is heard: the question is how. Hidden transcripts, as Scott reminds us, are notoriously difficult to decipher (132, 137-38). In dystopias what makes them even more hermetic is the extensive control elites exercise over their subjects. In *The Handmaid's Tale* their power over the public transcript is used to script personae so thinly constructed that they flatten the humanity of their subjects. Their powers of surveillance are used to constrict the backstage sites where fuller humanities might be enacted. And because ordinary life is allowed so little purchase in dystopias, no common acts of friendship and love remain just that—they become transgressions, potential sites of rebellion.

Offred is a survivor whose various disciplines of survival implicate her in sites where collective resistance is being carried out. But for Offred neither the Moira nor the Ofglen story are crafted solidly enough to withstand the sordidness of Jezebel's or the brutality of the Salvaging where a coconspirator is killed. The site she seems most fully able to inhabit, the one in which she and Nick are lovers, is (paradoxically for one who calls herself a coward) literally and figuratively the most dangerous one of all (366). It is the site where Offred's sensuality is least under discipline; where her stories lack exactitude, become more incoherent, and finally break apart in their inability to capture the ephemeral, unmediated language of orgasm.

The sensuality—and the exactitude—that has fueled Offred's solitary meditations seem not to have withstood the pressures of the collectively constructed backstage sites that riddle Gilead. The precisely crafted selves she has constructed in solitude offer no bridgework to the cruder arenas where Moira and Ofglen act. At the end, the stories she is trying to tell break into fragments "like a body caught in crossfire or pulled apart by force" (343).

And in the ambiguous and richly ironic last chapter, the anthropologists and archivists who seem to be the final recipients of her story busily flatten the fragments still further as they enact their own "public transcript." Papers are delivered on appropriately academic subjects as "Krishna and Kali Elements in the State Religion of the Early Gilead Period" and "Problems of Authentication in Reference to *The Handmaid's Tale*" (380). Amid reminders that the "handmaid" tapes were not the first such discovery, that they might be a forgery, that the audience must be cautious about passing moral judgment upon the Gileadeans (such judgments are always culture-specific), the reader is led to wonder whether those who make a profession of the past always trivialize it so thoroughly when urgencies of survival and resistance are removed.

In this torrent of language we never learn what happens to Offred, Nick, or the Commander. The listeners Offred wanted to address were those who had escaped "in the future or in heaven or in prison or underground, some other place" (344). The audiences the author supplies her with can't see her through the academic paraphernalia that appears to constitute not only the official transcript, but the only one. But is it? Or are there other audiences present?

"Because I'm telling you this story I will your existence. I tell, therefore you are" (344). The Cartesian dictum is reformulated to assert a more precarious form of identity. The exercises that make up Offred's private acts of resistance, stories hard won for all their ambiguities, do appear to have been flattened into inconsequentiality. But the audience of readers created by Atwood's narrative (different, to be sure, from Offred's imagined audience) has no stake in, indeed has never heard of Krishna and Kali elements in the state religion. Such exercises, added to the meticulously documented debate over which of two almost interchangeable figures has the better claim to be Offred's Commander, suggest that it is perhaps not Offred but the twelfth symposium on Gileadean Studies that is being flattened into inconsequentiality.

Who, finally, is the audience for Offred's very private acts of resistance? Clearly not the speaker who rhetorically acknowledges that it is difficult to decipher voices from the darkness of the past in the "clearer light of our own day" (394-95). He ends by asking his academic audience, "Are there any questions?" (395). To which, perhaps, may be best juxtaposed the distinctly uncomfortable realization that Atwood leaves *her* audience with very few answers.

From *Utopian Studies* 5, no. 2 (1994): 56-70. Copyright © 1994 by Society for Utopian Studies. Reprinted by permission of Society for Utopian Studies.

Notes

1. Scott acknowledges that "the total abolition of any social realm of relative discursive freedom" would result in conditions under which a hidden transcript cannot be generated among subordinates. These conditions, approximated in a few penal institutions, thought-reform camps, and psychiatric wards, require the almost total isolation of their subjects. He notes that such conditions do not even remotely approximate the conditions in any real society as a whole. The Draconian isolation, the intensity and minuteness of the surveillance, are requirements so stringent that they do not apply to the large scale forms of domination with which Scott is concerned (83-5).

On two occasions Atwood has referred to *The Handmaid's Tale* as "speculative fiction," bringing her dystopia closer to Scott's work than might first be imagined (Freibert, 291). While such stringent conditions do not prevail in Gilead, the handmaids, once indoctrinated, aside from publicly prescribed salutations, live in almost total linguistic solitude. When personal speech is silenced, the handmaids use the formal scripts of officialdom to communicate. "The crimes of others are a secret language among us. Through them we show ourselves what we might be capable of, after all" (335).

2. To the extent that public transcripts offer rigidly schematized personae, the manipulative acting out of such personae may constitute forms of empowerment for subordinates and may also generate some of the energy for backstage transcripts. "The practice of domination," in Scott's words, "*creates* the hidden transcript" (27; cf. 33ff).

In *The Handmaid's Tale,* "salvagings," similar to Orwell's two-minute hates, are district-wide women's events in which they witness the execution of female traitors. Salvagings can be followed by "particicutions" at which a male traitor is torn apart live by the handmaids (356ff.). The advantages of offering subordinates such collective retaliation is, of course, the complicity it induces. Conversely, as Scott notes, the experience (even in isolation) of faking participation, of refusing to comply with the official transcript, can be empowering.

3. Offred's isolated offstage site is a small room with a ceiling relief ornament in the shape of a wreath, once the decorative frame for a chandelier. The chandelier removed (a possible suicide opportunity), Offred repeatedly sees the wreath's center as a blind plaster eye. It suggests both surveillance and its absence: the security and the restrictions of a site where suicidal thoughts (for lack of any means to realize them) remain just that (9, 49, 68, 125, 242-3).

4. Offred is aware of the singularity of her position: the handmaids of her age are a transitional generation. The next generation will lack the experience of a lived past different from the present (151, 283). The problem is noted by Plato who contemplates dealing with it by rusticating the population above the age of ten. Plato (262-63; VII.540-541).

5. With fine irony, Offred muses on the fate of the other two companion cushions: hope and charity (140).

6. The one dimensional character of the handmaids' public persona is graphically illustrated by the punishments they could incur. Punishments were first inflicted on the feet, then the hands. "Remember," said Aunt Lydia. "For our purposes your feet or your hands are not essential" (118; cf. 124, 176). In her study of Atwood, Barbara Rigney relates the cognate imagery of shoes, dangling from corpses in *The Handmaid's Tale*, to the film "The Red Shoes" in which the dancer Moira dances herself to death (Rigney, 117).

7. An earlier litany explores the difference between *lie* and *lay* (49). Other litanies entail the pleasant exactitudes of scripture (which the instructors systematically mangle and Offred corrects in her head [60, 115]) and a novel reformulation of Marx: "From each according to her ability; to each according to his needs" (151).

8. Like mirrors, names both identify and mask their carriers. Offred digs up her real name, like a buried treasure, an imagined charm that has survived from the distant past (108). But her "shining name" fails as a talisman when Nick uses it in a plea for trust in the final crisis (376).

Ketterer cites the possible plays on Offred's name: "offered," "afraid," "off-red," referring to her red habit, or "off-read" in the sense of "misread" (148; cf. Rubenstein, 101).

9. A number of feminist dystopias end on similarly ambiguous notes. Cf. Russ, Lessing and Peel's commentary on Lessing. Marge Piercy's utopia, *Woman on the Edge of Time*, ends with a literal public transcript (the history of Connie's hospital commitments) which stands in ironic and poignant contrast to the more fully evolved private identity of the protagonist. On Atwood's ending cf. Davidson, 113-121; Malak, 9-15.

Works Cited

Atwood, Margaret. *The Handmaid's Tale*. New York: Fawcett, 1986.

Davidson, Arnold E. "Future Tense Making History in 'The Handmaid's Tale.'" *Margaret Atwood: Vision and Forms*. Ed. Kathryn VanSpanckeren and Jan Garden Castro. Carbondale: Southern Illinois UP, 1988. 113-121.

Freibert, Lucy M. "Control and Creativity: The Politics of Risk in Margaret Atwood's 'The Handmaid's Tale.'" *Critical Essays on Margaret Atwood*. Ed. Judith McCombs. Boston: G. K. Hall, 1988. 281-291.

Ketterer, David. *Canadian Science Fiction and Fantasy*. Bloomington: Indiana UP, 1992.

Malak, Amin. "Margaret Atwood's 'The Handmaid's Tale' and the Dystopian Tradition." *Canadian Literature* 112 (Spring, 1986): 9-16.

Peel, Ellen. "Feminist Narrative Persuasion: The Movement of Dynamic Spatial Metaphor in Doris Lessing's 'The Marriages between Zones Three, Four, and Five.'" *Sociocriticism/Sociocritique* 4-5 (1987): 115-42.

Piercy, Marge. *Woman on the Edge of Time*. New York: Alfred A. Knopf, 1976.

Plato. *The Republic of Plato*. Ed. Francis Cornford. New York: Oxford UP, 1945.

Rigney, Barbara Hill. *Margaret Atwood*. London: Macmillan Education Ltd., 1987.

Rubenstein, Roberta. "Nature and Nurture in Dystopia: 'The Handmaid's Tale.'" *Margaret Atwood: Vision and Forms*. Ed. Kathryn VanSpanckeren and Jan Garden Castro. Carbondale: Southern Illinois UP, 1988. 101-112.

Russ, Joanna. *The Female Man*. New York: Bantam Books, 1975.

Scott, James C. *Domination and the Arts of Resistance: Hidden Transcripts*. New Haven: Yale UP, 1990.

Scott, James C. *Weapons of the Weak: Everyday Forms of Peasant Resistance*. New Haven: Yale UP, 1985.

"We Lived in the Blank White Spaces":
Rewriting the Paradigm of Denial in
Atwood's *The Handmaid's Tale*
Danita J. Dodson

While Margaret Atwood's *The Handmaid's Tale* brandishes partial portraits of human-rights violations around the globe—especially in Iran, India, Germany, South Africa, Guatemala, and the former Soviet Union—it is quite clear that Gilead is most wholly the U.S.A., embodying its past, its present, and its potential future. This novel is Atwood's first foray into an extended representation of America (Stimpson 764-67). *The Handmaid's Tale* illuminates the deplorable irony that a nation established upon the utopian principle of "liberty and justice for *all*" has also been a dystopia for those humans sequestered and tortured because of differences from mainstream culture. As casualties of a patriarchal-based empire within the national borders, Native Americans, African Americans and women are all examples of peoples who have been historically locked away from the utopian American Dream. Amy Kaplan asserts that American history is built upon the huge myth that the U.S.A. is anti-imperialistic because of its documented opposition to the totalitarianism of "evil empires" around the world (12). Such a "paradigm of denial" has caused numerous American citizens to ignore how "imperial relations are enacted and contested within the nation" (13). Atwood shatters this paradigm of denial and forces us to recognize how seriously "American imperialism and nationalism account for the repressive order which becomes the Republic of Gilead" (Hengen 55). Within *The Handmaid's Tale* lies the powerful suggestion that progress toward global human rights will never be possible until nations of "freedom" face their own incarcerated dystopian realities.

To come to terms with the confusing reality that domestic imperialism and enslavement characterize a nation that pledges "liberty and justice for all," the first section of my essay briefly discusses America's foundational dichotomy of utopia/dystopia. The next section surveys the violent legacy of the Puritans' divine mission; God's perfect kingdom in the New World was constructed through dystopian methods of capturing, ousting, and silencing apostates against the patriarchal communal vision, especially women dissidents—e.g., Anne Hutchinson, Tituba, and Mary Webster. Within this historical context, *The Handmaid's Tale*, emphasizing the terror that drives men to subjugate women, illustrates how rescuing the promised land from the subversive Mother/Other becomes the divine mission of Gilead's conservative reformers. My evolving argument is that Atwood evokes background memories of this Puritanical exorcistic tendency to accentuate and develop her major American genre reenactment: the narrative of the enslaved black mother. Focusing finally upon a specific comparison/contrast of Offred's tale with the slave narrative of Harriet Ann Jacobs, the paper moves to a discussion of the confessional purposes of *The Handmaid's Tale*.

By understanding how Offred ultimately develops a discourse with slavery, we witness the incredible power behind one individual's confession of her former indifference to the concept of American freedom. The major task of *The Handmaid's Tale* is "to portray convincingly . . . how the abridgement of freedom evolved in the United States" (Woods 134). Atwood suggests that an intimate and painful association with the history of this abridgement will help us attend to current global horrors; a better world that truly recognizes human rights will transpire only when we empathetically descend to the Other's hell and then reawaken to the atrocities of the present. Lest we allow ourselves to be culturally defined by a "paradigm of denial" (Kaplan 13)—like the scholars who meet at the University of Denay (Deny) for the Gileadean Studies Symposium—we must look at the skeletons in the closet of our own national history.

Atwood and the American Dichotomy of Utopia/Dystopia

Any contemplation of our postmodern world must involve an examination of the instability of deconstructive tensions. Thus, current reflection upon such a country as the U.S. must move beyond the stereotypical icon of a free eagle and toward an awareness of how the national symbol has also been fettered and forced into extinction. To understand the dichotomous images of liberty/captivity and justice/inhumanity in our native ideology, we must first recognize how both "utopia" and "dystopia" have been at the heart of the American experience both in historical events and in literary expression.

Vernon Louis Parrington, Jr., in *American Dreams*, discusses America's characteristic tradition of "planning a new world" based upon the "American dream" of freedom (3). The names of the cities and regions in America suggest recurring ideas of rebirth and hope: New England, New York, New Haven. In a seminal edition of essays on utopian literature, Kenneth Roemer asserts that the word "America" is often synonymous with that of "Utopia"; he states that "to understand . . . to know America, we must have knowledge of America as utopia" (14). The following are examples of the American heritage of idealism: "Winthrop's 'City upon a Hill,' Jefferson's Declaration of Independence, the possibilities for rebirth in the 'virgin' West, the idealism of youth and civil rights movements, New Deals, New Frontiers, and Great Societies" (Roemer 14).

However, though Europeans established the land of the free and the home of the brave out of the Renaissance concept of the "good place," the name "America" also conjures up vivid images of dystopia, or the "bad place." While to some Columbia signified heaven, to others it represented hell; with Columbus's dream of a terrestrial paradise came excruciating horrors of "discovery." Ernest Tuveson and John May both argue that a sense of dystopian apocalypse has always been apparent in America, running as a strong countercurrent to visions of a New Eden. Richard Slotkin has also written that ominous violence is one of the major themes of our national literature (4). Thus to know America, according to the revelations in its literature, is also to have a knowledge of "the dystopian aura of the 'howling wilderness,' the genocide in the name of Manifest Destiny, the horrors of slavery, the nightmares of rampant commercialism, technology, urban squalor, Vietnam" (Roemer 14).

Recognizing the apocalyptic effects of a national history characterized by a failed sense of utopian achievement, Atwood deals with cultural tensions as she defines America as dystopia in *The Handmaid's Tale*. Leslie-Ann Hales has delineated the dystopian elements of Atwood's "darkening vision" (257-262). The novel is a stark caricature of an American Dream gone bad, a vision of hope that has dwindled into "a nightmare of unbridled power and industrial alienation, of moral purposelessness and individual anomie" (Kumar 98). Exposing the rotten rafters that support the house of American ideals, Atwood warns of the maddening consequences of imposed utopianism, as she illustrates the horrors of building a perfect empire from which some will be barred (Dodson 103).

Such historical truth-telling is common in dystopias, which explore historical conflicts (Ruppert 104). Atwood delves more deeply into such conflicts than most fellow dystopianists, for her futuristic tale exceeds a clever prediction. It is a recollection of specific atrocities of the American experience, atrocities that Atwood authenticates by reviewing the imagery of containment evident in Puritan ideology and horridly intensified in the slave accounts of black females. The Handmaid's story about a "Gothic-dystopian land" (Banerjee 88), therefore, works hard to shatter what Kaplan calls "the paradigm of denial" by presenting a once-privileged 20th-century woman's quantum leap through ignored parts of the American experience.

Puritan America: Atwood's Truth about God's Perfect Empire

As she told me in a recent interview, Atwood, a citizen of Canada, has attempted to understand her own heritage in America (Dodson 97). Though Canada has its own background of conservative and intolerant movements, she chooses to focus her attention upon another nation and another history that she also claims as her own; thus, her commentary is offered both as an outsider and as an insider. Having studied for years in New England under Puritan scholar Perry Miller, Atwood has explored the obscure history of her colonial American ancestors—ultimately learning that one of her Puritan forebears, Mary Webster, was sentenced to hang as a witch but curiously survived her execution. *Survival*, Atwood's earliest long work of literary criticism, is the product of her prolonged scholarship on the psychological and social consequences of North-American colonialism.

Atwood's concern about the continual effects of American colonialism is most strongly addressed in *The Handmaid's Tale*. Here she labors to show how the repressive order of Gilead exhibits internal elements of the colonial agenda historically associated with America's numerous policies of domination. According to Atwood, the historical mistreatment of those marginalized in America because of race, religion, or gender is a direct ramification of an unjustified sense of national superiority. Believing that societal institutions are responsible for promulgating ideas of bigotry, she asserts that Americans have been given a false sense of importance by an educational system that breeds attitudes of supremacy and intolerance: "'They' had been taught that they were the centre of the universe, a huge, healthy apple pie, with other countries and cultures sprinkled round the outside, like raisins" (*Second Words* 87-88). The result of such indoctrinated supremacy is a system in which the One is opposed to the Other, with dire consequences played out on the homefront itself. This cultural system is clearly reflected in the national literature; Slotkin states that "at the source of the American myth there lies the fatal opposition, the hostility between two worlds, two races, two realms of thought and feeling" (17). Pitted against each other have been the tensions of civilization and savagery, progress and primitivism, dominant Christianity and alternate Christianities, white and black skin, English and Spanish.

The Handmaid's Tale defines how the false binary system of Gileadean politics is saturated in intolerant beliefs that result in the abuse of "raisins," who are seen as objects that either help or hinder the goal of a New Colony, the "centre of the universe" (Atwood, *Second Words* 87-88). Handmaids are considered the personal property of Commanders who use them to produce progeny. Also, the Children of Ham (African Americans) and the Sons of Jacob (Jewish-Americans) are regarded as hindrances to the creation of a superior race and a superior religion, so they are sequestered and sent to neo-containment camps.

Eager to illuminate unvoiced truths about the mission of those who sought to build a "Citty upon a Hill," Atwood parodies Puritanism as she delineates Gilead, as Cathy Davidson has noted (24-26). Sandra Tomc argues that the author satirizes not only "the persistence of a puritan strain in modern American culture but a tradition of American studies that celebrates Puritan intransigence as quintessentially representative of the American spirit" (80). In a 1994 interview with me, Atwood emphasized that American legends are based upon a denial of truth, for they have been falsely crafted out of "the fairy tale version" of why the Puritans came to the New World: to establish a democracy, a land of equal opportunity where no voice is considered a dissenting one (Dodson 97). She contends, "They were not interested in democracy. In fact, it wasn't even a notion at that time. They were interested in a theocracy" (Dodson 97). Thus, religion became the utopian basis of the nation's first government, and Protestantism a propelling force behind colonization.

Atwood's attention to the connection between church and state points a bold finger back to the obdurate tenets of the first Protestant movement in America, tenets that led to the persecution of "basically anybody who didn't agree with them [the Puritans] religiously"

(Dodson 97). As a result of the Puritan policy of persecuting the religious dissenter, many people in 17th-century America, like Atwood's ancestor, were burned or hanged for purported witchcraft, while others were exiled and locked away from the colony. Puritan settlement was actually based upon an exclusive goal, to set up a New World colony for only the chosen and righteous people of God, as prophesied in the Bible, so that the kingdom of Israel could be theirs.

Of course, this meant the dispossession, eradication, and/or incarceration of those not considered chosen ones by the dominant group. The Puritan missionary spirit ultimately gave way to the military spirit, and the Puritans defined their relationship to the New World in terms of violence and warfare. Donald Pease states that "the vision of the New World as potentially a second Eden will inspire the genocide of its first inhabitants whose difference from the Europeans is noted" (45). The journals of such Puritans as John Winthrop attests God's Providence in the removal of Others: "[We pray] that the Lord our God may blesse us in the land whether [wherever] wee goe to possesse it" (Winthrop 199). Even Thomas Jefferson's subsequent document of national unity, "The Declaration of Independence," associates "the merciless Indian savages" with the enemy who deserves to lose authority in the New World.

Atwood, by highlighting the background of violence in a colonial empire-building culture, forces us into an intertextual rereading of both American history and American literature as we read Offred's tale. Just as the 17th-century Puritans did, the Protestant reformers who have created Gilead have violently ousted, hanged, or enslaved—and ultimately silenced—those dissenting against their religious and racial ideology. *The Handmaid's Tale*, thus, challenges any former reading of the Puritan story as a utopian mission dedicated to divine justice for all and exposes the domestic imperialism that has long been denied by such traditional American Studies' intellectuals as Perry Miller (Kaplan 3-11). Karen Stein asserts that the Gileadean Symposium's Professor Pieixoto is a caricature of Miller, for both, in "explicating and valorizing the texts they interpret . . . ignore the deeply misogynist strain of Gileadean and Puritan cultures" (61). As Annette Kolodny shows, the European colonizers and the progenitors of American Studies both referred to the New World as a "virgin land" in order to ideologically deny Indian removal, frontier violence, government theft, land devastation, class cruelty, racial brutality, and misogyny (4).

To rewrite the story of Puritanism in the novel, and to tell the truth about its dystopian legacy of intolerance and violence, Atwood focuses upon the stories within the American tradition that emphasize slavery. If we read Offred's story in conjunction with American literature's stories of enslavement, as I do in the next section, it becomes evident that Atwood shows, as does Slotkin in his critical study of the American tradition, that the Puritan way of thinking regularly reasserts itself in American thought (564). The original Puritanical fear of the Other, exemplified in recorded views about the Native American, is responsible for exorcistic tendencies that have occurred periodically in the cultural history of the United States, wherein is enacted "the hunting down and slaying of rabid beasts embodying all qualities of evil" (Slotkin 154).

While men were slaying beasts on the outskirts of the colony, women were encouraged to manufacture tales about savages. The most culturally-sanctioned writing by females during the period was the captivity narrative, which was ultimately used by the dominant culture for the purposes of imperialism. Attempting to document justifiable reasons why the Native Americans should be dispossessed of their territory, captivity narratives show how white Puritan women are pursued and kidnapped by fiends who take them on long journeys into the wilderness. Mary Rowlandson's tale, for example, is exemplary of colonial texts focusing on the Native Americans as sons of the Devil who remove a daughter of Zion into Satan's lands. Atwood underlines this political, imperialistic use of language by inverting the Indian captivity narrative; she situates the white neo-Puritan Gileadean males as the true "rabid beasts."

The Handmaid's Tale, a tale of a new captivity, presents itself as an interpolation of the untold story about the "beasts" of history, whose imperialistic legacy is reenacted in Gilead, a regime reverting to, and actually exceeding, the prejudice of the original Puritans. Existing as an outgrowth of a utopian attempt to purify American culture and obliterate liberal tendencies identified with the wilderness, the Gileadean regime views females—who are associated with the "Mother" Earth— as "dark" and "native" forces threatening traditional patriarchal rule. As Sherry Ortner notes, women since colonial times have been given a "pan-cultural second class status," being considered a part of nature and thus identifiable with primitive races (73). Driven by a view that, according to Ortner, is as old as history itself, Protestant reformers of Gilead undertake the divine mission of freeing the land of the dangers of the subversive Mother/Other, and the original utopian "errand into the wilderness" waxes into a dystopian project. Though many men in the regime also lack any real choice, their plight is not as severe as that of women, who are either Handmaids (sexual slaves), Marthas (cleaning slaves), Unwomen (enslaved workers in a toxic-waste camp), Wives and Daughters (properties of Commanders), or Jezebels (underground prostitutes). The Eyes of the regime have tried to eliminate any liberal tendencies in American thought resulting from the 1970s feminist movement, which was identified as a type of witchcraft.

By illustrating how women are primary targets of Gilead's reform movements, Atwood intimates a historical fact of the Salem witch trials conducted by Puritans in the 1690s: more women than men were tried as witches because "witches were assumed to be lascivious creatures who freely indulged their passions and liked to cavort in the wild country beyond civilization's pale" (Pike 6). Because women were viewed as wild and libidinous creatures threatening patriarchal control, they were hunted down, caged, then annihilated. According to bell hooks, "Such treatment was a direct consequence of misogynist attitudes toward women that prevailed in colonial American society" (*Ain't I a Woman?* 29). Woman, hooks asserts, was portrayed as "an evil sexual temptress, the bringer of sin into the world. [This] led to the development of anti-woman sentiment" (29).

Looking back to the Puritan legacy, Leslie Fiedler writes that beneath American literature's gothic imagery lies a dominant patriarchal fear of the evil associated with women, which he calls the "maternal blackness" (132). Though Fiedler refers to the extreme trepidation that men had about women in general, his terminology indicates a double marginalization apparent as early as the 1600s, wherein women of color were the first to be equated with witches in Salem. Tituba, a black slave in the household of Reverend Samuel Parris, was one of the earliest accused, setting up an enduring pattern of domination and oppression to be enacted throughout history. Even a study of the label "witch," generally applied to women in the 17th-century, must not deny the reality that the pioneering patriarchs' fears were extremely complex, revealing much more than overt misogynist anxieties; their frenzied reactions were also racially motivated.

Understanding that both sexual and racial fears were integral factors contributing to social tensions in America's first settlements, Atwood alludes to gender and race issues in Offred's story of enslavement. It is true that Offred is a white woman in forced servitude, but her decision to make ongoing references to the black woman's slave narrative signals her recognition of the double enslavement that women of color have endured for centuries. She reveals the lesson she has learned: subvert the "paradigm of denial" by confessing her own compliant role in a domestic imperialism that ultimately turns women against women.

The Handmaid's Dialogue with the 'Black Mother'

Like Atwood's Puritan ancestor, Mary Webster, who survived her death sentence in spite of the rope placed around her neck, some women have lived to tell the horrors that exposed them to violent ceremonies. The narrator of *The Handmaid's Tale* is one who survives to speak her "tale." Although the story we read is language in print, it is crucial to remember that Offred first transmitted her narrative on audiotape, and to her it will always be vocalized. As Mario Klarer shows, "In Gilead, being a woman means to become *pre*-literate" (132). Offred asserts that this "pre-literate" medium is the only viable one for telling her story: "Tell, rather than write, because I have nothing to write with and writing is in any case forbidden" (52). Offred proceeds to take pride in the power of oral autobiography, her means to a subjective creation of reality: "Because I'm telling you this story I will your existence. I tell, therefore you are" (344). By presenting the narrator's tale in an innovative manner—oral transcription from tapes—Atwood reminds us of the rawness and originality of the slave narrative, a distinctively American form of prose (Dixon 298; Stepto 225-241; Lauter 1201). She also shows orality as a woman-centered means of survival for those not in possession of the tools of literacy. As hooks argues, "Until masses of women in this society read and write, feminist ideas must also be spread by word of mouth" (*Feminist Theory* 109).

When *The Handmaid's Tale* is explored in terms of its oral history, it becomes evident that Offred's recording reveals a metaphorical discourse with the autobiographical narratives of black female slaves of antebellum America. Examples of such narratives include Harriet Ann Jacobs's *Incidents in the Life of a Slave Girl* (1861), Kate Drumgoold's *A Slave Girl's Story* (1882), and Lucy Delany's *From the Darkness Cometh the Light* (1892). Linda Kauffman discusses the relationship between Offred's tale and the records of black women's experiences, noting that "The closest corollary to the Gileadean system is slavery in the American South, when black women were similarly prized and priced as breeders" (234). Janet Larson states that by "imaginatively yoking her post-biblical, Caucasian servant-woman with the biblical, Black slave-mother who survives, Atwood meditates on . . . what freedom means when others are in chains" (53). When I asked Atwood whether or not she agrees with such assertions about her intended application of the slave narrative in the novel, she said "Absolutely" (Dodson 101).

Atwood uses an implicit corollary to condemn the evil forces of American imperialism that are responsible for the silencing of marginalized peoples. The Gileadean regime has continued the traditional Puritanical treatment of cultural and racial Others: obliteration of that which is different. People of color in this novel have been deported and colonized, thereby literalizing the nation's segregational politics: "'Resettlement of the Children of Ham is continuing on schedule,' says the reassuring pink face, back on the screen. 'Three thousand have arrived this week in National Homeland One, with another two thousand in transit'" (83). Only Caucasians inhabit Gilead. Those who are not white have their own tales of exile and slavery, but these are tales silenced and unrepresented in the Gileadean Symposium at the novel's end.

Not only have the "Historical Notes" displaced the histories of the people of color, but they further reveal the Gilead period in American history as one of overt white supremacy and bigotry, for the Symposium on Gileadean Studies falls under the isolated rubric of "Caucasian Anthropology" (379). Furthermore, the word "Caucasian" is stressed five times throughout the notes of the authoritative male scholar, who himself colonizes Offred's voice. Discussing the Gileadean epoch as if it were a second antebellum era, Professor Pieixoto purposely employs historical vocabulary that is representative of America's 19th-century racist ideology: "lynchings," "racist politics," "diaries," "Underground [Rail]road" (387). The Puritanical intolerance at the root of American history has helped to sustain the aura of the Gileadean era: "Its racist politics . . . were firmly rooted in the pre-Gilead period, and racist fears provided some of the emotional fuel that allowed the Gilead takeover to succeed as well as it did" (387). This statement, alluding to why the Children of Ham become the victims of a New Diaspora, provides implicit reminders of American policies that called for the containment of both Native Americans and Japanese Americans.

Though victims of racial differences have been categorized and displaced from Gilead's dominant culture, fertile Caucasian females remain within it, used as objects at the discretion of powerful males. Having been first hunted down as though they were the witches of Old Salem and then governmentally classified as "Handmaids," women with working wombs are branded as different from males and from other females. The surface similarities between the female protagonists of slave narratives and the Handmaids of Gilead are underlined by the legal role of the patriarchal white male in reproduction: "As in slavery, despite the woman's labor, the white slave-holders, like the men in Gilead, retain legal property rights over the product of the woman's body" (Kauffman 234).

This legal control over the woman's body and its offspring can best be explained by the striking resemblance between the tale of the Handmaid and Harriet Ann Jacobs's *Incidents in the Life of a Slave Girl* (1861), an autobiographical work that politicizes the physical exploitation of female slaves in the pre-Civil War South. *Incidents* is generally regarded as the best-known and most-discussed female slave narrative, especially because Jacobs was the only African-American writer of the period to explicitly direct her writing to women (Foster 83). Her treatment of conflict, dominion, and power is more complex and varied than that of male slave narrators like Frederick Douglass (Foster 95).

To tell her own story of sexual violation, Jacobs creates Linda Brent, an alter-ego who narrates her history in the first person, as Offred does. Brent's tale is chiefly her own sexual history, as is that of Atwood's narrator, and both storytellers illuminate the plight of being female chattel by confessing their lives as fallen women and by revealing the scarlet "A" written upon their chests by neo-Puritanical communities. Hazel Carby has written that women's slave narratives are commonly associated with illicit sexuality (38-39). When society labels Brent and Offred as sinful because of their involvement in sexual slavery and illicit procreation, it declares them unfit mothers and thereby dispossesses them of their children. Roberta Rubenstein asserts that Offred's name encodes "her indentured sexuality" in that it is akin to "offered" (103). Like Brent, the Handmaid realizes that the next child she bears must be offered to the rich patriarch who impregnates her, her Commander. Commissioned to not only bear a child in captivity, Offred also loses a daughter to slave hunters: "I can see her . . . holding out her arms to me, being carried away" (97). Her story centers on her painful contemplation of an "inability to mother" (Hansen 22).

Offred and other Handmaids are treated as chattel, goaded by the Aunts with "electric cattle prods" (4). The story of the Handmaid's commodification is based upon an awareness that she shares with Brent, who remarks, "I was a piece of merchandise" (*Incidents* 1726). Offred similarly says, "I wait, washed, brushed, fed, like a prize pig" (69). From the beginning of her narrative, the Handmaid asserts that she is literally a prisoner, tattooed with a chattel number: "Four digits and an eye. . . . It's supposed to guarantee that I'll never be able to fade, finally, into another landscape. I am too important, too scarce, for that. I am a national resource" (4-5). She faces deportation to the Colony of the Unwomen if she fails to bear a child on her third try. Similarly, if an African-American slave woman proved infertile she would be sold since her worth as a resource was diminished (Jennings 49-51). Both narrators give eye-witness testimonies about how the concepts of empire and colonization have been applied to woman's body (Kolodny 4-6; Lewes 66-73).

Despite these overt similarities that Atwood wants us to see, it must be noted that nowhere does she claim that Offred as a white indentured servant has an equivalent or identical subject position to the black slave woman, nor does she argue that all women's oppression is the same. Even as her tale employs a metaphorical play on the enslavement trope, Offred's discourse with slavery uncovers major differences that are strongly emphasized throughout the tale. Atwood ultimately reveals that the narrator is not so naive that she believes rapprochement between privileged white women (even if enslaved as walking wombs) and marginalized women of color is readily and wholly possible. The novelist remains conscious of the warning given by black feminists to white women writers: "[T]o gloss over differences, to argue, for example, as did nineteenth-century white feminists that the social situations between themselves and black slaves were parallel, is to grossly distort reality" (Foster 13). Offred's tale observes these differences, admitting that sexual servitude was more physically and psychologically oppressive for a black woman like Brent, for whom the onset of sexual maturity was fraught with danger.

Though Offred periodically refers to her current "reduced circumstances" (10, 141), she realizes that her coming-of-age was not defined by violence and oppression, though other women around her had suffered; her servitude began in her 30s. She further indicates that she will not have to face the maltreatment during pregnancy that black slave women historically suffered. As hooks notes, "Breeding was oppressive to all fertile black slave women. Undernourished, overworked women were rarely in a physical condition that would allow for easy childbirth" (*Ain't I a Woman?* 41). In fact, slave women were kept at fieldwork for up to the last three weeks of pregnancy and were expected to return to work no later than three weeks after delivery (Bush 198). Offred realizes that she, as a Handmaid, has even fewer physical burdens than in her former life, and she discusses how her labors were confined to shopping and the monthly Ceremony, noting with embarrassment how free time, in fact, caused her boredom (89). In her comparative discourse, recognizing that antebellum slave women suffered from many gynecological complaints and received no prenatal care (Bush 148), Offred spends pages emphasizing her privileged trip to the gynecologist during captivity (77-80). She says, "I'm taken to the doctor's once a month, for tests: urine, hormones, cancer smear, blood test" (77). Furthermore, apparently noting that malnutrition was common among slave women of other times (Steckel 48-51), Offred emphasizes that she was "fed like a prize pig" (90) and given daily vitamins (140-141).

At the center of Offred's "prize pig" status is Commander Fred, a figure that Atwood relates to the patriarchs of the Old South. Once again by comparing Offred's discourse to Jacobs's slave tale, we recognize how the Commanders of Gilead similarly use biblical precedents to justify involvement in the widespread cultural system of chattel slavery. Focusing upon the images of "brushed silver hair" and "sober posture" (86), Atwood fleshes out Offred's "Master" as the caricature of the white patriarch of an old aristocratic code, much as Jacobs presents Dr. Flint as the "epitome of corrupt male power" characterizing the domestic imperialism of the antebellum period (Carby 57).

Each man, a bearer of the patriarchal "Word," undertakes his plan of seduction in a room filled with books, as if to flaunt his power against the indentured female's prohibition of reading; similar to the Commander's "command" that Offred illicitly meet him in his library, Brent confesses Dr. Flint's mandate, "I was ordered to come to his office" (17-29). Furthermore, just as Dr. Flint tempts Linda Brent by passing her illicit notes, Commander Fred gives Offred forbidden magazines to read. In the manner of the importunate seducer in sentimental novels, both patriarchs attempt to bribe the heroine into capitulating. According to hooks, "[M]ale slaveowners usually tried to bribe black women as preparation for sexual overtures so as to place them in the role of prostitute. As long as the white slaveowner 'paid' for the sexual services of his black female slave, he felt absolved" (*Ain't I a Woman?* 25). The Commander allows Offred to play the forbidden Scrabble, to read fashion magazines and to use black market lotion, but he later expects her to accompany him to the house of Jezebels, associating her with Gilead's underground prostitute ring.

However, after Atwood sets up this surface similarity between the Commander and a patriarch like Flint, she shows us that they simply cannot be conflated. The differences are clearly intimated when Offred argues that her Commander has no real evil sexual intentions by inviting her to meet him in the library: "[H]e hasn't brought me here to touch me in any way, against my will. He smiles. The smile is not sinister or predatory" (178). Offred, thus, recognizes that Commander Fred, even though he may wish her to provide him something like love, does not pose a direct physical threat to her. This is in important contrast to

Jacobs's situation, wherein the slave woman is subjected to terrible violence, potential rape, and constant sexual harassment. As Carolyn Sorisio says, "Flint's desire to rape Linda is far more sinister than his need to increase his stock in slaves" (6). Claire Robertson states that sexual abuse was "the ultimate oppression" for black slave women (24). Offred discusses how the threat of harassment, rape, and violence toward women are eliminated by the regime, almost in utopian-like form: "[N]o man shouts obscenities at us, speaks to us, touches us. No one whistles" (33).

Though Atwood engages in an important discourse about the various differences of women's oppression by men, perhaps the most crucial and most complex point of dialogue that she allows us between *The Handmaid's Tale* and a slave narrative like Jacobs's *Incidents* lies in her representation of the Master's Wife. Like Jacobs's portrayal of Mrs. Flint, Offred's tale places specific attention on the background figure of the patriarch's refined spouse—the genteel Southern belle who envies her Handmaid's relationship with her husband. Serena Joy, the Wife of the Commander to whom Offred is currently assigned, recognizes her helplessness to do anything to stop the sexual "Ceremony" that occurs monthly within her house. Atwood places this act in high relief by having the Commander's Wife, through customs of Gilead, present when the act of procreation transpires. Similarly, the Southern wives of colonial patriarchs were often silent observers of the sexual abuse of enslaved black females.

While everything in her somber world seems void of emotion and romantic attachment, Serena Joy herself exhibits a saddened discomfort with the fact that her husband is having sex with "the outside woman" (210). Love, as in Orwell's *Nineteen Eighty-Four*, is implicitly outlawed in this destitute dehumanizing world, but Serena Joy still attempts to claim her man: "As for my husband, she said, he's just that. My husband. I want that perfectly clear. Till death do us part" (16). Offred notices early the jealousy that Serena Joy has toward her: "She doesn't speak to me, unless she can't avoid it. I am a reproach to her"

(13). Brent similarly says, "[E]veryday it became more apparent that my presence was intolerable to Mrs. Flint" (17-29).

Because of her recognition that Mrs. Flint has been hurt by Dr. Flint's infidelity, Brent asserts, "I, whom she detested so bitterly, had far more pity for her than he had.... I never wronged her, or wished to wrong her; and one word of kindness from her would have brought me to her feet" (17-29). Offred likewise recognizes how Serena Joy is another woman in pain, and she feels, or would like to feel, some kinship with the Wife, who so obviously detests the sight of her. The Handmaid comes into Serena Joy's house with the dream that sharing their plight might strengthen them: "I wanted, then, to turn her into an older sister, a motherly figure, someone who would understand and protect me.... I wanted to think I would have liked her, in another time and place, another life" (15-16). However, she is soon discouraged by her recognition of the division between them: "I didn't ask what I was supposed to call her, because I could see that she hoped I would never have the occasion to call her anything at all. I was disappointed" (15).

Perhaps Offred can ultimately feel no real connection to Serena Joy due to the sharp gap between the "haves" and the "have-nots" in Gilead, for a scale of dissonances, with degrees of oppression and liberty, is set up even within the female gender. While the Handmaid longs for the small luxuries of lotion and cigarettes, Serena Joy waves "the large diamonds on the ring finger" (14), a material sign of difference. This delineation of the differences between the elite female and the enslaved one is one of the most apparent statements of Atwood's novel. Offred, looking back at her mother's feminist protests in the 1960s, remarks that at last there is a "women's culture" that the radical feminists had so badly wanted (164). Inherent in this despairing, sarcastic cry is the implication that the dystopian society of Gilead results, among other things, from women's failure to bond across class and color lines. Evident symbols of this exist in the fact that the Wife (who flaunts her diamonds) wears blue and the Handmaid (so impoverished that she has no personal belongings of her own) wears red.

By creating a symbolic caricature of the external color gaps between women, Atwood, in fact, "offers a cruel refutation of [female] separatism," according to Gayle Greene, who says that *The Handmaid's Tale* "carries the warning that feminists must not lose sight of the larger issues" (14). Larger issues like class and race have not been noticed by feminists of the generation of Offred's mother, and Gilead is, in part, a result of the failure of feminism to effect social change for *all* women. According to black feminist Barbara Smith, feminism "is the political theory and practice that struggles to free *all* women. . . . Anything less than this vision of total freedom is not feminism, but merely female self-aggrandizement" (49). Some women have been segregated from "mainstream" women's ideology because of race or class, their voices are forced into silence, so the women's movement itself has had totalitarian moments. Gayatri Spivak argues that Western feminism goes to great extremes to disavow the "other woman" (*In Other Worlds* 134-53). The black woman, Atwood implies, is totally disavowed, remaining alien to Gilead—doubly oppressed, remote, silent, and engulfed in the larger phrase "Children of Ham." Though we cannot see her in National Homeland One, we can assume that there she endures abuses inflicted by an openly racist culture of domination. Offred, in her own way, tries to invoke a coded discourse with/about this silent woman of Ham and her maternal forebears.

Since the antebellum period, black women, hooks argues, have been culturally portrayed as the "Other" who embodies the "dark" sexually wanton side of the female persona, and feminism has done very little to address this intensification of black women's oppression (*Ain't I a Woman?* 31-34). Solidarity has not existed, for the most part, between black and white women in the United States due to racial divisions that occurred in the time of slavery, when a longstanding religious conception of women as the source of bodily sin was transformed through the creation of a racial dichotomy between the sexual images of white and black women (36). The white male slaveholder idealized and controlled white women by denying their sexuality, and he rationalized his sexual exploitation of black female slaves by declaring the black woman as the embodiment of primitive, overt sexuality (Carby 27). This contrast between the pure white woman and the licentious black woman still prevails today in America as part of the general devaluation of black women (hooks, *Ain't I a Woman?* 31-34). Once again, U.S. feminism has employed a paradigm of denial centered upon a domestic ideology that continues to enslave black women.

Offred, in her maturing consciousness, slowly opens a "tiny peephole" (31) of resistance to the privileged white women's order, identifying herself with the Other Woman who is posed as antithetical to the dominant image of the True Woman. She says, "I am the outside woman" (210). The "cult of True Womanhood" was the most popular social convention of female sexuality during the antebellum period (Welter 21-41). By showing us a world where privileged white women suddenly become licensed licentious females, Atwood shatters the racist ideology that historically separates and contrasts white and black females in America. She begins her discourse by addressing the opposing credos of womanhood represented by the dualities of slave woman and mistress that were apparent during the 19th century (Carby 20-39). Atwood works from the understanding that one of the most popular female images in antebellum America was of "a Jezebel character . . . [who] was the counter-image of the mid-nineteenth-century ideal of the Victorian lady" (White 28-29).

The ideal of the True Woman privileged the "pale, delicate, invalid" mistress and promulgated purity, piety, domesticity, and submissiveness (Foster 112). The central axiom of purity denied that True Women had sexual drives: "Love of home, children and domestic duties are the only passions they feel" (Berg 84). Offred quickly recognizes the cultural definition of True Woman placed upon Serena Joy, the angel with a pious and pure voice: "She was ash blond, petite, with a snub nose and huge, blue eyes which she'd turn upwards during hymns" (22). Clearly opposing the sterile and sexless mistress, Offred focuses upon her own absence of the virtue of purity, without which "she was, in fact, no woman at all, but a member of some lower order" (Welter 23). The regime has classified her as unvirginal, and thus of lower status than Serena Joy; the title of Handmaid is given to women who are in their second marriages and who are fertile by proof of previous childbearing.

Like Brent, Offred decides to survive through an act that literalizes her loss of virtue, placing herself outside the parameters of the conventional heroine of sentimental fiction. According to the doctrine of the True Woman, death is preferable to the loss of innocence (Foster 131). Brent chooses to survive in an impure state, entering a voluntary sexual liaison with a white lover named Sands rather than submit to Dr. Flint. Though Offred has the choice to make herself the sexless Unwoman, sent to the Colonies to die a martyr's death, she confesses how she embodied her subversive association with the Unpure Woman through taboo sexual practices (liaison with Nick, Scrabble games with the Commander, trips to the Jezebel house). Her chosen rebellion against the so-called "women's culture" lies in her resistance to the stereotypes of the original feminist ideology.

In considering how Atwood discusses the discriminatory ideology of the slave woman and mistress, our dialogue between Offred and Brent must also note her recognition that Jacobs attempted to change women's stereotypes by using elements of popular fiction. Foster has documented the conventional pressures that shaped the slave narrative to conform to the demands of the reading public (135). The sentimental novel was employed as a typical framework for the black female's slave narrative (Yellin 1725; Smith, *Self-Discovery*, 212-26). Using the pattern not only of autobiographers like Jacobs, but also of such novelists as Harriet E. Wilson (*Our Nig*, 1859) and Frances Harper (*Iola Leroy*, 1892), Atwood superficially portrays the enslaved Handmaid as the helpless heroine who is abused by a gothic villain. Banerjee has written about the classic seduction element of Atwood's novel: "The basic situation is familiar: a woman, totally helpless in a strange environment, continuously finds herself in a variety of situations where a menacing alien power is spectacularly displayed" (83). Offred's seducer is the governmental machine who represents the misogynist/racist principle that seeks to capture and control the body of the Other.

The historical use of the elements of sentimental fiction within the frame of the slave narrative served a confessional function: "to shock the bourgeoisie into an awareness of what a chamber of horrors its own smugly regarded world really was" (Fiedler 135). The political design of writers such as Jacobs was to teach white women about the horrors of the institution of slavery and the ideology of white racism (Yellin 1725). Valerie Smith notes that Jacobs, as a strategy for educating elite women readers about the historical circumstances of marginalization, "couches her story in the rhetoric and structures of popular fiction" (36). Such narrators as Jacobs affirm and legitimize their psychological autonomy by telling the story of their lives, for "in their manipulation of received literary conventions they also engage with and challenge the dominant ideology" (V. Smith 2). It is appropriate, then, as Sorisio notes, that Jacobs chooses to use the discourse of sentimental fiction (6), for this genre "represents a monumental effort to reorganize culture from the woman's point of view" (Tompkins 83). In *Incidents* the author labors to reorganize the women's culture, attempting "to write across the color line, to mediate between the races" (Foster 96). Offred's tale, like Jacobs's, ultimately becomes a testimony about the need for women to cross borders, to discover each other's voices, and to intersect but not conflate their stories.

Understanding the 'Blank White Spaces': The Handmaid's Confession

By using the slave-woman trope to tell her story, Offred, at the same time, comments upon and critiques her own rhetorical procedures, offering a silent revolt to the political problems that the rhetoric entails. She warns us of the dangers inherent in the oversight of apparent differences in various women's tales of oppression, as she learns that both her former and current status do not compare to the historical atrocities of many other women. Invoking the sentimental novel frame of black women's slave narratives, the Handmaid ultimately confesses her own contribution to the dystopian situation in Gilead. Jill LeBihan notes that Offred is "a confessional journal-style first person narrator" (106). This narrator is the white, once-privileged, once-complacent woman whose past reveals her numbness to the voice of the marginalized female. Before the revolution she lived comfortably in the midst of the mainstream in Cambridge, never identifying with the cause of feminism, never noticing the struggles of American women who were less fortunate because of income or color, never taking seriously her activist friend Moira. Peter Stillman and S. Anne Johnson have noted Offred's emblematic complacency throughout her life (70-86). Glenn Deer also argues that the narrator's confessed complacency causes her to become, to some extent, complicit in the violent story she tells (230).

Through an agonizing process of recording details about her own enslavement, Offred discovers that she had, even in her own history, denied that the stories of other women were important. She had segregated their voices from the realm of her own, and nothing inspired her toward a global/multiracial vision of womanhood. Taking her former liberty for granted, Offred had turned a deaf ear toward those enslaved by horrific conditions in American culture. As she makes her confession, she shows that she is beginning to understand the repercussions of her complicit actions. hooks writes about this process: "Women must begin the work of reorganization with the understanding that we have all (irrespective of our race, sex, or class) acted in complicity with the existing oppressive system" (*Feminist Theory* 160).

Stillman and Johnson accuse Offred of being chiefly guilty of "the complicity of ignoring" (77). The narrator acknowledges this shortcoming by delineating numerous past instances in which she had maintained an active negligence toward the plight of other women. Alluding to her dangerous denial of the violence leading up to the coup, Offred confesses how she saw other less-privileged women as "corpses" and "dreams," thereby refusing their reality:

> We [the privileged] lived, as usual, by ignoring. Ignoring isn't the same as ignorance, you have to work at it. . . . There were stories in the newspapers, of course, corpses in ditches or the woods, bludgeoned to death or mutilated . . . but they were about other women. . . . The newspaper stories were like dreams to us, bad dreams dreamt by others. . . . We [privileged white women] were the people who were not in the papers. We lived in the blank white spaces at the edge of print. It gave us more freedom. (74)

Offred here discloses that her acquiescence to the sexual and racial imperialism of contemporary America was based on a false sense of the freedom that comes from "ignoring." Uncovering the "we"/"they" dichotomy of the American mindset, she makes an extremely crucial admission of her former racism, denoting that the stories of other women were in "black" because they were in "print"—as opposed to her distanced bourgeois position in the "blank white spaces" at the edge of the story (74).

Offred further recalls the former lethargy she once felt as she watched movies about "the rest of the world," wherein Third World women were enslaved as colonial subjects both in reality and on film:

> women in long skirts or cheap printed cotton dresses, carrying bundles of sticks, or baskets, or plastic buckets of water, from some river or other, with babies slung on them . . . looking squint-eyed or afraid out of the screen at us. . . . Those movies were comforting and faintly boring. They made me feel sleepy. (151)

Such confessions of her sleepy indifference to national and international news about other women underline Offred's maturing recognition of her failure to understand the social and political context of America, which she saw "only as a story" (86). Her apathy is implicit of a "paradigm of denial" within which dominant members of her culture hide in comfort.

Now, through the description of her loss of freedom, and thus the privilege of ignoring, the narrator attempts to redress her own contribution to the former conditions of other women around the world and to the current conditions of the Handmaids. She, toward the end, speaks in an embarrassed and reparative tone: "I am coming to a part you will not like at all, because in it I did not behave well, but I will try nonetheless to leave nothing out. After all you've been through, you deserve whatever I have left, which is not much but includes the truth" (344). Here Offred assumes a confessional style remarkably like Brent's: "I come to a period in my unhappy life, which I would forget if I could. The remembrance fills me with sorrow and shame. It pains me to tell you of it; but I have promised to tell you the truth, and I will do it" (*Incidents* 1733). Once again, this allusion to Jacobs's chosen confessional mode indicates Offred's own modest but "monumental effort to reorganize culture" (Tompkins 83).

Once Offred has told the truth about the costs of her lethargy, she endeavors to reorganize the past by summoning a sisterhood with women who have "been through" hell and who, therefore, "deserve . . . the truth." Understanding that women's conditions cannot be conflated, Offred directly promises others that she will no longer ignore stories based on differences: "I will bear yours . . . if I ever get the chance, if I meet you or if you escape, in the future or in heaven or in prison or underground" (344). Within her own space, the room allotted to her by the regime, she discovers a new zeal for history inscribed by the woman before her. "Nolite te bastardes carborundorum"—which means "Don't let the bastards grind you down"—is a sororal encouragement for survival through language (69). Offred accepts the challenge to decipher words communicated by "unknown" women: "It was a message, and it was in writing, forbidden by that very fact, and it hadn't yet been discovered. Except by me, for whom it was intended. . . . It pleases me to ponder this message. It pleases me to think I'm communing with her, this unknown woman" (69). In turn, leaving her own message, Offred recognizes that her story is only one in a huge number by women: "*Dear You*, I'll say. Just *you*, without a name. . . . *You* can mean more than one. *You* can mean thousands" (53). Although thousands of women of color have been removed to National Homeland One, Offred implies a readiness to exchange tales if she ever gets the chance, if she meets them or they escape (344). As hooks writes, "Women must explore various ways to communicate with one another cross-culturally if we are to develop political solidarity" (*Feminist Theory* 58).

Offred's expression of desired solidarity with other women signals her maturing consciousness about the immense power of language. Admitting her former insouciance with language, she understands that words could have been her most powerful weapons against the social injustice toward the women who were "in the papers" (74). Offred admits the ridiculousness of her former wordplay, which provided only amusement in her empty time in confinement, and she ultimately confesses her folly, "I've been wasting my time" (293). Though her deconstructions occasionally opened up "tiny peepholes" (31) for interpretation, meaning, and critique, the Handmaid soon learns that they have represented no real verbal action. She remembers, with horror, how she played with the phrase "date rape" in college, only to trivialize the horrors of other women (50).

Immediately following Offred's disclosure of her apathy with words, she begins the mysterious new confinement within which her story is recorded. She never tells us where she is. We learn from the "Historical Notes" that she moves through an Underground Femaleroad, sequestered, as was Brent, in small rooms along the way. Regardless of her final destiny, Offred has arrived at a state of reinscription into a world from which she has been amputated (Lacomb 3-20). Her repossession of language—though "limping and mutilated" because of the challenges posed to literacy—underlines Atwood's assertion that the most important movement toward achieving decolonization and ending oppression is to give voice to suppressed histories. Offred learns that to suppress her story, and ultimately the stories of others, is to aid the dominant force in the promulgation of its imperialistic cultural myths. As Atwood has said elsewhere, "The aim of all suppression is to silence *the voice*, abolish the word, so that the only voices and words left are those of the ones in power" (*Second Words* 350). That which Gayatri Spivak terms as an "inaccessible blankness" in the dominant text is made accessible by narrators like Offred, who speak the voice that history has eclipsed ("Can the Subaltern Speak?" 294). Atwood sees blankness as a territory free of imperial order (Tomc 76). She fills in "the blank white spaces," making them less obviously white.

It is true that the colonization of Offred's body can be linked with the colonization of her voice—even in the end another has imperial control of it, has taken it out of its pure oral form and published it in "his" symbols, as both Arnold Davidson (113-121) and Sandra Tomc (82) note. Thus, when we read the "Historical Notes" at the close of the novel, we are reminded that history, in written form, has most frequently censored the experience of the Other for the purposes of the One. We are also left to wonder whether there are other unspeakable horrors "told" by Offred that have been amputated from the manuscript.

Nevertheless, we are able to discern that however distorted the Handmaid's tale, "her story" has managed to survive even the abuses of history. Overcoming complacency, Offred takes pride in the power of even a "limping and mutilated" narrative, realizing that she speaks a story from which she had distanced herself before the regime colonized her body. By deconstructing Gilead Offred, in turn, constructs her own subjectivity through language as a mode of survival (Russell 143-152). Her "hidden transcript" is a survival technique to resist the "public transcript" of the regime (Hansot 56-69). Working in this secret territory free from imperial order (Tomc 86), Offred makes a "tiny peephole" in the solid prison of a dominant history and "decanters the central image of... the [dominant power's] eye" (Givner 73). Through the Handmaid we learn that the personal tale is a political one, that agency can be found, established, and liberated even in the buried structures of historical silence. Showing us that genuine emancipation occurs only when we open ourselves up to the gaps in the dominant national myths, *The Handmaid's Tale* helps us to face the truth about the horrid paradox at the heart of the American experience, forcing us to meditate on "what freedom means when others are in chains" (Larson 53). Anything less is denial.

From *Utopian Studies* 8, no. 2 (1997): 66-87. Copyright © 1997 by Society for Utopian Studies. Reprinted by permission of Society for Utopian Studies.

References

Atwood, Margaret. *The Handmaid's Tale*. Boston: Houghton Mifflin Company, 1986.
_____. *Second Words: Selected Critical Prose*. Toronto: Anansi, 1982.
_____. *Survival: A Thematic Guide to Canadian Literature*. Toronto: Anansi, 1982.
Banerjee, Chinmoy. "Alice in Disneyland: Criticism as Commodity in *The Handmaid's Tale*." *Essays on Canadian Writing* 41 (Summer 1990): 74-92.
Berg, Barbara. *The Remembered Gate: Origins of American Feminism*. Oxford: Oxford UP, 1978.
Bush, Barbara. "Hard Labor: Women, Childbirth, and Resistance." *More Than Chattel: Black Women and Slavery in the Americas*. Ed. David Barry Gaspar and Darlene Clark Hine. Bloomington: Indiana UP, 1996. 193-217.
Carby, Hazel. *Reconstructing Womanhood: The Emergence of the Afro-American Woman Novelist*. New York: Oxford UP, 1987.
Davidson, Arnold E. "Future Tense: Making History in *The Handmaid's Tale*." *Margaret Atwood: Vision and Forms*. Ed. Kathryn VanSpanckeren and Jan Garden Castro. Carbondale: Southern Illinois UP, 1988. 113-121.
Davidson, Cathy. "A Feminist '1984': Margaret Atwood Talks about Her Exciting New Novel." *Ms* 14: 8 (February 1986): 24-26.
Deer, Glenn. "Rhetorical Strategies in *The Handmaid's Tale*: Dystopia and the Paradoxes of Power." *English Studies in Canada* 18.2 (June 1992): 215-33.
Dixon, Melvin. "Singing Swords: The Literary Legacy of Slavery." *The Slave's Narrative*. Ed. Charles T. Davis and Henry Louis Gates, Jr. Oxford: Oxford UP, 1985. 298-317.
Dodson, Danita J. "An Interview with Margaret Atwood." *Critique* 38.2 (Winter 1997): 96-104.
Fiedler, Leslie. *Love and Death in the American Novel*. New York: Doubleday, 1960.
Foster, Frances Smith. *Written by Herself: Literary Production by African American Women, 1746-1892*. Bloomington: Indiana UP, 1993.

Givner, Jessie. "Names, Faces and Signatures in Margaret Atwood's *Cat's Eye* and *The Handmaid's Tale*." *Canadian Literature* 133 (Summer 1992): 56-75.

Greene, Gayle. "Choice of Evils." *The Women's Review of Books* 3.10 (July 1986): 14.

Hales, Leslie Ann. "Genesis Revisited: The Darkening Vision of Margaret Atwood." *The Month* (July 1987): 257-262.

Hansen, Elaine Tuttle. "Mothers Tomorrow and Mothers Yesterday, but Never Mothers Today." *Narrating Mothers: Theorizing Maternal Subjectivities*. Ed. Brenda Daly and Maureen Reddy. Knoxville: U of Tennessee P, 1991. 21-43.

Hansot, Elisabeth. "Selves, Survival, and Resistance in *The Handmaid's Tale*." *Utopian Studies* 5.2 (1994): 56-69.

Hengen, Shannon. "'Metaphysical romance': Atwood's PhD Thesis and 'The Handmaid's Tale.'" *Science-Fiction Studies* 18 (March 1991): 154-57.

hooks, bell. *Ain't I a Woman? Black Women and Feminism*. Boston: South End Press, 1981.

_____. *Feminist Theory: From Margin to Center*. Boston: South End Press, 1984.

Jacobs, Harriet Ann. *Incidents in the Life of a Slave Girl*. The Heath Anthology of American Literature. Vol. 1. Ed. Paul Lauter. Lexington, MA: D. C. Heath, 1990. 1726-50.

Jennings, Thelma. "'Us Colored Women Had to Go Through a Plenty': Sexual Exploitation of African-American Slave Women." *Journal of Women's History* 1.3 (Winter 1990): 45-74.

Kaplan, Amy. "Left Alone with America: The Absence of Empire in the Study of American Culture." *Cultures of American Imperialism*. Ed. Amy Kaplan and Donald Pease. Durham: Duke UP, 1993. 3-21.

Kauffman, Linda. "Special Delivery: Twenty-First Epistolarity in *The Handmaid's Tale*." *Writing the Female Voice: Essays on Epistolary Literature*. Ed. Elizabeth Goldsmith. Boston: Northeastern UP, 1989. 221-44.

Klarer, Mario. "Orality and Literacy as Gender-Supporting Structures in Margaret Atwood's *The Handmaid's Tale*." *Mosaic* 28.4 (December 1995): 129-42.

Kolodny, Annette. *The Lay of the Land*. Chapel Hill: U of North Carolina P, 1975.

Kumar, Krishan. *Utopia and Anti-Utopia in Modern Times*. Oxford: Basil Blackwell, 1987.

Lacomb, Michele. "The Writing on the Wall: Amputated Speech in Margaret Atwood's *The Handmaid's Tale*." *Wascana Review* 21.2 (Fall 1986): 3-20.

Larson, Janet. "Margaret Atwood and the Future of Prophecy." *Religion and Literature* 21 (Spring 1989): 27-61.

Lauter, Paul, ed. *The Heath Anthology of American Literature*. Vol. 1. Lexington, MA: D. C. Heath, 1990.

LeBihan, Jill. "*The Handmaid's Tale*, *Cat's Eye*, and *Interlunar*: Margaret Atwood's Feminist (?) Futures (?)." *Narrative Strategies in Canadian Literature*. Ed. Coral Ann Howells and Lynette Hunter. Buckingham: Open UP, 1991. 93-107.

Lewes, Darby. "Nudes from Nowhere: Pornography, Empire, and Utopia." *Utopian Studies* 4.2 (1993): 66-73.

May, John R. *Toward a New Earth: Apocalypse in the American Novel.* Notre Dame: U of Notre Dame P, 1972.

Ortner, Sherry. "Is Female to Male as Nature Is to Culture?" *Woman, Culture, and Society.* Ed. Michelle Zimbalist Rosaldo and Louise Lamphère. Stanford: Stanford UP, 1974.

Parrington, Vernon Louis, Jr. *American Dreams: A Study of American Utopias.* New York: Russell & Russell, 1964.

Pease, Donald. "New Perspectives on U.S. Culture and Imperialism." *Cultures of American Imperialism.* Ed. Amy Kaplan and Donald Pease. Durham: Duke UP, 1993. 23-37.

Pike, Fredrick B. *The United States and Latin America: Myths and Stereotypes of Civilization and Nature.* Austin: U of Texas P, 1992.

Robertson, Claire. "Africa into the Americas: Slavery and Women, the Family, and the Gender Division of Labor." *More Than Chattel: Black Women and Slavery in the Americas.* Ed. David Barry Gaspar and Darlene Clark Hine. Bloomington: Indiana UP, 1996. 3-40.

Roemer, Kenneth M. "Defining America as Utopia." *America as Utopia.* Ed. Kenneth M. Roemer. New York: Burt Franklin & Company, 1981. 1-15.

Rubenstein, Roberta. "Nature and Nurture in Dystopia: *The Handmaid's Tale.*" *Margaret Atwood: Vision and Forms.* Ed. Kathryn VanSpanckeren and Jan Garden Castro. Carbondale: Southern Illinois UP, 1988. 101-112.

Ruppert, Peter. *Reader in a Strange Land: The Activity of Reading Literary Utopias.* Athens: U of Georgia P, 1985.

Russell, Elizabeth. "Acts of Defiance in *The Handmaid's Tale*: Constructing the Subject, Deconstructing Gilead." *Revista Española de Estudios Canadienses* 2.1 (May 1994): 143-152.

Slotkin, Richard. *Regeneration Through Violence: The Mythology of the American Frontier, 1600-1860.* Middleton, CT: Wesleyan UP, 1973.

Smith, Barbara. "Racism and Women's Studies." *But Some of Us Are Brave.* Ed. Gloria Hull, Patricia Bell Scott, and Barbara Smith. New York: Feminist Press, 1982. 47-56.

Smith, Valerie. *Self-Discovery and Authority in Afro-American Narrative.* Cambridge: Harvard UP, 1987.

Sorisio, Carolyn. "'There Is Might in Each': Conceptions of Self in Harriet Ann Jacobs's *Incidents in the Life of a Slave Girl.*" *Legacy* 13.1 (1996): 1-18.

Spivak, Gayatri. "Can the Subaltern Speak?" *Marxism and the Interpretation of Culture.* Eds. Cary Nelson and Lawrence Grossberg. Urbana: U of Illinois P, 1988. 271-313.

_____. *In Other Worlds.* New York: Methuen, 1987.

Steckel, Richard H. "Women, Work, and Health Under Plantation." *More Than Chattel: Black Women and Slavery in the Americas.* Ed. David Barry Gaspar and Darlene Clark Hine. Bloomington: Indiana UP, 1996. 43-60.

Stein, Karen. "Margaret Atwood's Modest Proposal: *The Handmaid's Tale.*" *Canadian Literature* 148 (Spring 1996): 57-73.

Stepto, Robert Burns. "I Rose and Found My Voice: Narration, Authentication, and

Authorial Control in Slave Narratives." *The Slave's Narrative.* Ed. Charles T. Davis and Henry Louis Gates, Jr. Oxford: Oxford UP, 1985. 225-241.

Stillman, Peter G., and S. Anne Johnson. "Identity, Complicity, and Resistance in *The Handmaid's Tale.*" *Utopian Studies* 5.2 (1994): 70-86.

Stimpson, Catherine R. "Atwood Woman." Review of *Handmaid's Tale*, by Margaret Atwood. *The Nation* 31 May 1986: 764-67.

Tomc, Sandra. "'The Missionary Position': Feminism and Nationalism in Margaret Atwood's *The Handmaid's Tale.*" *Canadian Literature* 138 (Fall 1993): 73-87.

Tompkins, Jane. "Sentimental Power." *The New Feminist Criticism.* Ed. Elaine Showalter. New York: Pantheon, 1985. 81-104.

Tuveson, Ernest. *Millennium and Utopia.* New York: Harper and Row, 1964.

Welter, Barbara. *Dimity Convictions: The American Woman in the Nineteenth Century.* Athens: U of Ohio P, 1976.

White, Deborah. *Arn't I a Woman? Female Slaves in the Plantation South.* New York: Norton, 1985.

Winthrop, John. "A Modell of Christian Charity." *The Heath Anthology of American Literature.* Vol. 1. Ed. Paul Lauter. Lexington, MA: D. C. Heath, 1990. 191-99.

Woods, Diane. "Bradbury and Atwood: Exile as Rational Decision." *The Literature of Emigration and Exile.* Ed. James Whitlock and Wendell Aycock. Lubbock: Texas Tech UP, 1992. 131-42.

Yellin, Jean Fagan. "Harriet Ann Jacobs." *The Heath Anthology of American Literature.* Vol. 1. Ed. Paul Lauter. Lexington, MA: D. C. Heath, 1990. 1723-25.

Margaret Atwood's *The Handmaid's Tale*: Resistance Through Narrating

Hilde Staels

In the futuristic novel *The Handmaid's Tale* the Canadian novelist Margaret Atwood presents a dystopian vision of a world in which the American neo-conservatives and the New Christian Right or New Puritans of the 1980s have seized power in a totalitarian theocratic republic named after the biblical land of Gilead. Like the New England Puritans of the seventeenth century, the rulers of Gilead establish a theocratic state in the area surrounding the city of Boston, Massachusetts, in the year 2000. The rulers of Gilead return to the Old Testament in a reaction against abortion, sterilization, and what they consider to be dangerous kinds of freedom of the modern welfare state.

The ideal which Gilead's 'Sons of Jacob Think Tank' devised is an imitation of the biblical land of Jacob and Laban, where Jacob restored hope and fertility with the help of a few Handmaids. Thus the regime uses Commanders who subject Handmaids to a monthly penetration in order to solve the problem of excessive and deliberate infertility in the past. The protagonist Offred, who is the Handmaid-slave of the Commander Fred and his infertile wife Serena Joy, is supposed to enact the biblical story of Rachel and Bilhah: 'Give me children, or else I die. Am I in God's stead, who hath withheld from thee the fruit of the womb? Behold my maid Bilhah. She shall bear upon my knees, that I may also have children by her' (*Genesis*, 30).

Margaret Atwood looks at the patriarchal biblical history from the perspective of its female 'victims'. All the women in Gilead are made to play subsidiary parts, the wives of Commanders included, as well as the elderly infertile women, the Aunts, who save their skins by collaborating and who train the Handmaids in self-suppression.

Gilead's victims can find refuge only in a secret Female Underground Road that leads from New England to Canada. Atwood here alludes to the escape route or the Underground Railroad by means of which the runaway slaves of the American South used to enter British-controlled Canada where slavery had been abolished in 1841. Historically, the underground is also a hiding place in the margin of society from which subversives attempt to disrupt the power of the regime above ground.

In my discussion of *The Handmaid's Tale*, I am particularly interested in recurring discursive forms, in the manner in which the first-person narrator delivers the story-material, and in the composition of the narrative text. For the investigation of the personal voice of the narrator, I use Roger Fowler's notion of 'mind-style'. Fowler was the first to introduce the concept into literary theory at the end of the 1970s. In *Linguistics and the Novel*, he defines mind-style as: 'the systems of beliefs, values and categories by reference to which a person comprehends the world'.[1] In *Linguistic Criticism*, he gives the following definition:

> Cumulative ideational structuring depends on regular and consistent linguistic choices which build up a continuous, pervasive, representation of the world. This is the major source of point of view in fiction. [. . .] Discussing this phenomenon in literary fictions, I have called it *mind-style*: the world view of an author, or a narrator, or a character, constituted by the ideational structure of the text. [. . .] I shall illustrate ideational structuring involving three different types of linguistic feature: *vocabulary, transitivity*, and certain *syntactic structures*.[2]

Mind-style is a formal feature of the narrative text that serves the author's technique of indirect characterization. The study of mind-style combines stylistics and narratology, linguistics and literary theory. Mind-style analysis involves a scrutiny of consistent linguistic choices with which the narrator puts ideas or experience into words. I shall give special consideration to lexical forms and syntactic patterns, but also to the metaphors that convey the first-person narrator's conscious and unconscious mental operations.

I shall focus on two types of discourse used by the narrative voice, the discursive law of the theocracy and the narrator's personal, aesthetic discourse with which she counters the authoritarian speech of Gilead. For the description and interpretation of these types of discourse, I rely on some concepts used by the French semiotician Julia Kristeva. In her theory of literary discourse, Kristeva distinguishes between a codified or dominant discourse and another discourse that transgresses the boundaries of dominant sign systems: 'The poetic word, polyvalent and multi-determined, adheres to a logic exceeding that of codified discourse and fully comes into being only in the margins of recognized culture. Bakhtin was the first to study this logic, and he looked for its roots in carnival'.[3] According to Kristeva, poetic discourse escapes the linguistic, psychic and social prohibitions of systematizing discourse. In poetic language, heterogeneity manifests itself, for instance, in non-calculable musical effects. Kristeva emphasizes that poetic discourse renovates language: it breaks through governing laws and ideologies and generates new meanings. It embodies a process between sense and non-sense, or that which does not yet signify, a rupturing of 'normal' communication rules or grammatical rules through rhythm. It is my contention that poetic language has a similar function in *The Handmaid's Tale*, as well as in Atwood's other novels.

The discussion of the narrator's mind-style is followed by an investigation of verbal forms used by the Cambridge dons in the epilogue to *The Handmaid's Tale*, entitled 'Historical Notes'. I am particularly interested in the historians' ironic repetition of Gileadean discourse. I would like to demonstrate that a critical evaluation of the scholarly discourse underlies the design of the text. The mind-style of the historians is judged or evaluated by the 'implied author'. Roger Fowler, among others, defines the implied author as follows: 'the design of a text situates the writer, and thus his reader, in a certain location relative to his represented content—the structure of the text contributes to the definition of its author'.[4]

1. Witnessing the Closed Morality of an Absolutist State

In *The Handmaid's Tale*,[5] Offred retrospectively witnesses her personal victimization as a Handmaid in Gilead's theocracy. The totalitarian regime forces the inhabitants to submit to the power of one (moral) law, one true religion, one language code. Gilead's Newspeak makes all other modes of thought impossible. The new regime legitimizes its own meaning system and demands an unconditional allegiance to it. Where meaning is singular and final, ambiguity of meaning and variety of experience are excluded. People are indoctrinated into so-called traditional values that are expressed in terms of universal truths, maxims or slogans. In a society that functionalizes language to the extreme, the potential polysemy of discourse is replaced by absolutely homogeneous, univocal signs.

Though modernity is judged to have been a threatening force, the rulers highly esteem the values of logocentrism and materialism that typify the capitalist spirit. Everything is coded, measured and regulated to an economic value. All human qualities are instrumentalized, and reduced to quantitative values of exchange. In other words, the new rulers equate the value of something and someone solely with validity, usefulness, functionality, economic profit.

Everything and everyone is substantified. People's identity is supposed to coalesce with the coded concepts and the predicated state by which they are defined. Handmaids are supposed to merely think of themselves 'as seeds' (p. 18), as objects with a procreative function that should save the world from the threat of sterility, as 'two-legged wombs, that's all: sacred vessels, ambulatory chalices' (p. 136). The 'deadly' regime paradoxically aims at creating new life.

The governing discourse of the absolutist state is an artificial, so-called Biblical speech. In the theocracy, a metaphysics of truth reigns that conveys the full presence of meaning in what is said to be the Word of God. The rulers have the power over the use and abuse of language whereas lesser human beings are granted the freedom neither to see nor to speak personally, in their own name. Handmaids, who must neither see, nor be seen as individuals, are therefore freed from self-reflection and self-affirmation. Freedom from too much knowledge and from choice are said to be the privilege of the meek. Mirrors are practically absent, because freedom from self-reflection saves one from the traditional search for identity. The ideal is freedom from the constitution of an identity and from the struggle for self-definition. It is part of Gilead's double-think to disguise as privilege people's mindless, wordless condition.

Handmaids are allowed to see only the flat surfaces of the present, i.e., a wall of rules and regulations. The eyes of Handmaids are not allowed to move beyond the prescribed edges. Gilead excludes all agency functions of the colonized individuals: 'The active, is it a tense?' (p. 97), Offred wonders. Whereas Offred remembers the 1980s as the time when one could freely communicate and 'squander' words, Gilead excludes all exchange of personal speech. In a society where social interaction is excessively mechanized and people are reduced to passive recipients of the law, the constitution of subjectivity through interaction between human beings has become obsolete.

As there is no room for a shifting of boundaries, any aesthetic, creative use of language is necessarily outlawed. A bureaucratic rationality that is completely dehumanized censors all dangerous personal, irrational and emotional elements that escape calculation. The ideal is the absolutely unified individual, whose inner life is gradually stultified and in the end totally and finally conditioned by Gilead's law. Thus Offred is supposed to be a soulless object: 'My self is a thing [...] a made thing, not something born' (p. 66), she says. She feels she is nobody in particular, a depersonalized 'it'. Gileadean logic mutes the flesh and numbs the blood. It mortifies the site of unconscious, 'irrational' feelings and desires; the site of heterogeneous elements. Offred says: 'That is how I feel: white, flat, thin. I feel transparent' (p. 85) or 'I too am disembodied' (p. 104).

The indoctrination sessions supervised by Aunts aim at excluding nostalgia for the past or a yearning for the future. Memories of the past, together with personal desires, are supposed to fade away. Whatever unconscious irrational or emotional forces may remain, in the form of aggression and frustration against the regime, they are drained off, or are guided into collective ritual events. Rituals, ceremonies or clock time dominate in the theocracy to keep the oppressed away from social disruption.

In Gilead, hands and feet are pronounced non-essential tools: 'Remember, said Aunt Lydia. For our purposes your feet and your hands are not essential' (p. 91): 'I feel as if somebody cut off my feet', says Offred (p. 178). With gloved, folded hands and encased feet, the Handmaid's body signals its dismembered condition. In the theocracy, the heart is supposed to be no more than a mechanical clock that counts time. The metaphor of cancelled hearts, hands and feet connotes uprootedness, or a soulless existence.

Ironically, the biblical land of 'healing balm' (Jeremiah, 8:22) appears in the new context as a waste land, a desolate area, whose inhabitants are spiritually and emotionally deadened. It is an 'unreal' place that resembles an infernal circle, a labyrinth without exit, the trails are dead-ends. Natural colours are 'a sickly yellow' (p. 82), white, grey, dim or fading. With nature put to sleep, the womb of the earth is a tomb, or a place where absolute stillness reigns. The lifeless heart or centre of Gilead is a metaphor for the numbed hearts or souls of its inhabitants. The air communicates the reign of violent suppression, inertia, boredom, total stagnation, infertility. In this context, the instrumentalized wombs of Handmaids mainly produce stillbirths.

2. A Tale of Silenced Voices

Offred's place of narration is an Underground Female Road that is associated with images of 'the dark realm within' (p. 295), 'some other place' (p. 268), a 'cellar' (p. 303), an 'attic hiding place' (p. 311), an 'obscure matrix' (p. 311). Metaphorically, the underground is the space in the margin of law and order from which the creative artist ideally expresses her own voice. The dark subterranean realm from which Offred witnesses events of the past is penetrated by light. The image of light associates the tale with the imaginative activity of the mind. 'I step up, into the darkness within: or else the light' (p. 295), says the retrospective narrator, who remembers the moment before she found a refuge in the 'Underground Female Road'.

By bringing into prominence a Handmaid's personal, aesthetic discourse spoken in the margin of a fundamentalist regime, the eyewitness account is both a report of and a challenge of the meaning system established by the rulers of the theocracy. Offred's tale is the personal expression of insights that move beyond the historical facts of Gilead, beyond the frontiers of Gilead's meaning system and, finally, beyond the identity of Handmaid-slave that the colonizing power imposed on her.

From the point of view of Gilead, personal discourse is disallowed, because it is considered too dangerous. However, among the colonized individuals, the total suppression of personal desire and personal speech causes an irrepressible yearning for gratification. In the margin of society, Offred articulates her muted insights and sacrificed feelings, and she evokes absent objects and meanings. Her individual speech produces a profusion of words and desires that are not allowed. Offred crosses the boundaries of accepted meaning by giving voice to an alternative perspective and an alternative discourse that continuously cut through the rigid logocentric texture of the superstructure.

By giving expression to her inner feelings and bodily sensations from her situation on the periphery of society, Offred breaks through the discursive Law of the theocracy. Gilead censors the threatening force of creative self-expression. Yet Offred defies the strict rules of authoritative discourse by giving life to a silenced discourse. She revives the capacity for individual spiritual and emotional life. In the margin, she speaks in her own name, the name that she was supposed to forget once and for all: 'I keep the knowledge of this name like something hidden, some treasure I'll come back to dig up, one day. I think of this name as buried' (p. 84). In Gilead, Offred used to silently repeat her hidden name (June) to maintain her existence: 'I want to be more than valuable. I repeat my former name, remind myself of what I once could do, how others saw me' (p. 97). By recalling her former name, June regenerates her creative energy. She is the grammatical subject and narrative agent of the tale, whereas Gilead reduced her position to that of (grammatical) object and patient.

In Gilead, where Offred is forced to lead a paralysed existence, she suffers from an almost uncontrollable physical desire to take in the smell of organic life—of earth, flowers and warm wet grass—that silently breaks through the hardened surface. She desires to feel alive and become united with the buried voice or life-cycle of the earth, in defiance of the power which the regime exercises over her. The narrator-witness reconstructs the will of the protagonist to survive, to liberate herself from the trap of 'here and now'.

The protagonist yearns spiritually and emotionally for a crossing of spatiotemporal boundaries. Offred wants to absorb the smell of objects that bring back to mind the context of the past. The connection with these memories, though it is a painful recollection, is necessary to her survival. She longs to move down, into and through the linear subdivisions on the surface of the petrified city. She desires to give expression to repressed corporeal and affective processes by opening up her hands and feeling the blood flow again through the cancelled hands, feet and heart. She gives voice to a want, to a personal desire for touch and for being touched. Against the reign of economic exchange value between commercially valid objects, she posits a desire to create a contiguous, free-flowing relationship with the elements and with other human beings. Remembering what she felt while standing close to the Commander's servant Nick, she says: 'Whether it is or not we are touching, two shapes of leather. I feel my shoe soften, blood flows into it, it grows warm, it becomes a skin' (p. 81).

The loving gestures contradict the reign of folded, gloved, coldly artificial hands. Offred wishes to regenerate subjectivity and undo frozen dichotomies in the object world. She wishes to resuscitate the life of the soul or the heart. She relates spatially and semantically polarized animate and inanimate objects in both/and relationships. From her own world of desire and in her own voice, everything becomes animated: 'Even the bricks of the house are softening, becoming tactile; if I leaned against them they'd be warm and yielding. It's amazing what denial can do' (pp. 153/4).

With her outstretched bare open hands, Offred communicates with the hidden organic, biological rhythm of nature that resurrects concealed corporeal and affective processes. She revives the exchange with ex-centric space in opposition to the sheer exchange between consumer objects in the centralized regime. Adverbials 'in', 'into', 'across', 'out', 'up' and 'through' point to the crossing of limits. The desire for warmth, fluidity, light and life ruptures the reign of cold, dead abstraction and violence.

The absolutist regime wants to abolish the past. Yet Offred re-enacts the past in the present. Her memory of the past brings back to life the excluded pole in Gilead, such as the existence of love and humanity. Offred's act of retracing the lost connection with her roots in the process of life is a desire to escape from the trap of paralysis and defeatism. It is an act of survival that saves her from despair and that resurrects the missing part of herself. 'I want to be with someone' (p. 104), says Offred, who desires to be 'someone' who calls 'someone' into existence where subjectivity is pronounced obsolete. By activating her silenced inner body,[6] she asserts her will to be visible.

The singularity of Offred's speech frees words from Gilead's communicative constraints of language, from denotative speech and from the sign as merely an element of commercial transaction. The narrator's poetic discourse resists the reduction of reality to coded concepts and of individuals to reified objects. In a society that censors aesthetic speech, Offred's poetic discourse reactivates the lost potential of language and the conditions for the production of meaning. She revitalizes an otherwise extinct language and inner life, deadened by the supremacy of codes. She resists Gilead's transparent, quantifiable products of meaning by creating heterogeneity.

Traces of unconscious processes are visible in the narrator's free flow of similes. She describes the posture of the Handmaid Ofglen as follows: 'Without a word she swivels, as if she's voice-activated, as if she's on little oiled wheels, as if she's on top of a music box. I resent this grace of hers. I resent her meek head, bowed as if into a heavy wind' (p. 43). Consider also Offred's description of the dead bodies of 'subversives' that hang on the wall surrounding Gilead: 'The three bodies hang there, even with the white sacks over their heads looking curiously stretched, like chickens strung up by the necks in a meatshop window; like birds with their wings clipped, like flightless birds, wrecked angels' (p. 277). Whereas the theocracy wants the gap between the word and its meaning to be filled, and the relationship paralysed, Offred compulsively opens up the gap by using an exuberant flow of similes.

Offred creates a contiguity between spatio-temporally and semantically discontinuous objects by an abundant use of metonymical speech and synaesthesia, as in: 'my hands; they fill with flowers of light' (p. 49); 'Time as white sound' (p. 69); 'a thin sound like the hum of an insect; then nearing, opening out, like a flower of sound opening, into a trumpet' (p. 111). Compare also: 'Aunt Lydia pressed her hand over her mouth of a dead rodent' (p. 55) and '[Janine's] transparent voice, her voice of raw egg white' (p. 129). The rhythmic features of her mind-style appear not only in semantic, but also in phonetic associations, as in: 'Sun comes through the fanlight, falling in colors across the floor: red and blue, purple. I step into it briefly, stretch out my hands; they fill with flowers of light' (p. 49).

Offred sets against the impersonal, denotative Scrabble game that she is made to play with the Commander, a personal connotative discourse that ideally unites the word and the flesh, that attempts to bridge the gap between language and feelings: 'I feel like the word *shatter*'

(p. 103); 'the [bullet] hole [...] the one flash, of darkness or pain, dull I hope, like the word *thud*, only the one and then silence' (p. 104).

Offred connects the concrete and the abstract; remembered objects, impressions and sensations of the past (censored events) and events in the present; the visible (the 'true' and 'real') and the invisible (declared 'unreal' and 'irrational'): conscious and unconscious events. She awakens a sense of things that she has never experienced before. The narrator opens tunnels inside herself that lead towards the unrecorded. As a protagonist, the danger of silently creating relations that are based on fantasy fills her with both pleasure and pain: 'In a minute the wreath will start to color and I will begin seeing things [...] things at the sides of your eyes: purple animals, in the bushes beside the road, the vague outlines of men, which would disappear when you looked at them straight' (pp. 128/9).

Whereas Aunt Lydia warns the handmaids against the word *Love*: 'Don't let me catch you at it. No mooning and June-ing around here, girls' (p. 220), June offers an alternative to the mechanized petrification by calling back to mind the power of ancient fertility (moon) goddesses. Offred remembers there once were primitive matriarchal societies that conceived of a goddess as the main element in the formation of the universe. The power of the Great Goddess, the Virgin-Mother who is renewed every month as moon-goddess, or once a year as earth-goddess, fills her with hope for renewal of life. The gift of creative life force which the Goddess offers counteracts the reduction of fertility to a functionalized procreative act. Thus Offred awakens an ancestral memory, a traditional world of culture and value. The Great Goddess is a recurring metaphor in Atwood's novels. She is the origin of life that can be reached only through death. The ancestral mother or Nature Goddess manifests herself in the novels as both a tomb and a womb. Through re-established contact with the Goddess, the protagonist retrieves the willpower to receive and to give new life.

Offred wants to make the 'unreal,' the 'irrational' and invisible happen, and make real fantasies of restored contact with the Great Goddess and creative energy. We read 'in the obscured sky a moon does float, newly, a wishing moon, a sliver of ancient rock, a goddess, a wink' (p. 97) and 'at the edges of my eyes there are movements, in the branches; feathers, flittings, grace notes, tree into bird, metamorphosis run wild. Goddesses are possible now and the air suffuses with desire' (p. 153). Above ground, the air communicates a smell that emerges from the womb of the earth, from the dark matrix that hides the power of the (moon) Goddess of fecundity. Sensations of warmth and life force (water) fill the air, because they know no boundaries: 'It's started to rain, a drizzle, and the gravid smell of earth and grass fills the air' (p. 111).

Offred, who creates an outpouring of words, the rhythm of which is a symptom of her oppressed inner life, notices how, in a similar vein, suppressed but inviolable natural space symptomatically disrupts the logocentric superstructure. From Offred's point of view, the garden of the Commander's wife Serena Joy communicates the invincible power of buried life energy. Offred says: 'There is something subversive about this garden of Serena's, a sense of buried things bursting upwards, wordlessly, into the light, as if to point, to say: Whatever is silenced will clamor to be heard, though silently' (p. 153). She associates breaks in the social structure with symptoms of silent rebellion of the oppressed.

The narrator recurrently uses the image of an egg, an object that seems to be no more than white and granular on the outside. The egg is an image for the barren surface of Gilead and for the condition of the protagonist's outer body, both of which are 'defined by the sunlight' (p. 110) or by the logocentrism of the rulers. Yet the egg glows red from the inside. Underground, a red, hot pulsing process of life is hidden. Red is the colour of organic, free-flowing blood that reveals the existence of life energy: 'the life of the moon may not be on the surface, but inside', Offred says (p. 110).

Against the prescribed mono-tone voice, the narrator creates a personal, multivocal tale: 'this sad and hungry and sordid, this limping and mutilated story' (p. 267). A range of feelings and responses calls into existence a vulnerable, breathing subject. The voice shifts from hatred to resentment, despair, outrage, mockery, from nostalgia for the past to compassion for fellow-victims. Sometimes, Offred gives voice to hope and belief in new life: 'It's this message, which may never arrive, that keeps me alive. I believe in the message' (p. 106); 'Out there or inside my head, it's an equal darkness. Or light' (p. 194). Spiritual and emotional revival resides in hope for change and belief in love and vitality that will defeat the reign of stasis: 'hope is rising in me, like sap in a tree. Blood in a wound. We have made an opening' (p. 169). Offred moves back through layers of history, opens the wounds and retraces the loss. Pain is still possible because of memory, and memory is what the narrator tries to keep alive. The destruction of memory, which Gilead aims at, involves a numbing of the site of personal desire and creative energy.

Offred's tale moves, emotionally, as well as rhythmically, in contrast with the deathly stillness that reigns above ground. In *The Handmaid's Tale*, the most striking traces of what Kristeva calls the 'semiotic' are rhythm and sound in poetic discourse. The rhythm of the text is symptomatic of traumatic events, and of excluded experiences. *The Handmaid's Tale* transforms or shifts the boundaries of the conventional dystopic genre. This defamiliarization of the traditional dystopia is an effect of the narrator's inner journey that results in the subject's creation of an alternative word and world to the everyday object world. Though the personal voice and perception (mind-style) of a female protagonist are at the centre of the tale, the language spoken from within the margin is not necessarily 'a woman's language', but the discourse of a socially marginalized individual.

3. The *Historical Notes*: Irony in Retrospect

On the twenty-fifth of June in the year 2195, academics organize a Symposium about the history of Gilead at the University of Denay,

Nunavit. The names 'Denay' and 'Nunavit' allude to the first Canadians, the native Eskimos and Indians, victims of a politics of colonization. The Indians prefer to be called 'Dene' and the Eskimos 'Inuit'. Both words mean 'the people'. 'Nunavut', the Northwest Territories (between Alaska and Greenland) is land claimed by the Eskimos in Canada. Yet Atwood alludes to the Canadian government which even today opposes the demands for autonomy. It also allows the territory of the Innu, who are a nomadic people, to be invaded by military exercises with airplanes that threaten animals and human beings by flying at low level (100 ft. only). The words 'Denay' and 'Nunavit' may also be Atwood's pun on 'deny none of it', which both applies to the victimization of the native Eskimos and Indians and to the colonization of the inhabitants of Gilead.

At the Symposium, two Cambridge dons, Professor Wade and Professor Pieixoto, are proud of having discovered some thirty fragments of a tale which they have subsequently transcribed. They have entitled the anonymous narrative *The Handmaid's Tale*. Offred's tale turns out to be an oral account and taped narrative that was excavated after having remained buried for about a century.

A spoken text is transcribed, which implies that the tonal voice is deleted (a voice that adds meaning to discourse) and the discourse further hardened. The hardening further removes the meaning of the speaker from the meaning of her discourse. Even though in the taped text Offred insists that neither the truth nor the exact context of her experience can be retraced, let alone pinpointed, the historians attempt to reconstruct the reality about Gilead. Whereas the tale claims neither to be a factual document, nor simply a report and eye-witness account, the historians nevertheless try to figure out what really happened. The joint paper of the scientists, 'Problems of Authentication in Reference to *The Handmaid's Tale*', indicates they are in search of closed interpretations. The narrator, however, repeatedly emphasizes that her tale is a reconstruction, an invention which necessarily involves the loss of the original story. At times, Offred explicitly states that she attempts to remember stories that went on inside her head while she was living above ground. The tale can never be an authentic account of lived experience or a mimetic representation of reality.

Offred asserts that the act of telling covers up the horror of reality, because lived experience is unnameable and irretrievable. Yet positivism pushes to the margins of experience what it cannot explain and control: the irrational and emotional elements that emerge from an 'obscure matrix' (p. 311). The self-satisfied Pieixoto and Wade trivialize the expressions of pain to 'a whiff of emotion' (p. 303). They exclude from their horizon of perception the act of telling as a re-articulation of reality, as an effort to give expression to inner sensations, or hope and faith in change. They aim at a reconstruction of the historical facts of a patriarchal history. They express more concern for the historical author of the tale and for the position assigned to her above ground, rather than for the unique narrating voice of 'someone' who speaks from within the periphery, and who draws strength from her marginalized position.

Proud of their own 'Enlightened days', the academics announce the return to, or the continuation of, a supreme rationalism that typifies Gilead. The connection between the mind-style of the narrator and the context is utterly misunderstood by the academics in their own context. They fail to consider the narrator as generator of meaning in their search for 'objective' truth. By endowing the non-measurable aspects of the narrative with a sheer decorative value, the academics merely create another subjectivity in relation to the same history. By ignoring the narrator's attempt to witness to the unspeakable horror, the academics also negate the work of art as a moral instrument. June, who wants her own voice to be heard and her inner life to be visible, is muted once again. In her relationship to the future listeners, the storyteller has failed to be rehabilitated as 'someone' who speaks to 'someone', for the male researchers turn a deaf ear to her personal voice. Offred fails to achieve her wished-for creative interaction between the 'I' who speaks and the 'you' who responds, as in: 'By telling you anything at all I'm at least believing in you. I believe you're there. I believe you into being. Because I'm telling you this story I will your existence. I tell, therefore you are' (p. 268). In the academic world, 'June' means nothing more than the month during which the Symposium takes place.

The mind-style with which the academics approach Offred's narrative is characterized by sheer logical reasoning. The scholars attempt to track down clues, proof, evidence that should lead to definitive knowledge about the original identity of the narrator; of the Commander (Waterford?); the place of narration; the original meaning of the tale and the whole context of Gilead. They are interested in as many measurable facts as possible. They are concerned with deciphering the tale precisely 'in the clearer light of our own day' (p. 311). This statement recalls the supremacy of 'the defining sunlight' (p. 110) or logocentrism in Gilead that fixes the position of everyone and everything. It is no accident then that the Commander Fred calls himself 'a sort of scientist' (p. 185). The academics investigate the tale so as to establish its stable meaning and to pinpoint cause and effect relationships: 'Supposing, then, the tapes to be genuine [. . .] If we could establish an identity for the narrator [. . .] to identify the inhabitants [. . .] to trace and locate the descendants [. . .] this trail led nowhere [. . .] we pursued a second line of attack' (p. 303); 'whatever the causes, the effects were noticeable [. . .] her original name [. . .] Offred gives no clue' (p. 305).

'Many gaps remain' (p. 310), says Pieixoto, who would love to see the gaps between the words and lived experience filled and the narrative ended. He would like to undo the ambiguities and indeterminacies and establish an original, transparent meaning instead. He ignores the narrator, who emphasizes the necessity to maintain the gaps between the words and reality, and to be well aware of the existence of unrecorded experience.

The desire of the scholars for univocal, transparent meaning ironically mirrors the authoritative word of Gilead. The logocentric, categorizing mental structures or speech types are analogous to the logocentrism that underlies the tyranny of the Gilead regime. The desire for a metaphysics of truth is equivalent to Gilead's dogmatism and its illusions of stable, given meaning. The academic scientists similarly exclude polyvalence and ambiguity in favour of essential meaning.

In the manner of Gilead, the scientists push into the margin the subject's creative individual utterances, the connotative speech of the (female) subject. They (consciously) overlook the narrator's self-expression and self-affirmation, the rhythmic pulsations, intuitions, the creative power that underlies her poetic speech. Even though the researchers compare Offred to Eurydice, the Creation-death goddess whose voice emerges from a far distance, Eurydice escapes as soon as they try to 'grasp' her, that is, understand and control her by looking at her from their own rational perspective. Her voice remains enigmatic and returns to the womb of the earth, where it lies buried. The personal voice is lost to those who do not wish to acknowledge its existence, or who fear to listen. They simply neglect the tale as a work of art, namely Offred's restructuring of the order of language and her re-visioning of reality. As a result, the historical listener radically fails to coincide with the implied, ideal listener.

The scholars ignore Offred's conscious effort to call the lost, loved ones back into existence. They do not try to comprehend the articulation of her inner world as a deliberate attempt at survival. Instead, they approach the text in a utilitarian way. From their perspective, more historical data and exhaustive material facts about Gilead would have made the tale a commercially interesting exchange object. Because the document does not provide the complete picture of Gilead, and has too many 'obscure' passages, it fails as a commodity. The restitution of the whole context and of the meaning of the theocratic model would have been more valuable than the evanescent personal utterances, the woman's expression of hidden feelings and desires that is a wasted effort in economic terms: 'What would we not give, now, for twenty pages or so of printout from Waterford's private computer! However, we must be grateful for any crumbs the Goddess of History has deigned to vouchsafe us' (p. 310).

The nightmare that underlies the Symposium has to do with the negation of Offred's tale as a timeless account, for the scholars trivialize the horror of which she speaks by simply regarding it as a moment in history, rather than comprehending it as a warning against the reification of a mental construct that may return at any time in history, in any form. Furthermore, the academics marginalize the narrator's personal mind-style, especially the pain, the hope and the belief in new life, the alternative world and word. Consequently, the novel affirms the survival of darkness, though the age is said to be enlightened.[7] Darkness survives as well in the refusal of male intellectuals, of those who establish a literary canon, to acknowledge the value of a woman's perspective on patriarchal history.

I hope to have shown that mind-style analysis throws an interesting light on the complex psychological and ideological stance of Atwood's protagonists. In addition, readers of Atwood's novels need to pay careful attention to the ironic mirroring of discursive forms, as it is a typical formal feature of her novelistic practice. In her fiction, Atwood uses this technique to critically evaluate or judge a particular perception of reality. The evaluation underlies the compositional structure of the narrative text. It is up to the reader to disclose the design of the text as the hidden signifier.[8]

Some readers apparently fail to do so. In her review of *The Handmaid's Tale*, the American author Mary McCarthy attacks Atwood for her failure to create a 'true' dystopia: 'the most conspicuous lack, in comparison with the classics of the fearsome-future genre, is the inability to imagine a language to match the changed face of common life. No newspeak. [. . .] This is a serious defect, unpardonable maybe for the genre: a future that has no language invented for it lacks a personality. That must be why, collectively, it is powerless to scare'.[9]

I consider such criticism to be unjust, for the literal application of biblical texts, the anachronistic use of scriptural phrases, and other such devices that aim at making other modes of thought impossible, are functionally analogous to Orwell's Newspeak. Moreover, not only is it highly questionable that Newspeak is a necessary ingredient of the dystopic genre, but McCarthy's criticism of Atwood's novel also seems to stem from the reviewer's neglect of the context or ex-centric spatial position from which the tale is narrated. It is my contention that by 'designing' the text in such a manner, Atwood precisely aims at shifting the boundaries of the conventional dystopic genre.

From *English Studies* 76, no. 5 (1995): 455-468. Copyright © 1995 by Taylor and Francis Ltd. Reprinted by permission of Taylor and Francis Ltd.

Notes

I would like to express my sincerest thanks to Professor R. Derolez for his critical advice.

1. Roger Fowler, *Linguistics and the Novel* (London, 1977), p. 130.
2. Roger Fowler, *Linguistic Criticism* (Oxford, 1986), pp. 150-1.
3. Julia Kristeva, 'Word, Dialogue, and Novel', in *Desire in Language: A Semiotic Approach to Literature and Art*, ed. Leon S. Roudiez (New York, 1980), p. 65.
4. Roger Fowler, *Linguistics and the Novel*, p. 7.
5. Margaret Atwood, *The Handmaid's Tale* (Boston, 1986). Page references in the text are to this edition.
6. In her writings, Margaret Atwood consistently distinguishes between an 'outer' and an 'inner' body. The outer body is the disciplined surface that is submitted to societal constraints, and it is one's reified image in the eyes of the other. The inner body is the space of feelings and sensations that is disruptive of the disciplined surface. It is also an image for the unstructured and pre-symbolic, pre-reflexive realm or in Julia Kristeva's terms, the fluid 'semiotic' body.
7. Arnold E. Davidson rightly speaks of the epilogue as the 'most pessimistic part of the book. Even with the lesson of Gilead readily at hand, the intellectuals of 2195 seem to be preparing the way for Gilead again.' In 'Future Tense: Making History in *The Handmaid's Tale*', in *Margaret Atwood: Vision and Forms*, eds. Kathryn Van Spanckeren and Jan Garden Castro (Carbondale, 1989), p. 120.
8. See Hilde Staels, *Margaret Atwood's Novels: A Study of Narrative Discourse* (Tübingen and Basel: Francke Verlag, 1995), p. 241
9. Mary McCarthy, 'Breeders, Wives', *The New York Times Book Review*, February 9, 1986.

A Body in Fragments:
Life Before Man and The Handmaid's Tale
Eleonora Rao

Described as a failed "attempt at social and domestic realism," *Life Before Man* has been regarded as Atwood's worst achievement.[1] Critics have seen it as a text dominated by a dark, pessimistic mood, where a static imagery conveys a sense of lack of change.[2] This reading is reinforced by the essential "sameness," or "similarities" of the characters involved.[3] To my mind, however, the interest of the novel does not lie in the development of plot. In *Life Before Man* the modernist contrast between objective and subjective time and the absence of plot, combined with a focus on the inner life of the characters, posit an emphasis on changes in the characters' development. In this respect the novel's vision is not static. Change does occur. However imperceptibly, it is, as a critic has noted, "constant and profound."[4]

In this section I shall analyse and contrast *Life Before Man* with *The Handmaid's Tale* as the former presents *in embrio* concerns that will receive further development and elaboration in Atwood's work of dystopic fiction. The two novels have a number of themes in common—the emphasis on the ever indefinite character of self-knowledge; the treacherous aspects of memory; the problematization of language as a medium which represents an objective and knowable reality; the self as a locus of change and contradictions. Both texts present images of the fragmented body regarded by psychoanalytic theory as a sign of a threat to the rational unity of the subject.

These topics are treated in a more complex way in *The Handmaid's Tale*, which was written four years later. Here the question of identity is closely related to metafictional reflections on the form of this tale itself. *The Handmaid's Tale* simultaneously encodes the narratives of autobiography or confessional writing and those of history. At the same time it addresses the fictionality of these forms, of biography, autobiography and history. The fragmented and iterative structure of the novel undermines the traditional realist narrative conventions of the inscription of the subject as continuous and coherent. It may, on the contrary, suggest that fragmentation and replication are also conditions of subjectivity. Similarly, the segmented narrative in *Life Before Man*, the plurality of narrative voices it contains, emphasize subjective interpretations of the real world and discontinuities of the self.

Life Before Man is structured around three distinct narrative voices: those of Elisabeth Schloendorf, her husband Nate, and Lesje, a younger woman who eventually becomes Nate's lover. The novel starts at one specific point in time, Friday, 29 October 1976 and ends at a later point in time, Friday, 18 August 1978. The narrative is chronologically arranged in a series of short sections, with the exception of two flashbacks, describing events or experiences from three different points of view, that of Elisabeth, of Nate and of Lesje.

From the point of view of action and plot, very little happens in this novel. The only "event" that marks the narrative is the suicide of Chris, Elisabeth's lover, which occurs before the novel starts. Marriage, which Lesje considers an "event" (p. 293), does not take place, nor does divorce.[5] Instead there is a dissolving and re-forming of relationships around the three members of the triangle.

Elisabeth and Nate, we understand, have been living together for some time for the sake of the children. They both have had a number of extramarital relationships. But the suicide of Chris, who demanded that Elisabeth leave her children and marry him, disrupts the precarious balance of their life together. Half-way through the novel Lesje leaves her partner William and becomes involved with Nate, who earlier in the narrative had terminated his relation with Martha.

This summary, however, does not do justice to the complexity of the novel, since it makes it sound like a "soap opera."[6] For the narrative mode of *Life Before Man* is reflective, and focuses on the characters' emotional states and "moments of being" in a manner that is very close to a modernist treatment of character and time. Objective time is marked at the beginning of each section, but it is of little importance.

The reader instead is confronted with the exploration of subjective, arbitrary inner time as experienced by the characters. The segmentation of the narrative into overlapping "chunks of time" (p. 308) serves the purpose of providing contrasting subjective perspectives on each event. This is only one of the interests the novel shares with modernist literature. As Gayle Greene notes, in *Life Before Man* "the structure problematizes time and reality; events are filtered through three consciousnesses in a way that draws attention to problems of interpretation; and Atwood's lyrically and imagistically textured style draws attention to itself rather than offering a transparent medium of a knowable reality."[7]

In a typically modernist manner the slow horizontal progression in time which occurs in the novel is accompanied by a vertical movement into the characters' inner life. The reader becomes acquainted with the tragedies of Elisabeth's childhood and adolescence, the memory of which still continues to haunt her; we follow the subtle changes that Lesje undergoes as she becomes slowly aware of her involvement with Nate, and Nate's personal anxieties and uncertainties.

This modernist mode of introspection results, on occasion, in abrupt shifts of focus in the narrative as the text attempts to register the characters' emotional reactions. One example is constituted by Nate, shortly after he has received a most amazing revelation from his mother. He is told that she has turned to political action not out of hope but despair, as an alternative to suicide after the death of his father. The presence of his young daughters in the house provokes another bitter "revelation"; he recognizes that one day they will leave him to "live with surly, scrofulous young men" (p. 287). The narrative register at this point changes quite abruptly to convey Nate's sense of lack, and loss. The image that is created as a result is reminiscent of Joyce's Leopold Bloom. "Motherless, childless, he sits at the kitchen table, the solitary wanderer, under the cold red stars" (p. 287). The echo of *Ulysses* reinforces the modernist focus in *Life Before Man* on the characters' subjective states.

The apparent lack of action in the novel at the level of plot is countered by the characters' altered perception of themselves and of their relations with one another. Of the three protagonists, Lesje is the one most affected by change.

As her involvement with Nate progresses she starts to question her previous attitude to life, and the nature of her feelings for her ex-partner, William: "She must have thought she could live with William for a million years and nothing in her would really be changed" (p. 222). Lesje begins to examine what "she means by being *in love*" (p. 126). She used to think she was in love with William "since it upset her that he did not ask her to marry him" (p. 126). By contrast, her feelings for Nate make her discover the composite and "painful" (p. 222) nature of love. At first the "simplicity," even the "bareness," of her life with William was something Lesje welcomed. But, now, as she reflects, "Nate has changed things, he has changed William. What was once a wholesome absence of complications is now an embarrassing lack of complexity" (p. 126).

When later Lesje meets William the question that she is prompted to ask is whether he has changed: "What she wants to ask him is: Have you changed? Have you learned anything? She herself feels she has learned more than she ever intended to, more than she wants" (p. 295). Similarly, Nate strives to avoid what he perceives as the constraints imposed by other people's fixed definitions of himself:

> . . . he's spent so much effort to avoid becoming: his mother's son. Which may be he is.
>
> But not only, not only. He refuses to be defined. He's not shut, time carries him on, other things may happen. (pp. 305-6)

As for Elisabeth, despite her active resistance to Nate's plan to leave her and move in with Lesje, she eventually recognizes that she welcomes the event. She realizes it will mean "freedom" from the set of unspoken rules, established for the most part by herself, that life with

Nate had come to represent (p. 206). She feels strong enough now, "she does not have to depend" (p. 140) on him. "Despite the wreckage" (p. 302) Elisabeth has a sense that she has salvaged something. "She is still alive . . . she's holds down a job even. She has two children—she's managed to accomplish a house. . . . She's built a dwelling over the abyss, but where else was there to build it? So far, it stands" (p. 302).

In the last section of the novel Elisabeth's imagination, prompted by the Chinese art exhibition which she has organized, is released by a fantasy of a better life. Her first reaction to the exhibition's catalogue was one of pronounced lack of interest. At the end, however, she surprises herself by noticing that she is moved by those pictures of happy peasants. She is aware that it is foolish. "This is propaganda. . . . China is not paradise; paradise does not exist" (p. 316). She is also forced to realize how alone she has been for the past years, and she has a sudden vision of a connection with other people. She knows that "China does not exist. Nevertheless she longs to be there" (p. 317).

This dream of displacement constantly haunts the protagonist of Atwood's dystopia *The Handmaid's Tale*. Like many of Atwood's characters Offred is "aware of finding herself trapped in the wrong place and with the wrong people."[8] The world of personal relations so deeply explored in *Life Before Man* is painfully part of the narrator's past in Atwood's dystopia. The novel stresses the deprivation or personal relationships imposed by the patriarchal oligarchy of the Gilead regime and the suffering it causes to the protagonist.

Like other examples of historiographic metafiction, *The Handmaid's Tale* is a narrative "that is intensely self-reflective art, but is also grounded in historical, social and political realities."[9]

In a manner which is predominantly ironic, *The Handmaid's Tale* recalls both fairy tales and more canonical texts.[10] As I mentioned in Chapter One, the use of intertextuality in Atwood's dystopia involves a wide range of reference. It underscores the many themes that are so skilfully interwoven in the text. Hawthorne's *The Scarlet Letter*, for example, and Zamyatin's dystopia *We*, are, to different extents, parodically echoed and revisited in terms of setting, theme and narrative frame.[11] Hawthorne's depiction of the destructive aspects of Puritanism in nineteenth-century New England echoes in the description of the futuristic regime in *The Handmaid's Tale*. In the State of Gilead, which represents a magnified version of the extreme tendencies of contemporary American society, a Fundamentalist conformity imposes a life of emotional repression, duty, and self-sacrifice on the handmaids. Analogies between *The Handmaid's Tale* and *The Scarlet Letter* are also found in the characterization of their protagonists, Offred and Hester.

Zamyatin's dystopic fiction *We* relates to *The Handmaid's Tale* in the emphasis on the precariousness of the self, and in the relation between happiness and freedom in totalitarian regimes that both novels investigate.

We is written in the form of a diary. The writing registers the protagonist's movement from conformity to rebellion and final psychological destruction operated by the regime. Here, as in Orwell's *1984*, writing is depicted as a subversive act against the dictatorships. In *The Handmaid's Tale* Offred's story likewise signifies a form of resistance and a creative act. There is, however, a significant difference between these examples of dystopic fiction and *The Handmaid's Tale*, one which adds to the complexities of Atwood's text. Offred's first person narrative takes the form of a "reconstruction," produced after she has escaped from Gilead. In the epilogue to the novel, a Symposium on Gileadean Studies set in the year 2195, the reader perceives that Offred's story has been constructed from a transcription of recordings produced by an unidentified narrator, recordings which lack any sequential ordering. This subsequent "reconstruction" carried out by the historians posits the question of how history itself is constructed and produced.

Offred's tale, which is initially related verbally, displays characteristic traits of oral narrative as it acquires a particular significance in its relation to life. A parodic version of Scheherazade,[12] Offred is the "obsessive" teller of this tale (p. 239), recurrently engaged in re-writing (re-telling) herself in an endless embroidering of herself as a character.

In *The Handmaid's Tale*, as in oral narratives, the act of telling conveys "both the superiority and the inferiority of art to living."[13] In Atwood's dystopia, Offred's fictional fabrications bring an alternative world into existence and create a refuge from the painful reality of her own life. As she muses, "I'm too tired to go on with this story. I'm too tired to think about where I am. Here is a different story, a better one. This is the story of what happened to Moira" (p. 138).

Stories appear to provide an escape, a salvation. Offred remarks,

> I would like to believe this is a story I'm telling. I need to believe it. Those who can believe that such stories are only stories have a better chance.
>
> If it's a story I'm telling, then I have control over the ending. Then there will be an ending, to the story, and real life will come after it. (p. 49)

On other occasions the act of telling becomes very painful. Offred observes, "Nevertheless it hurts me to tell it over, over again" (p. 279); "I don't want to be telling this story" (p. 237; p. 285). But, of course, she does.

The quality of Offred's narrative establishes a close interrelation between her life and her "story," by presenting her life *as* a story. In the text's frequent paradoxes, this tale becomes both a fabrication and a form of witness to Offred's painful experience as a handmaid. "It isn't a story I'm telling. It's also a story I'm telling, in my head, as I go along" (p. 49).

Her narrative is repeatedly defined as a "reconstruction" (p. 144, p. 114). In the fictive reality of the text Offred's tale is inscribed as a kind of unconventional autobiography, recorded on tape rather than composed in writing. Offred's personal narrative illustrates the inescapably fictive nature of the autobiographical text. The quality, the richness of the lived experience, she observes, cannot be adequately expressed.[14] The act of "writing the self" is represented as closely linked to a process of invention which in itself is integrated as constitutive part of the truth.[15] The self is shown to be unable to produce a faithful narrative of itself and identity becomes an "elusive" construct.

The use of intertextuality in *The Handmaid's Tale* underscores this concern. It denotes an idea of the self as dispersed and plural, in a manner similar to that employed in *Lady Oracle*. Offred's identity is scattered in a series of projected fairy-tale figures, which convey a notion of a splintered subjectivity. Offred muses, that, like Cinderella, "I must be back at the house before midnight; otherwise I'll turn into a pumpkin, or was that the coach?" (p. 266). Like the protagonist in *Lady Oracle*, Offred identifies with victimized Rapunzel-like figures, with whose experiences she contrasts her own struggle for survival.[16] And it is precisely her survival that highlights her difference from these doomed characters.

Portrayed as a parodic version of "Little Red Riding Hood," Offred is forbidden to stray from the prescribed path during her daily walk. However, as in the fairy story, she takes the risk of diverging from it and encounters danger. As Offred remarks, perceiving her image in the mirror, "If I turn my head . . . I can see . . . myself in it like a distorted shadow, a parody of something, some fairytale figure in a red cloak, descending towards a moment of carelessness that is the same as danger" (p. 19). She agrees to the plan of Serena Joy, the Commander's wife, to engage in sexual intercourse with the chauffeur Nick, in the hope of conceiving a baby. This is already dangerous for her. She will go further, however, and will see Nick secretly, "time after time," without Serena knowing it (p. 280). Unlike the protagonist in the fairy tale, Offred finds in risking that danger a reason for existence.

I mentioned earlier that the "scarlet" dress of the handmaids in this novel and the forced seclusion imposed on them by the Puritanical regime echoes Hawthorne's *The Scarlet Letter*. Like Hester, Offred is barred from forming spontaneous relations with people. In Atwood's novel the handmaid's red dress reveals, as we read in *The Scarlet Letter*, "a mystic sisterhood" of fallen women, since it is a symbol of

A Body in Fragments

"woman's frailty and sinful passion."[17] Once Offred has become a handmaid, her face is sadly altered in a manner that is reminiscent of Hester. As Atwood's narrator observes, "There is supposed to be nothing entertaining about us, no room is permitted for the flowering of secret lusts . . . there are to be no toeholds for love" (p. 146).[18]

However, Offred's dress and what it denotes do not signify a complete change in character. Atwood's treatment of this theme is quite complex. As in Zamyatin's *We*, the author touches on the relation between happiness and freedom. In *We* "The United State" has tried to induce in its subjects the belief that loss of freedom is the only way to happiness. In *The Handmaid's Tale* despite the fact that Offred struggles against the brain-washing operated by the régime, she suffers during these unspecified years as handmaid (perhaps three years) a weakening of her sense of autonomy, of her desire for freedom. As she observes, "Already we were losing the taste for freedom, already we were finding these walls secure" (p. 143). And later, when she has started to see Nick regularly, "The fact is that I no longer want to leave, escape, cross the border to freedom. I want to be here, with Nick, where I can get at him. . . . Truly amazing, what people can get used to, as long as there are a few compensations" (p. 283).[19]

This is one of the contradictions that characterize Offred. As I shall discuss in more detail in Chapter Three, the narrator in *The Handmaid's Tale* has produced a text of her own, a text which, by presenting paradoxes and contradictions, problematizes the possibility of locating truth. The emphasis the text places on its status as "fiction" undermines the trust in the speaking I. Atwood had already employed this device in *Surfacing*. In the latter, however, the reader towards the end recognizes the fictive nature of protagonist's fabrications. In *The Handmaid's Tale* the device has a more unsettling effect as the reader cannot verify Offred's different, contrasting versions of events.

Like Rennie in *Bodily Harm* who fictionalizes the reality of her cancer, Offred frequently transforms her life into "fictions." Characteristic of Offred's narrative and of her fabrications is a resistance to, and at times a rejection of, definite meanings (p. 150; p. 273). The presence of these contradictory episodes suggests not the permanence of an "identical" self but the energies of a "prospective" one.

"Text" and "self" are presented here in close conjunction, as the interrelation between Offred's life and her story discussed earlier suggests. Both "text" and "self" are inscribed as essentially incomplete. Offred's tale is discontinuous and fragmented in its very materiality, and lacks a conclusive ending. The absence of closure is, however, also attributable to Atwood's choice of the futuristic genre of dystopia. A narrative projected into the future, as *The Handmaid's Tale* is, cannot know any definite ending, although its novelistic form demands some such ending.[20] The novel's self-reflexive epilogue does not supply any answers in relation to the protagonist's destiny, but both points at and undermines the conventionality of novelistic closure.

In *The Handmaid's Tale*, both the "self" and the "text" are shown to be in constant construction and conflict. The narrator's interrogation of the nature of her tale explores the processes and contradictions of its own production. The gaps and ambiguities in Offred's tale and its emphasis on being a "story" suggest the impossibility of full representation and thus problematize the mimetic function of the text. The close interrelation between self and text invites a further consideration. A loss of or an ambivalence towards representation has been interpreted by Paul De Man as indicating a parallel ambivalence or loss in the sense of selfhood.[21]

As Roberta Rubenstein has noted, the narrative provides a plethora of images of fragmented bodies, starting from the handmaids themselves who are, in the perception of the régime, "two-legged wombs." During her medical inspection Offred is aware that the doctor "deals with a torso only" (p. 70). The bodies hanging from the Berlin Wall-like structure are portrayed in fragments. The ceiling ornament in Offred's room is like "the place in a face where the eye has been taken out" (p. 17). When Offred is fired from her job and deprived of political and legal rights, she feels as if someone had "cut off [her] feet"

(p. 188), an image that brings to mind another form of social control of women, Chinese footbinding.[22] These disturbing representations of mutilated bodies highlight not only the fact that in Gilead the female body is considered exclusively as a tool for reproduction; they underscore the violent and cruel objectification of bodies and people carried out by the régime.

It is, however, the narrative itself to be defined in terms of fragments and compared with a mutilated body. Reference to the fragmented nature of this story punctuate the discontinuous narrative: "I'm sorry there is so much pain in this story. I'm sorry it's in fragments, like a body caught in a crossfire or pulled apart by force. But there is nothing I can do to change it" (p. 279).

Psychoanalytic theory draws a link between perception of the body and notions of self. The connection existing between self/text/body is indicated by the fact that the story itself is described in anthropomorphic terms: "But I keep on with this . . . limping and mutilated story" which has no "shape" (p. 279). These representations of corporeal disintegration that recur in the text can be seen as a threat to the unity of the self.[23] Psychoanalytic theory corroborates the connection between bodily fragments and the dissolving ego. The total image of the body is seen as the moment of production and structuration of identity through the mediation of the body image. According to Jacques Lacan, for example, "the image of the total body is necessary to the creation of a rational unity."[24] On the other hand, representations of bodily fragmentation indicate that the unified and transcendent ego is threatened with dissolution.

Images of segmented bodies are also coded into *Life Before Man*, Atwood's earlier novel. Nate feels his body has become "stiff fragments held together by his spine and his screwtop head. Segmented man. . . . But what if she discovers the truth? What he suspects is the truth. That he's patchwork, a tin man, his heart stuffed with sawdust" (p. 244; p. 246). In Elisabeth's recollections the image of her suicidal lover Chris has become only a set of discrete parts: "Scraps. All that's left of Chris, whom she can no longer remember whole" (p. 151). Similarly, as she tries to negotiate the stairs to meet her children, Elisabeth is turned into a "Nude descending the staircase, in cunning fragments. Stewed, descending the staircase" (p. 248). The extratexual reference here is, of course, Marcel Duchamp's notorious painting "Nude Descending a Staircase" (1911), where in a "static representation of movement" the human form is fragmented in the multitude of its parts.[25]

In *The Handmaid's Tale* fragmentation, discontinuity and contradictions characterize the narrative. Such features suggest a sense of a lack of a rationalizing and unifying entity at work in the text. Although in a more tentative and simple manner, these themes are introduced in *Life Before Man*. In the latter the split point of view between an "I" and a "She," in the section focussing on Elisabeth, denotes the lack of the identification of consciousness with a synthetic unity of mental action. The device produces a narrative of split perceptions which conveys a sense of cleavage between body and mind, an erosion of the ego and a loss of body image boundaries.

> She is not in. She's somewhere between her body . . . lying sedately on the bed . . . and the ceiling with its airline cracks. She can see herself there, a thickening in the air, like albumin. . . . She can't move her fingers. She thinks about her hands, lying at her sides, rubber gloves: she thinks about forcing the bones and flesh down into those shapes of hands, one finger at a time, like dough. (p. 12)[26]

In *The Handmaid's Tale* the lack of a synthetic unity is stressed by the fact that the text's fictive reality creates a "tale" without an author. As a norm, the presence of the proper name acts as a guardian of identity. But here, as for the protagonist of *Surfacing*, there is no name to guarantee identity.

To an extent also memory contributes to give a sense of unity and coherence to the self. In Atwood's *Life Before Man* memory occasionally fades or proves to be unreliable (p. 276; p. 313). *The Handmaid's Tale* explores to a further degree of complexity the treacherous and fallible nature of memory.

Atwood's use of conventions belonging to confessional writing questions the unity and authenticity of the narration compared to the "real life" that it aims to reconstruct. The manner in which Offred's narrative describes her experience as handmaid, as well as aspects of her former life, disclose the tortuous ways with which the act of remembering operates. The narrative foregrounds the deceptive nature of memories and presents the need of the individual to elaborate the past with imagination (p. 113; p. 281).

Offred's verbal text is punctuated by doubts, re-thinking, and retelling of what has already been presented as true. Such a device suggests that for a subject retracing his past, who can say which is more real, the actual event itself, or its imaginative transformations?

Memory and identity have vague outlines in this text. The former includes imagination and desire; the latter is elusive, and like the image in the mirror, cannot be grasped.

From *Strategies for Identity: The Fiction of Margaret Atwood* (New York: Peter Lang, 1993): 73-85. Copyright © 1993 by Peter Lang Publishing, Inc. Reprinted by permission of Peter Lang Publishing, Inc.

Notes

1. Sherrill Grace, *Violent Duality: A Study of Margaret Atwood* (Montreal, 1980), p. 135.
2. Frank Davey, *Margaret Atwood: A Feminist Poetics* (Vancouver, 1984), pp. 81-85.
3. Grace, *Violent Duality*, p. 136; Sherrill E. Grace, "'Time Present and Time Past': *Life Before Man*," *Essays on Canadian Writing* 20 (Winter 1980-81); Ildikó de Papp Carrington, "Demons, Doubles, and Dinosaurs: *Life Before Man*, *The Origin of Consciousness*, and 'The Icicle'," in *Critical Essays on Margaret Atwood*, ed. Judith McCombs (Boston, 1988), p. 223.
4. Gayle Greene, "*Life Before Man*: 'Can Anything Be Saved?'" in *Margaret*

Atwood: Vision and Forms, eds. Kathryn VanSpanckeren and Jan Garden Castro (Carbondale, IL, 1988), p. 67. However, the novel's vision is rather pessimistic. This is perhaps due to the fact that *Life Before Man* does not seem to convey any sense of belief in change through political action. There seems to be no remedy for the social injustice that Nate and his mother contemplate. As Greene suggests, the novel seems to indicate that "the most we can hope for is a ... private salvation, some connection to another human being, some shelter from the void. Build houses, cultivate our gardens, raise families to stem the tide ... harness our imaginations to creative rather than destructive uses—and perhaps do some political work in the hope of making a better world, knowing that our efforts will be futile" (*Ibid*, p. 67).

5. "Marriage is an event, a fact, it can be discussed at the dinner table. So is divorce. They create a framework, a beginning and an ending. Without them everything is amorphous, an endless middleground, stretching like a prairie on either side of each day" (p. 192).

6. Jeremy Rosenberg, *Margaret Atwood* (Boston, 1984).

7. Greene, "*Life Before Man*," p. 66.

8. Patrick Parrinder, "Making Poison," *London Review of Books*, 8, 5 (20 March 1986): 20.

9. Linda Hutcheon, *The Canadian Postmodern* (Toronto, 1988), p. 13.

10. Atwood shares Northrop Frye's contention that ironic modes are the most appropriate ones for serious fiction. (Margaret Atwood, "Northrop Frye Observed," in *Second Words: Selected Critical Prose*, ed. Margaret Atwood [Toronto, Anansi, 1982], p. 406. Northrop Frye, *The Secular Scripture: A Study of the Structure of Romance* [Cambridge, MA, 1976], p. 134).

11. Linda Hutcheon, *A Poetics of Postmodernism* (Toronto, 1988), p. 139.

12. The lack of synchronicity between the time of the narrative and the time of narration excludes an identification with the protagonist of *The Thousand's and One Nights*, as a critic has suggested. (Lucy M. Freibert, "Control and Creativity: The Politics of Risk in Margaret Atwood's *The Handmaid's Tale*," in *Critical Essays on Margaret Atwood*, ed. Judith McCombs [Boston, 1988].)

13. Robert Kellogg, "Oral Narrative, Written Books," *Genre* X, 4 (1977): 656.

14. "When I get out of here, if I'm ever able to set this down, in any form, even in the form of one voice to another, it will be a reconstruction then too, at yet another remove. It's impossible to say a thing exactly the way it was, because what you say can never be exact, you always have to leave something out, there are too many parts, sides, crosscurrents, nuances; too many gestures, which could mean this or that, too many shapes which can never be fully described, too many flavours, in the air or on the tongue, half colours, too many" (p. 144).

15. On this topic see Paul De Man, "Autobiography as Defacement," in *The Rhetoric of Romanticism* (New York, 1984); P. J. Eakin, *Fictions in Autobiography* (Princeton, 1985); Atwood herself has elsewhere aligned autobiography and interviews to the realm of fiction (Hancock).

16. In *Survival* Atwood writes that the Rapunzel syndrome, patterned on the Grimm brothers' fairy tale, is a recurring pattern in realistic fiction. The Grimm's tale provides the basic story line. The witch who wants the heroine in prison, the tower in

which she is imprisoned and the Rescuer, a "handsome prince of little substantiality who provides momentary escape" (Margaret Atwood, *Survival: A Thematic Guide to Canadian Literature* [Toronto, Anansi, 1973], p. 52).

17. Nathaniel Hawthorne, *The Scarlet Letter* (Harmondsworth, 1970), p. 192; p. 104.

18. As we read in *The Scarlet Letter*, there is "no longer anything in Hester's face for Love to dwell upon" and nothing in her that "passion would ever dream of clasping in its embrace" (p. 182).

19. Similarly Offred is terrified by the possibility of change in her situation that would ensue upon the doctor's offer to help her conceive a child. "Why am I frightened? I've crossed no boundaries, I've given no trust, taken no risk, all is safe. It's the choice that terrifies me. A way out, a salvation" (p. 71).

20. Fredric Jameson, "Progress versus Utopia: Or, Can we Imagine the Future?," *Science-Fiction Studies* 27 (July 1982).

21. Paul De Man, "Lyric and Modernity," *Blindness and Insight* (London, 1983).

22. Roberta Rubenstein, "Nature and Nurture in Dystopia: *The Handmaid's Tale*," in *Margaret Atwood: Vision and Forms*, eds. Kathryn VanSpanckeren and Jan Garden Castro (Carbondale, IL, 1988).

23. Julia Kristeva, *La Révolution du langage poétique* (Paris, 1974) [*The Revolution of Poetic Language*], trans. Margaret Waller, intr. Leon S. Roduiez (New York, 1984).

24. Allon White, *L'éclatement du sujet: The work of Julia Kristeva* (Birmingham, 1977), p. 10.

25. Marcel Duchamp [1946], "Painting . . . at the service of the mind," in *Theories of Modern Art*, ed. H. Chipp (Berkeley, 1968).

26. The theme of the blurring or erosion of the borders of identity is, according to a critic, underscored by the novel's epigraph taken from Andrei Sinyavsky's fantastic short story, "The Icicle," in which the narrated self undergoes a series of transformations and literally blurs and merges into other selves. According to this reading, characters often identify or take each other's roles. As a result of this interplay between the characters identity becomes a shifting construct. In De Papp Carrington's view, Atwood's novel "is not about the discovery of identity as a permanently defined construct, but about the characters' daily, existential experiencing of identity as a constantly shifting pattern of alteration, attrition, and inevitable loss" (De Papp Carrington, "Demons, Doubles and Dinosaurs," in *Critical Essays on Margaret Atwood*, ed. Judith McCombs [Boston, 1988], p. 242).

Margaret Atwood's *The Handmaid's Tale*: Scheherazade in Dystopia

Karen F. Stein

Margaret Atwood's novel *The Handmaid's Tale* is narrated by a Scheherazade of the future, telling her story to save her life. But whereas the Sultan of the *Arabian Nights* asks for Scheherazade's stories, Atwood's handmaid is locked into silence; to tell her tale is to risk her life. Her narrative itself is a criminal act, performed in secret and lost for many years. By narrating the story of the repressive republic of Gilead, the handmaid inscribes both her victimization and her resistance. Built on a woman's desire to tell her story, the novel is a provocative inquiry into the origins and meanings of narrative. Among the issues it explores are, first, the narrator's relation to her tale: the simultaneous fear and desire to narrate one's story, and the attempt to create a self through language; second, the nature of narrative itself: the ambiguity of language, and the multiplicity of interpretation.

In the novel Atwood brilliantly juxtaposes the feminist project—the desire to 'steal the language' of/from patriarchy—and the postmodern critique of language. The novel emphasizes the constraint and limitation Gilead imposes, and the narrator's growing resistance. The novel begins by describing two enclosed and silent living spaces, the 're-education center' and the handmaid's small room. The narrator, Offred, speaks of herself as 'in reduced circumstances' (10). (In a text where puns carry a weight of meaning, the similarity of re-education and reduction in Gilead is noteworthy.) Just when the narrator's tale seems to promise larger possibilities, it is silenced. Thus the dilemma of Scheherazade is revised, revisioned.

Feminists are particularly interested in stories, because, as a marginal group in society, women have often been the objects rather than the creators of narrative: their stories have often been untold. People on the margins of societies often find they are denied access to the discourses that confer power and status. A substantial body of work focuses on the theoretical and practical implications of women's problematic relations to these discourses. Adrienne Rich writes of women's need to explore 'how our language has trapped as well as liberated us, how the very act of naming has been till now a male prerogative' (35). Elaine Showalter describes women's writing as a 'double-voiced discourse' that draws from both the 'dominant' men's and the 'muted' women's 'social, literary, and cultural heritages' (263). According to Linda Hutcheon, both Blacks and feminists have 'linked racial and/or gender difference to questions of discourse and of authority and power that are at the heart of the postmodernist enterprise in general and, in particular, of both black theory and feminism' (21).

To speak, to write, is to assert one's personhood, inscribe one's subjectivity. According to Emile Benveniste, 'the basis of subjectivity is the exercise of language' (226). Hence, to lose language is to lose subjectivity. Not surprisingly, feminist dystopias often deal with women's loss of language. *The Handmaid's Tale* participates in the current theoretical debate about women's vexed relation to discourse. The narrative is both shaped and threatened by political repression, interpretation, and the fundamental instability of language itself.

Atwood's novel begins—with the handmaid's narrative—exploring silence and speech, oppression and resistance. The novel ends—with a male scholar's narrative—questioning the limits of narrative and interpretation. The subtexts of both narratives are the respective narrators' (handmaid's and scholar's) meditations on storytelling and meaning. Both face the storyteller's paradox: they are eager to communicate, but anxious about the limits of communication; they find language simultaneously empowering and constraining. This article is a critic's tale that rereads and reinterprets the novel.

Offred

Atwood's novel inscribes a contemporary nightmare, the erasure of speech. Government restriction of speech and storytelling is an important theme in twentieth-century dystopian fiction, as in George Orwell's *Nineteen Eighty-Four* or Ray Bradbury's *Fahrenheit Four Fifty-One*. Gilead, the patriarchal, fundamentalist society in Margaret Atwood's dystopian novel, has silenced women and rendered them invisible. The narrator, whose birth name we never learn, creates her subjectivity through her narrative. Although she is marginalized by her society, her use of narrative opens a space for her within the cramped quarters of Gilead.

Reading the handmaid's tale, we are drawn into complicity with her in the illegal act of narrative: our reading validates her narrative and her subjectivity. Yet, at the same time, all readings also distort and change her narrative, as we shall see. The story moves by flashback, meditation, and present-tense narration as the narrator pieces together what she remembers of her past life and knows of her present situation. Through her storytelling, she grows more politically aware and self-conscious. She resists the reduction of Gilead (her 'reduced circumstances') by small acts of self-assertion, by fantasies of becoming strikingly visible (she imagines stripping in front of the guards at the barriers) and by the act of narrating her tale and thereby constructing a self. Offred's storytelling violates the rules of Gilead, for handmaids are supposed to be not only speechless but invisible as well. Yet, dressed in their red robes and white wimples, they are highly visible. Colour-coded in this way, the handmaids become interchangeable, identified only by their biological function, child-bearing.

To complete their loss of individuality, the handmaids lose their names as well. Each is labelled as a possession of the Commander she serves. When a new handmaid replaces Offred's neighbour, Ofglen, she answers Offred's surprised query: 'I am Ofglen' (363). This casual acknowledgment of their infinite interchangeability seems to me the most chilling moment of the novel. Forbidden to acknowledge their names, their selves, they must submit to their use as objects, possessions.

As their names are erased, so is their discourse. They are denied access to writing, and restricted in their use of speech. Tokens replace money, and pictorial signs appear instead of written words on storefronts. Although the handmaids are most severely repressed, private discourse is constrained at all levels of Gileadean society, replaced by a shallow and hypocritical rhetoric. One of the controls on women's speech is the institution of the Aunts, a quasi-police institution which runs the 'reeducation' centers where divorced or remarried young women with viable ovaries are trained to become handmaids. The Aunts' speech consists of platitudes, admonitions, and iterations of codes of behaviour such as 'modesty is invisibility,' 'pen is envy.' The Aunts transmit the words of the patriarchal government, and they silence unwanted speech. They script the authorized speech of the handmaids, 'testifying,' a kind of brainwashing in which women are required to revise the narratives of their past lives: for example, blaming themselves for the rapes they suffered (92-3). In this discourse, both the Aunts and the young women must rewrite their stories to fit the political demands of Gilead.

When the handmaids are posted to their Commanders' homes, their discourse is officially limited to stock phrases and responses, as in the greeting rituals which stress passive receptivity.

'May the Lord open.'
'Praise be.'
'We are given good weather.'
'Which I receive with joy.' (26)

To speak with each other about larger issues is forbidden. When Ofglen and Offred do speak briefly, Ofglen warns, 'keep your head down. . . . Don't talk when there's anyone coming' (218).

Not only the handmaids have lost control over discourse; the women of the ruling class are also silenced. Serena Joy, the wife of Offred's Commander, was a public speaker advocating woman's place in the home. Now, Offred observes ironically, 'she doesn't make speeches any more. She has become speechless. She stays in her home, but it doesn't seem to agree with her' (61).

The restrictions on women's speech are a part of the larger limitation of discourse throughout Gilead. Thinking of her Commander's life, Offred muses 'it must be hell, to be a man, like that. . . . It must be very silent' (114). The powerful elite are themselves constrained by the repression they impose on others. Political repression, fear, caution, contribute to the silence of Gilead. But emotional repression is the root of silence. When the Commander asks her what the creators of Gilead overlooked, Offred's answer is simple: 'Love' (284). In a puritanical, totalitarian state where love, passion, and desire are repressed, the context for private discourse is attenuated. Political rhetoric drives personal speech underground.

In a world where language is taboo for women, the narrator finds solace in her meditation, and her play with words. She 'composes' herself by meditating on language, punning, and playing with words such as 'invalid,' 'Mayday,' 'habit,' 'lie/lay.' She takes great pleasure in finding a message scratched into the floor of her cupboard. Although she does not know the meaning of the words (a schoolboy's Latin joke—*nolite te bastardes carborundorum*), they are a link to another woman who lived here before she did (69). When the Commander begins a clandestine relationship with the narrator, he lures her with a game of Scrabble. Because writing is forbidden, the game is eroticized (179-80) (whereas the obligatory sexual ritual retains no vestige of pleasure).

Through her appropriation of language, Offred constitutes herself as a subject, and makes herself visible to the reader. 'My self is a thing I must now compose, as one composes a speech' (86). Implicit in the storytelling impulse is the wish to communicate and thereby to connect with others, a problematic activity in Gilead. Offred commits the rebellious act of communication: 'A story is like a letter. . . . I'll pretend you can hear me' (53). In storytelling she creates a self and an other, a listener.

Offred does reach listeners in Gilead. As she questions the regime in secret phrases murmured to her counterparts, she becomes a rebel. Her rebellion apparently saves her life. Eager to gain the child Offred is supposed to produce, Serena Joy arranges a sexual encounter for her with the chauffeur, Nick. Although it is potentially dangerous for all of them, Offred continues to meet him. In the course of their affair, she possibly becomes pregnant, and she divulges her name. Revealing her name, she reveals herself to him, and becomes vulnerable. But Nick may be more than just a servant. As a possible Eye, a secret agent, he apparently has the power to rescue her.

Atwood's book creates for Offred a theft of language and possible flight from Gilead. The narrative critiques a patriarchy which denies women control of language and their bodies. If the novel ended here, we would see the triumph of the Scheherazade figure saving herself through her body/sexuality and her narrativity. But counterposed to Offred's narrative is another story which calls its utopian possibilities into question. Turning to this part of the novel, we will discover that the framing story explores the ambiguities of interpretation, and compels us to reconsider the handmaid's tale.

Pieixoto's Tale

The book closes with a flash-forward to a post-Gileadean society. Atwood's frame for the handmaid's narrative is a panel on sociocultural interpretations of Gilead at an interdisciplinary conference (at the University of Denay, Nunavit). In this postscript, Atwood both satirizes academic pretensions and suggests a less utopian outcome for Offred's story. This device calls into question Offred's fate, and makes her story the text of a male interpretation.

Because women in Gilead were denied writing implements, Offred recorded her narrative on an audiotape which is found and transcribed by an archivist—Professor James Darcy Pieixoto—long after Gilead has been destroyed. His talk at the conference creates a new context and a new reading of Offred's tale. Michele Lacombe terms the novel a palimpsest in which Pieixoto reinscribes Offred's tale (Lacombe 5). The relationship of narration to interpretation is problematized here. In retelling Offred's tale, Professor Pieixoto both resurrects and reinterprets it, as do all readers—including the author of this article. Without the reader, the text is dead, but each new reading creates a new tale.

The scholar's project is to find out if the tapes are authentic: did Offred really exist? If so, who was she? His next question is: what happened to her after the tape ends? Most of Pieixoto's questions remain unanswered: thus the irony of his final words, 'Are there any questions?' He suggests alternative versions of her life after Gilead, just as Offred herself poses alternative versions of events in her life and the lives of friends. Thus, without closure, the ending of Offred's story continues to be deferred, untold.

The relationship between the handmaid's narrative and the scholar's tale raises the question of language and power in a new context. Here again, the words of a woman are subjected to interpretation by a male authority figure, an academician, a master of language. Her desires—for love, for the freedom to choose—are interpreted through the prism of his desires—for status, for knowledge, for achievement. He is long-winded and given to sexist puns. He is eager to promote his reputation and perhaps more concerned with the form of the narrative than its substance. In Gilead and in the hands of the scholar (just as in the American society of her previous life), she is reduced to her utility value (Hammer, 43). In Gilead she is a 'walking womb,' an incubator of children for high-ranking officials. For the scholar, she is a stepstone for professional advancement, and a possible source of information about his real interest, the male elite of Gilead. The contrasting styles of their discourses inscribe the status difference of male professor and female handmaid. Her narrative is tentative, fragmentary, sensuous, moving loosely by stream of consciousness, by revision. The scholar's narrative is logical, abstract, polished. Both, however, make frequent use of puns. Although privileged in his society, the scholar may be viewed as a voyeur, a parasite. He is to Offred as Sigmund Freud is to 'Dora' (the subject of his analysis of hysteria). Both men depend on the woman to provide material for interpretation; their reputations rest on their power to fix meaning and to explain the women (Bernheimer and Kahane). But just as Freud failed to resolve the problems Dora raised, so Pieixoto fails to discover who Offred was and what became of her. Further, both men use the women's texts for their own purposes, looking through the texts to satisfy their own desires.

And yet—Pieixoto reconstructs the story, which would have been lost without his intervention. Thus, the novel remains deliberately ambiguous: it first constructs, then reverses an optimistic conclusion to the tale.

Offred

Moreover, the novel questions the role of the storyteller and the limits of language itself. Offred has told her tale and inscribed her voice. But presence in discourse turns out to be problematic because language, the medium through which we experience our existence, is imperfect. In the late twentieth century, we have become acutely aware that language mediates all knowledge, all the manifestations of political, economic, and social power, and our subjective existence. Yet language is a system of conventional symbols; it can only point to, or suggest, meanings. Therefore, gaps always remain between intention and expression, the signified and the signifier.

When we reread Offred's tale in the light of the 'Historical Notes,' we realize that she must have written the entire tale some time after the events it narrates and not, as the present-tense narration implies, during the time the events were occurring. This fact immediately distances the narrator from her tale, and thus it renders her version suspect. Her use of present tense for recollection of the past suggests fiction, perhaps even trickery, deceit. Furthermore, her memory may not be exact: can we be sure that each event occurred exactly as she retells it? Because her tale is obviously a recreation after the fact, it is closer to fiction than to diary.

But Offred herself problematizes the narrative. Throughout her tale, she plays with and questions the limits of language and of storytelling. Even while telling her tale, she deconstructs it. This is accomplished within Offred's narrative by the use of word-play and metafictional interventions.

Her word-plays expose the multiple meanings of words and point to the impossibility of finding exact equivalents between language and experience. Words become counters in the games she plays with herself, survival games. (For examples of such word-plays, see her discussion of 'work out' [293-4]; of word derivations, see her discussion of 'Mayday' [58]).

The metafictional interventions are Offred's revisions of her story: her attempts to write, rewrite, and re-create experience. In these passages, she questions the possibility of representing experience. We have seen that for political reasons the handmaids are forced to revise the narratives of their previous lives. Under the political pressures of Gilead, they must disclaim their memories and rescript them to fit the demands of their society. But any narration is set into a particular context, hence shaped by both external as well as internal needs; a narrative is composed according to the narrator's awareness of both audience and self. Offred's revisions of her tale stem from semiotic pressures: as she retells her story, she questions the limits of narration, of memory, of language itself.

Some of her revisions are prompted by limited knowledge. Because she does not know her husband's fate, she imagines three versions (132-5). Similarly, she wishes she could complete the story of Moira according to her fantasy (325). However, the revisions of her first encounter with Nick point to the difficulties of remembering and reconstructing one's own experience: 'All I can hope for is a reconstruction: the way love feels is always only approximate' (340). In this passage, the narrator undercuts any claims to a special truth of experience. Her role becomes that of the novelist who must construct the events she describes. Thus, the boundaries between character and author, between truth and fiction, between past and present are blurred (Hutcheon, 16).

Yet, Offred's multiple versions of her story function in another way, as well. They subvert 'the linear logic of the system which controls her . . . and . . . assign[s] her one function and one vocabulary' (Letcher, 95). In her story she chooses more roles for herself (lover, author, speaking self) than Gilead offers her. In her word-plays and puns, she extends her vocabulary and enlarges the allowable definitions. In the revisions and reconstructions of her story, she suggests a larger realm of possibility. If there are many versions, the tale can never achieve closure. If we never learn the end of her story, all endings are possible (Letcher, 95).

Offred is both eager to tell her story and reluctant: 'I don't want to be telling this story' (291). Her narrative is a game, a story, an inscription of the self:

> I would like to believe that this is a story I'm telling. I need to believe it. I must believe it. . . . If it's a story I'm telling, then I have control over the ending. . . . It isn't a story I'm telling. It's also a story I'm telling, in my head, as I go along. (52)

The story is one of marginality: 'We were the people who were not in the papers. We lived in the blank white spaces at the edges of print. It gave us more freedom. We lived in the gaps between the stories' (72). Storytelling is thus a paradoxical project. While it appears to provide some degree of control and agency for the teller, it remains suspect, even dangerous. To be fixed in words is to be vulnerable, visible, and, therefore, less free than those who live in the gaps. Paradoxically, however, if meaning is unstable the story is never completed; its meanings are always in flux, the author may lose control of the ending, or avoid ending entirely.

We have already seen that the book remains problematic on the level of plot: the narrator is both oppressed victim and resisting agent; we cannot be sure whether or not she successfully escapes from Gilead. More significantly, the novel presents Offred's narrative as a theoretical problematic as well. Is storytelling enough? Can women gain power through language alone? After all, years later, in the conclusion, it is a male scholar who excavates and interprets the handmaid's tale; his voice is the last word of the story. Offred's tale has become his possession:

> We may call Eurydice forth from the world of the dead, but we cannot make her answer; and when we turn to look at her we glimpse her only for a moment, before she slips from our grasp and flees. . . . The past is a great darkness, and filled with echoes. Voices may reach us from it; but what they say to us is imbued with the obscurity of the matrix out of which they come. (395)

In the carefully crafted, allusive language of the scholar (far removed from the sensuous immediacy of Offred's narration), Pieixoto distances himself from the handmaid and recapitulates the difficulties of interpretation.

Atwood's Tale

Margaret Atwood is of course a Scheherazade herself; she is the invisible teller of all the book's tales. She has juxtaposed the voices of Offred and Pieixoto. *The Handmaid's Tale* has been termed a palimpsest (Lacombe, 5), but I will suggest the more complex image of a series of multiply reflecting mirrors in which storytellers and interpreters continually inscribe and reinscribe the narrative.

To begin with, Offred herself tells two stories which reinscribe and comment on each other: the story of Gilead and the story of America. As many readers of the novel have pointed out, Gilead replicates American society's oppression of women. Both of Offred's tales illustrate censorship and sexual repression: Gilead builds on American foundations.

Women in both societies participate in their own repression. The Aunts, as we have seen, limit and rescript women's discourse. However, feminists from America also participated in censorship: Offred's mother joined other women to burn pornographic magazines (50-1). The novel thus establishes a continuum of repression: once people begin to burn books, the door is open for further censorship.

Offred's memories of pornography, sex shops, and frequent rapes provide a thematic link between her past and present. Despite the Aunts' doctrine of 'freedom from' (as opposed to America's 'freedom to'), the women of Gilead are *not* free from rape or violence. Rather, rape has been institutionalized. Sexuality in Gilead is politicized; it has lost its emotional, communicative value and become a function of one's status. Yet, Offred implies that the separation of sexuality and love in Gilead is merely an exaggeration of conditions in the time before. Indeed, as Stephanie Hammer points out, Offred's position in Gilead as part of a sexual triangle replicates her previous position as Luke's mistress before he divorced his first wife (41). Further, as we have seen, Hammer suggests that Pieixoto's use of Offred's tale repeats the use men in both America and Gilead make of women to further their own purposes.

Just as the plots of Offred's two stories mirror each other, her narrative technique is built on doubling, through its puns and through the strategy of revising and postulating multiple versions. Tina Letcher discusses doubling of characters in Offred's tale as a means of deconstructing and reconstructing Offred's subjectivity.

Similarly, punning is a way of insinuating connections between apparently different words. The origin of the word 'pun' in the Latin root 'pug,' meaning 'to strike with the fist' (as in pugilist), supports the idea of contestation, struggle, inherent in the term. Puns are distorting mirrors of language, used here to suggest the slipperiness of meaning, the endless possibilities of language.

To Offred's doubled, punning narrative, Atwood adds the next layer, Pieixoto's reinscription at the University of Denay, Nunavit, a satirical version of an American university. This future is, like the America of Atwood's tale, another mirror of Gilead. The scholar speaks sympathetically and eloquently of Gilead's women, yet his puns (handmaid's tale/tail; 'enjoy' the Arctic Chair) suggest his reduction of women to sexual objects. Here again, puns and multiple versions point to the difficulties of fixing meaning. By setting Pieixoto's version in the post-Gilead future, Atwood implies that Offred's is a tale which—like Scheherazade's—needs to be told and retold because repression is a continuing condition of human society.

Offred's tale and Atwood's novel are cautionary tales, warning of the consequences of silencing and repressing others, of turning an other into an it (249). But at the same time that the tale describes constraint and entrapment, it also suggests an escape from limitation through the strategies of storytelling. As this study argues, Offred's storytelling enables her to create a more complex subjectivity than Gilead allows, and to become a visible presence for us.

Thus, the tale becomes one of hope as well as of caution. This is yet another of the paradoxes of the storyteller's art. The act of storytelling itself, for Scheherazade, for Offred, for Pieixoto, for Atwood (and, indeed, also for Stein) is a gesture of hope, of love, of reaching for connection with other readers and hearers. But once the storyteller makes this gesture, the story achieves an independent existence. Others will reread, reinterpret, critique it (or, worse, they will not reread, reinterpret, critique it). A diagram might look like this:

Offred < Pieixoto < Atwood < (critic <) reader

The book asks disturbing questions which are at once political and discursive. Its concluding sentence: 'Are there any questions?' is ironically appropriate. What is the status of a woman's narrative in a society where men often control the interpretation of texts? To what extent can any narrator/narrative escape or resist interpretation? Is discourse itself an adequate form of political action? What possibilities does narrative open, what doors does it close? In asking these questions, the novel compels us to read beyond the ending. Through its multiple narrators and theoretical self-reflexivity, it addresses serious issues for feminist, postmodern, and narrative theory.

Atwood has written an open-ended text, (play)fully conscious of the possibilities of deconstruction, reconstruction, and reinterpretation. By deliberately inserting gaps in the text, by punning and playing with words, and by suggesting multiple versions, she engages in metafictional commentary on the storytelling process—at the same time that she tells a good tale. By the time the critic/reader arrives at the text, Atwood has already told and retold the story, questioned and hedged, changed the context, deconstructed and reconstructed the narrative.

As Offred's/Atwood's stories are reread and reinterpreted, the ending is postponed, rewritten. Readers and critics join Atwood in the process she has already begun, the project of reinscribing the text. Scheherazade tells her tale(s) in spite of, or because of, the Sultans, the Commanders, and the scholars who seek to silence her or to rewrite her words.

From *University of Toronto Quarterly* 61, no. 2 (1991): 269-280. Copyright © 1991 by University of Toronto Press. Reprinted by permission of University of Toronto Press Incorporated.

Note
Bernice Lott and Melita Schaum read early versions of this article and offered suggestions for revision. At a final stage of revision, I benefited from reading Tina Letcher's unpublished dissertation.

Works Cited
Atwood, Margaret. *The Handmaid's Tale*. New York: Fawcett Crest 1985.
Benveniste, Emile. *Problems in General Linguistics*. Miami: University of Miami Press 1971.

Bernheimer, Charles, and Claire Kahane, eds. *In Dora's Case: Freud—Hysteria—Feminism*. New York: Columbia University Press 1985.
Bradbury, Ray. *Fahrenheit Four Fifty-One*. New York: Simon and Schuster 1967.
Freud, Sigmund. *Dora: An Analysis of a Case of Hysteria*. Ed Philip Rieff. New York: Macmillan 1963.
Hammer, Stephanie Barbe. 'The World as It Will Be? Female Satire and the Technology of Power in *The Handmaid's Tale*.' *Modern Language Studies* 20:2 (Spring 1990), 39-49.
Heilbrun, Carolyn. *Writing a Woman's Life*. New York: W.W. Norton 1988.
Hutcheon, Linda. 'Beginning to Theorize Postmodernism.' *Textual Practice* 1:1 (Spring 1987), 10-31.
Lacombe, Michele. 'The Writing on the Wall: Amputated Speech in Margaret Atwood's *The Handmaid's Tale*.' *Wascana Review* 21:2 (Fall 1986), 3-12.
Letcher, Tina. 'In the Belly of This Story: The Role of Fantasy in Four American Women's Novels of the 1980s.' Diss. University of Rhode Island 1991.
Orwell, George. *Nineteen Eighty-Four*. New York: Fawcett Crest 1955.
Rich, Adrienne. 'When We Dead Awaken: Writing as Re-Vision.' 1971; repr Rich. *On Lies, Secrets and Silence: Selected Prose*. New York: W.W. Norton 1979.
Showalter, Elaine. 'Feminist Criticism in the Wilderness.' In Showalter, ed. *The New Feminist Criticism*. New York: Pantheon 1985.

The Handmaid's Tale as Scrabble Game
Joseph Andriano

In *The Handmaid's Tale*, Margaret Atwood uses the game of Scrabble as a pervasive controlling metaphor. The familiar crossword game becomes a trope for the whole text, which actually comprises several subtexts, or "crosscurrents" (134). To make a play in Scrabble is to attempt to gain an advantage with words, to counteract, to cross. It is a game of text/countertext.

I: Text as Scrabble Game

> How do you learn to spell? . . .
> your own name first,
> your first naming, your first name,
> your first word.
> (Atwood, "Spelling" 64)

In this poem, published a few years before *The Handmaid's Tale*, Margaret Atwood suggested that spelling is a kind of naming. Most people are very particular about the proper spelling of their names, perhaps because, as the poem suggests, one's first name is the first word one learns to spell. It therefore casts a spell. The narrator of *The Handmaid's Tale* has not merely had her name misspelled; she's had it erased by the state. Her real name "has an aura around it, like an amulet, some charm that's survived from an unimaginably distant past" (84).

While it is true, as Harriet Bergmann has shown, that the narrator accepts her new name, "Offred," viewing her old one as "something hidden, some treasure [she]'ll come back to dig up, one day" (Atwood, *Handmaid's Tale* 84), she has deliberately buried that treasure in her text for those who reread it to find (Bergmann 848). Furthermore, her patronymic undercuts itself, for it is impossible for most readers not initially to mispronounce it: we want to say "off red" rather than "of Fred." Since the colour red in the context of the new order has come to be associated with the handmaids ("red: the color of blood, which defines us" [8]), to be "off red" is to be resistant to complete absorption in the wavelength of the Gileadites. The narrator's patronymic, then, becomes a sort of shibboleth: we who mispronounce it are the Ephraimites to these new Gileadites.[1] In order to pronounce the word the way the Gileadites would, we must work at it. We must train our eyes and ears away from the two words we immediately see and hear–*off* and *red*—and force the reading *Of Fred*. To do so, however, is implicitly to accept the sexist order of the society. I will therefore dig up the buried treasure, and call the narrator June rather than Offred.

The handmaids living at the Red Center whose names are listed at the end of the first chapter are all accounted for except June. This is the narrator's way of intimating to the reader what her real name is.[2] It is her first Scrabble play against the Gileadites. Names and words are her only weapons against the state. As the state attempts to erase her identity by renaming her, she reasserts it by slipping her real name in at the end of the first chapter. She knows attentive rereaders will catch it. This is the first of many exchanges between her and the reader. One's own name is a magic spell that creates the sense of self, of individuality, we need to keep us sane. Notice that June never tells us her daughter's name; she was absorbed by the state before she ever had a chance to spell her name, to become a person.

As Gilead constructs its horizontal text, June constructs a vertical one to cross it. She is constantly undercutting the power structure, creating "crosscurrents, nuances . . . gestures" not only to keep herself as sane as possible in such an insane world, but also to sabotage the game (134). Biblical fundamentalism is based not on words but on the Word, carved in stone, and though Gilead's Sons of Jacob unwittingly illustrate that the Bible may be interpreted in any way that is convenient to justify the most outrageous practices, they *think* they are taking the Bible literally. The Word has only one meaning as far as they're concerned. So our narrator, June, to undercut the Word, is constantly playing with words, bringing up multiple meanings, whose existence shatters the monolithic Word.

June does this, for example, with the word *job*. She invokes all its meanings, many of which have nothing to do with each other, crossing the Book of Job with a dog doing a job on the carpet (173). She sits in her chair and thinks of the word *chair* and all its various unrelated meanings, describing the exercise as one of the "litanies" she goes through to "compose [her]self" (110). It is a counter-ceremony in which she attempts to cross and annul the grotesque Ceremony that decomposes her self. June scrabbles to keep herself from being erased.

The Handmaid's Tale is filled with crossword patterns. Gilead spells out its text; June crosses it. Another way she accomplishes this is by continually conjuring up the voice of Aunt Lydia, one of the nunlike women who train the handmaids at the Red Center. Brainwashing has made Aunt Lydia's voice Offred's conscience, but June, in a heroic effort to erase the brainwashing, conjures it to undercut it. "Blessed are the meek," says Aunt Lydia. June's comment: "She didn't go on to say anything about inheriting the earth" (64). "Think of yourselves as pearls," says Aunt Lydia. "Pearls are congealed oyster spit," thinks June (114; cf. 117). At night before bed she recites the prayer Aunt Lydia taught her, only to cross it with her own (194), in which she says to God that she does not believe for a second that Gilead's activities are what God intended human activities to be. "There Is a Balm in Gilead" becomes "There Is a Bomb in Gilead" (218). At the Prayvaganza, June remembers a bathroom graffito scratched on the wall: "*Aunt Lydia sucks*." "It was like a flag waved from a hilltop in rebellion," a semaphore scrabbling to counteract Aunt Lydia's words (222). Then she conjures up her friend Moira's voice to cross Aunt Lydia's. Remembering Moira's nastiest comments, she says, "There is something powerful in the whispering of obscenities, about those in power. . . . It's like a spell, of sorts" (222). Spelling casts a spell that makes her forget, if only momentarily, the horrible reality of her actual existence. Atwood used this pun several years before in her poem "Spelling," in which the speaker's daughter is playing with plastic letters, "learning how to spell, / spelling, / how to make spells" (63).

Gilead knows the power of words. The handmaids are forbidden to read anything, even the Bible. In its efforts to achieve the ultimate logocentrism—a whole society constructed on the Word—the logocracy must erase other words that might create aporia. The clothing store for the handmaids is called "Lilies of the Field," but the lettering on its sign has been effaced. The Gileadites "decided that even the names of shops were too much temptation for us" (25). So June litters her text with the phrase "Lilies of the Field," always referring to the perfume, another forbidden fruit. Pictures have replaced words on all the signs of the stores frequented by handmaids. June restores the words and frequently puns on them to assure multiplicity of meaning. An anarchy of words, as on a Scrabble board, is infinitely preferable to a rigidly inscribed monolithic text. The latter is a monotonous litany; June creates "break[s] in the chant" (124).

In every chapter the pattern persists: text/countertext. The Soul Scrolls, computer printouts of prayers "going out endlessly," are secretly known as "Holy Rollers" (167). Immediately after making this pun, June adds that when she and her shopping partner start asking dangerous questions ("Do you think God listens . . . to these machines?") she puns again: her exchange with Ofglen is "Subversion, sedition, blasphemy, heresy, all *rolled* into one" (168; emphasis added). The speech act for her, as she tells her tale on tape, is a kind of unholy rolling.

One last example of text as Scrabble game: in the closet in her room, June finds some writing on the wall, "a message," "in writing, forbidden": "*Nolite te bastardes carborundorum*" (52)—fake Latin, she later learns, for "Don't let the bastards grind you down." Before she knows what it means and where her predecessor learned it, the graffito becomes her scripture, a countertext to the Commander's. She recites it to herself when she is supposed to be praying just after the Commander has read from the Bible in preparation for the Ceremony. And she keeps returning to it, touching it as though it were Braille, calling it a "command" to cross the Commander (147).

II: Scrabble Game as Text

The system empowers the Commander to undercut the system. This catch-22 is the crack in the tablet that assures the ultimate crumbling of Gilead. The forbidden Scrabble games the Commander plays with the narrator provide a vivid image of the collapse: the monolithic Word, the tablet of stone, crumbles into Scrabble tiles, a scattering of letters that form a myriad of words having only accidental semantic and syntactic elements.

Driven to assert himself as an individual rather than a mere cell in an organism he knows but cannot admit is sick, the Commander uses June to weaken it further. Handmaids are forbidden to be alone with Commanders; June is for breeding purposes only, not for pleasure, not a concubine or courtesan (136). Furthermore, since handmaids are not allowed to read, when the Commander says to June, "I'd like you to play a game of Scrabble with me" (138), he is breaking two rules at once. The games are intimate, and she must read to play them. She reads not only letters and words, but also the Commander.

June learns from the Scrabble games that "context is all" (144). In the pre-Gilead past, Scrabble to her was "the game of old women, old men, in the summers or in retirement villas, to be played when there was nothing good on television. Or of adolescents, once, long ago" (138). Now it is like kinky sex, a forbidden fruit, "dangerous . . . indecent. Now it's something he can't do with his Wife. . . . It's as if he's offered me drugs" (138-39). "Offered" is a key word here: she has been the offered, as her patronymic implies. Now Fred has "compromised himself," for surely there is some danger to him in this transgression (139). He offers her the chance to play on an equal footing, at least within the game, to play at something, anything, that might break the monotony of her existence as a vessel, a chalice, a womb, a nonperson. Playing a game, she becomes the illusion of an individual. And judging from the words she makes, most Scrabble players would consider her a formidable opponent.

When she wonders what she will have to do in return for this luxury, she uses a word that she has already carefully and calculatedly loaded: *exchange*. This word is used in *The Handmaid's Tale* almost always in the context of surreptitious or forbidden discourse and behaviour (for example, 4, 10-11, 133, 139, 192, 214). It suggests the free interplay and interchange of ideas between equals. This is precisely what begins to happen between the Commander and June over the Scrabble board. Since it's all a game, however, it is only the illusion of a true exchange. In reality, the Commander has all the power.

The first night, they play two games. The first word June tells us she spells is *larynx*, a metonym for voice, intimating that voice is primary. She thus asserts her voice in yet another way; in a broader context, she continuously asserts her voice in the speaking of her tale. She also makes the words *valance*, *quince*, and *zygote*, inviting readers to play with them as we would do if we were making them on the Scrabble board, but in the context of her tale (139). June takes pleasure in the tiles themselves, "the glossy counters with their smooth edges.... The feeling is voluptuous. This is freedom, an eyeblink of it." But counters create countertexts: she spells the word *limp*, enjoying the making of the word, even though the word itself comments on the nature of her freedom (139).

She wins the first game, and she lets the Commander win the second. Or so she thinks. On the next evening they play two more games, during which she realizes that he had let her win the first time (156). Although the words she makes demonstrate her ability to play the game well, she admits that it's a struggle, like trying to walk without crutches after relying on them for a long time. "It was like using a language I'd once known but had nearly forgotten.... [M]y mind lurched and stumbled, among the sharp *R*'s and *T*'s, sliding over the ovoid vowels as if on pebbles" (156). She is a better player than she thinks, however, as she makes the words *prolix, quartz, quandary, sylph,* and *rhythm* (155). (Notice that *quandary* is an eight-letter word that would have given her a fifty-point bonus.) All the words become part of the context of *The Handmaid's Tale*: June is in a quandary because she cannot fathom the Commander's motivation for the clandestine games; something more than the goodnight kiss he asks for seems at stake. The other words can also be played with: *prolix* suggests a weedlike proliferation of words, *quartz* is rock, and *sylph* anticipates Jezebel's (the nightclub). A text so filled with puns and free associations invites such play. The vowels are egglike (ovoid); June's role in society is dictated by her eggs, but the eggs become pebbles under the dictatorship of the Word, *Logos*, which in Gilead has completely quashed Eros. But the monolithic tablet also becomes pebbles as repressed Eros returns; June feels that the Scrabble game is kinky, naughty, "a violation too in its own way" as perverted as whips and chains (155). "Does he have a pony-whip, hidden behind the door?" she wonders (231).

The Bible is scrabbled into *The Story of O*. Handmaiden is just a euphemism for slave girl. The letter Ø becomes the numeral zero. June is null and void: "The squares on the board in front of me are filling up: I'm making my penultimate play of the night. *Zilch*, I spell, a convenient one-vowel word with an expensive Z" (183). June keeps finding herself in the situation of having too few vowels, too many consonants. The latter have greater value in Scrabble. Perhaps the ovoid vowels are feminine, the consonants masculine. In a patriarchal society, the consonants overpower the vowels, reducing their value to zilch, even though men realize they can form no words without vowels. This movement from *zygote* to *zilch* becomes even clearer when June is in her room looking up at the wreath on the ceiling where a chandelier used to be, until her predecessor hanged herself from it. The wreath is "a zero. A hole in space where a star exploded." She sits there staring at it as she waits for "the arrival of the inevitable egg" (200).

It is during one of the Scrabble games that June learns both the fate of her predecessor and the meaning of her Latinate message—not only its literal meaning, but its subtext as well. The woman had also played forbidden Scrabble games, and had learned the elementary-school Latin she used in her message from Fred (187). She, too, must have felt delight at first in tasting the forbidden fruits of reading and spelling again, until she realized, as June does, that such freedom is only an illusion. Fred is still the one in power. When he sees the word *zilch* on the board, he is not sure it's an acceptable word, but when June offers to look it up, he says "I'll give it to you" (183). (It is an acceptable word.) But sexual politics demand that *he* have the power to decide, not some extrascriptural text. At first, the Scrabble games give June the illusion of an intimate relationship; but ultimately she feels merely pampered, like a pet (187). The most genuine feeling she has during the games is the desire to murder Fred for reducing her to Offred, zero, zygote, zilch, null, and void (140). "I am a blank, here," she says, "between parentheses" (228).

June's tale is the filling in of the blank. "Whatever is silenced will clamor to be heard" (153). Telling her tale keeps her from killing herself, which would be the only other way to counter Gilead. She realizes that the Commander's offerings of forbidden fruit are calculated to make her life bearable to her because that would validate the way of the Gileadites, making him feel that "what they're doing is all right after all" (187). She does have one thing on him—"the possibility of [her] own death" (188). If handmaids keep killing themselves, Gilead will collapse. No words can be made without vowels.

Unfortunately, there is a third player in this Scrabble game: Professor Pieixoto, author of "Historical Notes," which is appended to *The Handmaid's Tale*. The text is "in fragments, like a body caught in crossfire" (267), for as June counters and crosses the Logos of the Gileadites, playing words to shatter the Word, so Pieixoto, in his turn, undercuts hers. Her puns, which she uses to make language polysemous again, are turned against her: the professor turns her pun on *chair* into a dirty, sexist joke (300), and he adds a few more of his own—which ominously reveal that though Gilead is no more, the seeds from which the weed grew are still alive.[3]

Pieixoto's speech also reminds us that *The Handmaid's Tale* is not only a speculative fiction about a possible future, but it also peers at the present through a glass darkly. How much worse is it, after all, to call a woman Offred than it is to call her Mrs. Frederick Waterford? Her first name, her essential identity, is still erased. Pieixoto continues the erasure by focusing his attention on the Commander rather than June. The last word is his, but it is like the last play of a loser in a Scrabble game. For those of us who reread this extraordinary book, June comes alive. It is only then that we realize the winner of the Scrabble game is the fourth player—Margaret Atwood.

From *Essays on Canadian Writing* 48 (1992/1993): 89-96. Copyright © 1992 by ECW Press Ltd. Reprinted by permission of ECW Press Ltd.

Notes

1. The term *shibboleth* originated in Judges (12.4-6). The Gileadites, at war with the Ephraimites, used the word to distinguish their own kind from fleeing Ephraimites. When someone tried during the war to cross the Jordan River to safety, the Gileadites forced that person to pronounce *shibboleth*. Since Ephraimites could not make the "sh" sound, they were killed if they mispronounced the word.

2. As far as I know, Harriet Bergmann was the first critic to notice this, but she still calls June "Offred" (853).

3. Cf. Bergmann (851-53) and Davidson (118-20). Many readers have commented on the bitter irony of the "Historical Notes." Pieixoto is a poor reader who attempts to apply "objective" historicism (a methodology outmoded in our own day) to Gilead, claiming that one should not condemn the Gileadites, but merely attempt to understand them. Atwood's text reveals, however, that we must not only condemn them, but also actively counter and cross them to prevent them from winning the game again.

Works Cited

Atwood, Margaret. *The Handmaid's Tale*. 1985. Boston: Houghton, 1986.

_____. "Spelling." *True Stories*. New York: Simon, 1981. 63-64.

Bergmann, Harriet F. "'Teaching Them to Read': A Fishing Expedition in *The Handmaid's Tale*." *College English* 51 (1989): 847-54.

Davidson, Arnold E. "Future Tense: Making History in *The Handmaid's Tale*." *Margaret Atwood: Vision and Forms*. Ed. Kathryn Van Spanckeren and Jan Garden Castro. Carbondale: Southern Illinois UP, 1988. 113-21.

RESOURCES

Chronology of Margaret Atwood's Life

1939	Margaret Eleanor Atwood is born in Ottawa, Canada, on November 18. During Atwood's childhood, her family divides its time between Ottawa and the wildernesses of northern Ontario and Quebec, where Atwood's father carries out entomological research.
1946	The Atwood family moves to Toronto, though they continue to spend summers in Ontario and Quebec.
1951-1957	Atwood begins attending school regularly in 1951. While at Leaside High School, she writes for the school newspaper. During the summers, she works as a camp counselor.
1957-1961	Atwood studies at Victoria College, University of Toronto, and earns B.A. in English. While at college, she writes poems and stories for the campus literary journal and designs posters and programs for the drama society.
1961	*Double Persephone* wins the University of Toronto E. J. Pratt Medal.
1961-1963	Atwood studies at Radcliffe College (which is later absorbed by Harvard University) with the support of a Woodrow Wilson Fellowship. She earns an M.A. in English and begins working toward a doctorate at Harvard.
1963-1964	Atwood leaves Harvard to return to Toronto, where she takes a job at a market research company and begins an unpublished novel. During the summer of 1964 she travels to England and France.
1964-1965	Atwood becomes a lecturer in English at the University of British Columbia. She writes a draft of *The Edible Woman* and numerous short stories and poems.
1965	Atwood returns to Harvard to continue work on a doctorate. She does not finish a thesis.
1966	*The Circle Game* is published. It wins the Governor-General's Award for Poetry the following year.

1967	Atwood married James Polk, a Harvard postgraduate student. The couple then move to Montreal, and Atwood takes a job lecturing in English at Sir George Williams University, which is today Concordia University.
1968	*The Animals in That Country* is published, and Atwood and Polk move to Edmonton, Alberta.
1969	*The Edible Woman* is published, and Atwood begins teaching creative writing at the University of Alberta.
1970	*The Journals of Susanna Moodie* and *Procedures for Underground* are published. Atwood and Polk live abroad in England and France.
1971	*Power Politics* is published. Atwood and Polk return to Canada and settle in Toronto. Atwood becomes Assistant Professor at York University and a member of Anansi Press's board of directors, a position that she holds until 1973.
1972	*Surfacing* is published. Atwood is invited to Massey College, Toronto, as a writer-in-residence.
1973	Atwood and Polk divorce, and Atwood moves to a farm in Alliston, Ontario, with Graeme Gibson, a novelist. Trent University, Ontario, confers upon her an honorary doctoral degree.
1974	*You Are Happy* is published. Atwood becomes a cartoonist for *This Magazine* and writes a television script, *The Servant Girl*, for the Canadian Broadcasting Corporation.
1976	*Lady Oracle* and *Selected Poems* are published. Atwood gives birth to a daughter, Eleanor Jess.
1977	*Dancing Girls, and Other Stories* and *Days of the Rebels, 1815-1840* are published.
1978	*Two-Headed Poems* and *Up in the Tree* are published. Atwood and her family move to Scotland, and Gibson spends three months as writer-in-residence at the University of Edinburgh.
1979	*Life Before Man* is published.

1980	*Anna's Pet* is published. The family moves back to Toronto, and the Writers' Union of Canada elects Atwood its vice president.
1981	*Bodily Harm* and *True Stories* are published. Atwood wins a Guggenheim Fellowship and becomes president of the Writers' Union of Canada.
1982	*Second Words: Selected Critical Prose* is published.
1983	*Murder in the Dark: Short Fictions and Prose Poems* and *Bluebeard's Egg* are published. The family moves to Norfolk and the following year to West Berlin.
1984	*Interlunar* is published. The family returns to Toronto, and the Canadian Centre of PEN International elects Atwood president.
1985	*The Handmaid's Tale* is published. It wins multiple awards, including the Governor-General's Award for Fiction and the Arthur C. Clarke Award for Best Science Fiction.
1986	*Selected Poems II: Poems Selected and New, 1976-1986* is published. Atwood spends the year at New York University as the Berg (Visiting) Chair.
1987	The Royal Society of Canada inducts Atwood as a Fellow.
1988	*Cat's Eye* is published.
1989	*Selected Poems, 1966-1984* is published.
1990	Volker Schloendorff's film adaptation of *The Handmaid's Tale* premieres at the Berlin Film Festival.
1991	*Wilderness Tips* is published. Atwood delivers the Clarendon Lectures at the University of Oxford, then spends the remainder of the year with her family in France.
1992	*Good Bones* is published.
1993	*The Robber Bride* is published.

1995	*Morning in the Burned House* and *Strange Things: The Malevolent North in Canadian Literature* are published.
1996	*Alias Grace* is published; it wins the Giller Prize.
1998	*Eating Fire: Selected Poems, 1965-1995* is published. The University of Oxford awards Atwood an honorary doctorate.
2000	*The Blind Assassin* is published; it wins the Booker Prize. Atwood delivers the Empson Lectures at the University of Cambridge. Poul Ruders's operatic adaptation of *The Handmaid's Tale* premieres in Copenhagen.
2001	The University of Cambridge awards Atwood an honorary doctorate.
2002	*Negotiating with the Dead: A Writer on Writing* is published.
2003	*Oryx and Crake* is published.
2004	*Moving Targets: Writing with Intent, 1982-2004* is published. Harvard University awards Atwood an honorary doctorate.
2005	*The Penelopiad* is published.
2006	*The Tent* and *Moral Disorder* are published.
2007	*The Door* is published.
2008	*Payback: Debt and the Shadow Side of Wealth* is published.

Works by Margaret Atwood

Long Fiction
The Edible Woman, 1969
Surfacing, 1972
Lady Oracle, 1976
Life Before Man, 1979
Bodily Harm, 1981
The Handmaid's Tale, 1985
Cat's Eye, 1988
The Robber Bride, 1993
Alias Grace, 1996
The Blind Assassin, 2000
Oryx and Crake, 2003
The Penelopiad: The Myth of Penelope and Odysseus, 2005

Short Fiction
Dancing Girls, and Other Stories, 1977
Bluebeard's Egg, 1983
Murder in the Dark: Short Fictions and Prose Poems, 1983
Wilderness Tips, 1991
Good Bones, 1992 (also known as *Good Bones and Simple Murders*, 1994)
Moral Disorder, 2006
The Tent, 2006

Poetry
Double Persephone, 1961
Kaleidoscopes Baroque: A Poem, 1965
Talismans for Children, 1965
The Circle Game, 1966
Expeditions, 1966
Speeches for Dr. Frankenstein, 1966
The Animals in That Country, 1968
What Was in the Garden, 1969
The Journals of Susanna Moodie, 1970
Procedures for Underground, 1970
Power Politics, 1971
You Are Happy, 1974

Selected Poems, 1976
Two-Headed Poems, 1978
True Stories, 1981
Snake Poems, 1983
Interlunar, 1984
Selected Poems II: Poems Selected and New, 1976-1986, 1986
Selected Poems, 1966-1984, 1990
Poems, 1965-1975, 1991
Poems, 1976-1989, 1992
Morning in the Burned House, 1995
Eating Fire: Selected Poems, 1965-1995, 1998
The Door, 2007

Nonfiction

Survival: A Thematic Guide to Canadian Literature, 1972
Days of the Rebels, 1815-1840, 1977
Second Words: Selected Critical Prose, 1982
Strange Things: The Malevolent North in Canadian Literature, 1995
Deux sollicitudes: Entretiens, 1996 (with Victor-Lévy Beaulieu; *Two Solicitudes: Conversations*, 1998)
Negotiating with the Dead: A Writer on Writing, 2002
Moving Targets: Writing with Intent, 1982-2004, 2004 (also known as *Writing with Intent: Essays, Reviews, Personal Prose, 1983-2005*, 2005)
Payback: Debt and the Shadow Side of Wealth, 2008

Edited Texts

The New Oxford Book of Canadian Verse in English, 1982
The Oxford Book of Canadian Short Stories in English, 1986 (with Robert Weaver)
The CanLit Foodbook: From Pen to Palate, a Collection of Tasty Literary Fare, 1987
The Best American Short Stories, 1989, 1989 (with Shannon Ravenel)
The New Oxford Book of Canadian Short Stories in English, 1995 (with Robert Weaver)

Children's Literature

Up in the Tree, 1978
Anna's Pet, 1980 (with Joyce Barkhouse)
For the Birds, 1990
Princess Prunella and the Purple Peanut, 1995 (illustrated by Maryann Kowalski)
Bashful Bob and Doleful Dorinda, 2004 (illustrated by Dušan Petričić)
Rude Ramsay and the Roaring Radishes, 2004 (illustrated by Dušan Petričić)

Bibliography

Andriano, Joseph. "*The Handmaid's Tale* as Scrabble Game." *Essays on Canadian Writing* 48 (1992/1993): 89-96.

Baccolini, Raffaella. "'What's in a Name?': Language and Self-Creation in Women's Writing." In *The Representation of the Self in Women's Autobiography*, ed. Vita Fortunati and Gabriella Morisco. Bologna: University of Bologna, 1993.

Banerjee, Chinmoy. "Alice in Disneyland: Criticism as Commodity in *The Handmaid's Tale*." *Essays on Canadian Writing* 41 (Summer 1990): 74-92.

Beran, Carol. *Living over the Abyss: Margaret Atwood's Life Before Man*. Toronto: ECW Press, 1994.

Bergmann, Harriet F. "'Teaching Them to Read': A Fishing Expedition in *The Handmaid's Tale*." *College English* 51 (1989): 847-854.

Bignell, Jonathan. "*The Handmaid's Tale*: Novel and Film." *British Journal of Canadian Studies* 8, no. 1 (1993): 71-84.

Bouson, J. Brooks. *Brutal Choreographies: Oppositional Strategies and Narrative Design in the Novels of Margaret Atwood*. Amherst: University of Massachusetts Press, 1993.

Cameron, Elspeth. *Atwood—The Edible Woman: Notes*. Toronto: Coles, 1983.

Carminero-Santangelo, Marta. "Moving Beyond 'the Blank White Spaces': Atwood's Gilead, Postmodernism, and Strategic Resistance." *Studies in Canadian Literature* 19, no. 1 (1994): 20-42.

Carrington, Ildikó de Papp. "Margaret Atwood." In *Canadian Writers and Their Works: Fiction Series*, Vol. 9. Toronto: ECW Press, 1987. 25-119.

_____. "A Swiftian Sermon." *Essays on Canadian Writing* 34 (Spring 1987): 127-132.

Christ, Carol P. "Margaret Atwood: Surfacing of Women's Spiritual Quest and Vision." *Signs* 2 (Winter 1976): 316-330.

Cooke, Nathalie. *Margaret Atwood: A Critical Companion*. Greenwood Press, Westport, CT: 2004.

Davey, Frank. *Margaret Atwood: A Feminist Poetics*. Vancouver: Talonbooks, 1984.

Davidson, Arnold E. "Future Tense: Making History in *The Handmaid's Tale*." In *Margaret Atwood: Vision and Forms*, ed. Kathryn Van Spanckeren and Jan Garden Castro. Carbondale: Southern Illinois University Press, 1988. 113-121.

Davidson, Arnold E., and Cathy Davidson, eds. *The Art of Margaret Atwood: Essays in Criticism*. Toronto: House of Anansi Press, 1980.

Dopp, Jamie. "Subject-Position as Victim-Position in *The Handmaid's Tale*." *Studies in Canadian Literature* 19, no. 1 (1994): 43-57.

Fee, Margery. *The Fat Lady Dances: Margaret Atwood's Lady Oracle*. Toronto: ECW Press, 1993.

Felski, Rita. *Beyond Feminist Aesthetics: Feminist Literature and Social Change.* Cambridge, MA: Harvard University Press, 1989.

Filipczak, Dorota. "'Is There No Balm in Gilead?' Biblical Intertext in Margaret Atwood's *The Handmaid's Tale*." In *Literature and Theology at Century's End*, ed. Gregory Salyer and Robert Detweiler. Atlanta: Scholars, 1995. 215-233.

Finnell, Susanna. "Unwriting the Quest: Margaret Atwood's Fiction and *The Handmaid's Tale*." In *Women and the Journey: The Female Travel Experience,* ed. Frederick Bonnie and Susan H. McLeod. Pullman: Washington State University Press, 1993.

Fitting, Peter. "The Turn from Utopia in Recent Feminist Fiction." In *Feminism, Utopia, and Narrative*, ed. Libby Falk Jones and Sarah Webster Goodwin. Knoxville: University of Tennessee Press, 1990. 141-158.

Florén, Celia. "A Reading of Margaret Atwood's Dystopia, *The Handmaid's Tale*." In *Gender, I-Deology: Essays on Theory, Fiction and Film*, ed. Chantal Cornut-Genille D'Arcy and José Angel García Landa. Amsterdam: Rodopi, 1996. 253-264.

Foley, Michael. "'Basic Victim Positions' and the Women in Margaret Atwood's *The Handmaid's Tale*." *Atlantis* 15, no. 2 (1990): 50-58.

_____. "Satiric Intent in Margaret Atwood's *The Handmaid's Tale*." *Commonwealth Essays and Studies* 11, no. 2 (Spring 1989): 44-52.

Freibert, Lucy M. "Control and Creativity: The Politics of Risk in Margaret Atwood's *The Handmaid's Tale*." In *Critical Essays on Margaret Atwood*, ed. Judith McCombs. Boston: G. K. Hall, 1988. 280-291.

Fullbrook, Kate. "Margaret Atwood: Colonisation and Responsibility." In *Free Women: Ethics and Aesthetics in Twentieth-Century Women's Fiction*. Philadelphia: Temple University Press, 1990. 171-193.

Givner, Jessie. "Names, Faces and Signatures in Margaret Atwood's *Cat's Eye* and *The Handmaid's Tale*." *Canadian Literature* 133 (Summer 1992): 56-75.

Godard, Barbara. "Telling It over Again: Atwood's Art of Parody." *Canadian Poetry* 21 (Fall/Winter 1987): 1-30.

Goldsmith, Elizabeth, ed. *Writing the Female Voice: Essays on Epistolary Literature.* Boston: Northeastern University Press, 1989.

Grace, Sherrill E. *Violent Duality: A Study of Margaret Atwood*. Montreal: Vehicule Press, 1980.

Grace, Sherrill E., and Lorraine Weir, eds. *Margaret Atwood: Language, Text and System*. Vancouver: University of British Columbia Press, 1983.

Gray, Francine du Plessix. "Margaret Atwood: Nature as the Nunnery." In *Adam and Eve and the City: Selected Nonfiction*. New York: Simon & Schuster, 1987.

Greene, Gayle. "Choice of Evils." Review of *The Handmaid's Tale*, by Margaret Atwood. *Women's Review of Books*, July 1986, 14-15.

Hales, Leslie-Ann. "Genesis Revisited: The Darkening Vision of Margaret Atwood." *Month*, 2d n.s. 20, no. 7 (July 1987): 257-262.

Halliday, David. "On Atwood." *Waves* 15, no. 4 (Spring 1987): 51-54.

Hammer, Stephanie Barbe. "The World as It Will Be? Female Satire and the Technology of Power in *The Handmaid's Tale*." *Modern Language Studies* 20, no. 2 (Spring 1990): 39-49.

Hengen, Shannon. *Margaret Atwood's Power: Mirrors, Reflections and Images in Select Fiction and Poetry*. Toronto: Second Story Press, 1993.

Hogsette, David S. "Margaret Atwood's Rhetorical Epilogue in *The Handmaid's Tale*: The Reader's Role in Empowering Offred's Speech Act." *Critique* 38 (1997): 262-278.

Howells, Coral Ann. *Margaret Atwood*. 2d ed. New York: Palgrave Macmillan, 2005.

——————. "Margaret Atwood: *Bodily Harm*, *The Handmaid's Tale*." In *Private and Fictional Words: Canadian Women Novelists of the 1970s and 1980s*. London: Methuen, 1987.

Howells, Coral Ann, and Lynette Hunter, eds. *Narrative Strategies in Canadian Literature*. Buckingham: Open University Press, 1991.

Ingersoll, Earl G. "Margaret Atwood's *The Handmaid's Tale* as a Self-Subverting Text." In *Cultural Identities in Canadian Literature*, ed. Bénédicte Mauguière. New York: Peter Lang, 1998. 103-109.

——————, ed. *Margaret Atwood: Conversations*. London: Virago, 1992.

Irvine, Lorna. *Collecting Clues: Margaret Atwood's Bodily Harm*. Toronto: ECW Press, 1993.

Jacobus, Lee A., and Barreca, Regina, eds. "Margaret Atwood Issue." *LIT: Literature Interpretation Theory* 6, nos. 3/4 (December 1995).

Johnson, Brian. "Language, Power, and Responsibility in *The Handmaid's Tale*: Toward a Discourse of Literary Gossip." *Canadian Literature* 148 (Spring 1996): 39-55.

Keith, W. J. "Apocalyptic Imaginations: Notes on Atwood's *The Handmaid's Tale* and Findley's *Not Wanted on the Voyage*." *Essays on Canadian Writing* 35 (Winter 1987): 123-134.

Kolodny, Annette. "Margaret Atwood and the Politics of Narrative." In *Studies on Canadian Literature: Introductory and Critical Essays*, ed. Arnold E. Davidson. New York: Modern Language Association of America, 1991. 90-109.

Lacombe, Michele. "The Writing on the Wall: Amputated Speech in Margaret Atwood's *The Handmaid's Tale*." *Wascana Review* 21, no. 2 (Fall 1986): 3-20.

Lecker, Robert, Jack David, and Ellen Quigley, eds. *Canadian Writers and Their Works: Essays on Form, Context, and Development*. Fiction Series 9. Toronto: ECW Press, 1987.

McCombs, Judith, ed. *Critical Essays on Margaret Atwood*. Boston: G. K. Hall, 1988.

——————. *Margaret Atwood: A Reference Guide*. Boston: G. K. Hall, 1991.

Malak, Amin. "Margaret Atwood's *The Handmaid's Tale* and the Dystopian Tradition." *Canadian Literature* 112 (1987): 9-16.

Mendez-Egle, Beatrice, ed. *Margaret Atwood: Reflection and Reality*. Edinburg, TX: Pan American University, 1988.

Miner, Madonne. "'Trust Me': Reading the Romance Plot in Margaret Atwood's *The Handmaid's Tale*." *Twentieth Century Literature* 37 (1991): 148-168.

Montelaro, Janet J. "Maternity and the Ideology of Sexual Difference in *The Handmaid's Tale*." *LIT: Literature Interpretation Theory* 6, nos. 3/4 (December 1995): 233-256.

Murray, Heather. "'Its Image in the Mirror': Canada, Canonicity, the Uncanny." *Essays on Canadian Writing* 42 (Winter 1990): 102-130.

Mycak, Sonia. *In Search of the Split Subject: Psychoanalysis, Phenomenology, and the Novels of Margaret Atwood*. Toronto: ECW Press, 1996.

Myhal, Bob. "Boundaries, Centers, and Circles: The Postmodern Geometry of *The Handmaid's Tale*." *LIT: Literature Interpretation Theory* 6, nos. 3/4 (December 1995): 213-231.

Nicholson, Colin, ed. *Margaret Atwood: Writing and Subjectivity*. London: Macmillan, 1994.

Nicholson, Mervyn. "Food and Power: Homer, Carroll, Atwood and Others." *Mosaic* 20, no. 3 (Summer 1987): 37-55.

Nilsen, Helge Normann. "Four Feminist Novels by Margaret Atwood." *American Studies in Scandinavia* 26, no. 2 (1994): 126-139.

Nischik, Reingard M., ed. *Margaret Atwood: Works and Impact*. Toronto: House of Anansi Press, 2002.

Norris, Ken. "'The University of Denay, Nunavit': The 'Historical Notes' in Margaret Atwood's *The Handmaid's Tale*." *American Review of Canadian Studies* 20, no. 3 (1990): 357-364.

Palmer, Carole L. "Current Atwood Checklist, 1988." *Newsletter of the Margaret Atwood Society* no. 5 (1988): 5-11.

Parker, Emma. "You Are What You Eat: The Politics of Eating in the Novels of Margaret Atwood." *Twentieth Century Literature* 41, no. 3 (Fall 1995): 349-368.

Pearlman, Mickey, ed. *Canadian Women Writing Fiction*. Jackson: University Press of Mississippi, 1993.

Perrakis, Phyllis Sternberg. "The Female Gothic and the (M)other in Atwood and Lessing." *Doris Lessing Newsletter* 17, no. 1 (1995): 1, 11-15.

Rao, Eleonora. *Strategies for Identity: The Fiction of Margaret Atwood*. New York: Peter Lang, 1993.

Raschke, Debrah. "Margaret Atwood's *The Handmaid's Tale*: False Borders and Subtle Subversions." *LIT: Literature Interpretation Theory* 6, nos. 3/4 (December 1995): 257-268.

Reesman, Jeanne Campbell. "Dark Knowledge in *The Handmaid's Tale*." *CEA Critic: An Official Journal of the College English Association* 53, no. 3 (Spring/Summer 1991): 6-22.

Reynolds, Margaret. *Margaret Atwood: The Essential Guide to Contemporary Literature*. London: Vintage, 2002.
Rigney, Barbara Hill. *Margaret Atwood*. Ed. Eva Figes and Adele King. Totowa, NJ: Barnes & Noble, 1987.
Rosenberg, Jerome H. *Margaret Atwood*. Boston: Twayne, 1984.
Rubenstein, Roberta. "Escape Artist and Split Personalities: Margaret Atwood." In *Boundaries of the Self: Gender, Culture, Fiction*. Urbana: University of Illinois Press, 1987. 63-122.
St. Pierre, P. Matthew. "Envisioning Atwood." *Cross Currents* 36, no. 3 (Fall 1986): 371-373.
Slonczewski, Joan L. "A Tale of Two Handmaids." *Kenyon Review* n.s. 8, no. 4 (Fall 1986): 120-124.
Sparrow, Fiona. "'This Place Is Some Kind of a Garden': Clearings in the Bush in the Works of Susanna Moodie, Catharine Parr Traill, Margaret Atwood and Margaret Laurence." *Journal of Commonwealth Literature* 25, no. 1 (1990): 24-41.
Staels, Hilde. *Margaret Atwood's Novels: A Study of Narrative Discourse*. Tübingen, Germany: Francke, 1995.
Stein, Karen F. "Margaret Atwood's *The Handmaid's Tale*: Scheherazade in Dystopia." *University of Toronto Quarterly* 61 (1991/1992): 269-279.
Suarez, Isabel Carrera. "'Yet I Speak, Yet I Exist': Affirmation of the Subject in Atwood's Short Stories." In *Margaret Atwood: Writing and Subjectivity*, ed. Colin Nicholson. New York: St. Martin's Press, 1994. 230-247.
Templin, Charlotte. "Atwood's *The Handmaid's Tale*." *Explicator* 49, no. 4 (Summer 1991): 255-256.
Updike, John. "Expeditions to Gilead and Seegard." *The New Yorker* 62, no. 12 (May 12, 1986): 118, 121-123.
VanSpanckeren, Kathryn, and Jan Garden Castro, eds. *Margaret Atwood: Vision and Forms*. Carbondale: Southern Illinois University Press, 1988.
Verwaayen, Kimberly. "Re-examining the Gaze in *The Handmaid's Tale*." *Open Letter* 9, no. 4 (1995): 44-54.
Wagner-Martin, Linda. "Epigraphs to Atwood's *The Handmaid's Tale*." *Notes on Contemporary Literature* 17, no. 2 (1987): 4.
Wall, Kathleen. *The Callisto Myth from Ovid to Atwood: Initiation and Rape in Literature*. Montreal: McGill-Queen's University Press, 1988.
White, Roberta. "Margaret Atwood: Reflections in a Convex Mirror." In *Canadian Women Writing Fiction*, ed. Mickey Pearlman. Jackson: University Press of Mississippi, 1993. 53-70.
Wilson, Sharon Rose. *Margaret Atwood's Fairy-Tale Sexual Politics*. Jackson: University Press of Mississippi, 1993.
_____, ed. *Margaret Atwood's Textual Assassinations: Recent Poetry and Fiction*. Columbus: Ohio State University Press, 2003.

Wilson, Sharon Rose, Thomas B. Friedman, and Shannon Hengen. *Approaches to Teaching Atwood's The Handmaid's Tale and Other Works*. New York: Modern Language Association of America, 1996.

Woodcock, George. *Introducing Margaret Atwood's Surfacing: A Reader's Guide*. Toronto: ECW Press, 1990.

Workman, Nancy V. "Sufi Mysticism in Margaret Atwood's *The Handmaid's Tale*." *Studies in Canadian Literature* 14, no. 2 (1989): 10-26.

York, Lorraine M. "The Habits of Language: Uniform(ity), Transgression, and Margaret Atwood." *Canadian Literature* 126 (Autumn 1990): 6-19.

_____, ed. *Various Atwoods: Essays on the Later Poems, Short Fiction, and Novels*. Toronto: House of Anansi Press, 1995.

CRITICAL INSIGHTS

About the Editor

J. Brooks Bouson is Professor of English at Loyola University in Chicago. In her book on Margaret Atwood, *Brutal Choreographies: Oppositional Strategies and Narrative Design in the Novels of Margaret Atwood* (1993), Bouson makes use of both feminist and psychoanalytic theory as she investigates the psychological and political concerns expressed in Atwood's fiction, and she also shows, through an analysis of the critical conversations surrounding Atwood's fiction, that Atwood's novels have the power to disturb and compel readers while calling attention to their preoccupation with form and design. Since the publication of *Brutal Choreographies*, Bouson has published book chapters and essays on Atwood, including an essay on Atwood's invocation of third-wave "power feminism" in *The Robber Bride*; on Atwood's borrowing from a popular genre, the confessional memoir, in *The Blind Assassin*; and on Atwood's satiric vision of a bioengineered and posthuman future in *Oryx and Crake*. In addition to her work on Atwood, Bouson has published essays and book chapters on a variety of authors (including Dorothy Allison, Saul Bellow, Emily Dickinson, Ted Hughes, Franz Kafka, Jamaica Kincaid, Toni Morrison, Edwin Muir, George Orwell, Richard Russo, and Christa Wolf), and she is the author of four other books—*Embodied Shame: Uncovering Female Shame in Contemporary Women's Writings* (forthcoming), *Jamaica Kincaid: Writing Memory, Writing Back to the Mother* (2005), *Quiet As It's Kept: Shame, Trauma, and Race in the Novels of Toni Morrison* (2000), and *The Empathic Reader: A Study of the Narcissistic Character and the Drama of the Self* (1989). Bouson's area of specialization is twentieth-century women's literature. Her other areas of interest include psychoanalysis and literature, feminist theory (especially the history of feminist theory), empathy and the novel, emotions and literature, shame in literature, and trauma and narrative.

About *The Paris Review*

The Paris Review is America's preeminent literary quarterly, dedicated to discovering and publishing the best new voices in fiction, nonfiction, and poetry. The magazine was founded in Paris in 1953 by the young American writers Peter Matthiessen and Doc Humes, and edited there and in New York for its first fifty years by George Plimpton. Over the decades, the *Review* has introduced readers to the earliest writings of Jack Kerouac, Philip Roth, T. C. Boyle, V. S. Naipaul, Ha Jin, Jay McInerney, and Mona Simpson, and published numerous now classic works, including Roth's *Goodbye, Columbus*, Donald Barthelme's *Alice*, Jim Carroll's *Basketball Diaries*, and selections from Samuel Beckett's *Molloy* (his first publication in English). The first chapter of Jeffrey Eugenides's *The Virgin Suicides* appeared in the *Review*'s pages, as well as stories by Edward P. Jones, Rick Moody, David Foster Wallace, Denis Johnson, Jim Shepard, Jim Crace, Lorrie Moore, Jeanette Winterson, and Ann Patchett.

The Paris Review's renowned Writers at Work series of interviews, whose early installments include legendary conversations with E. M. Forster, William Faulkner, and Ernest Hemingway, is one of the landmarks of world literature. The interviews received a George Polk Award and were nominated for a Pulitzer Prize. Among the more than three hundred interviewees are Robert Frost, Marianne Moore, W. H. Auden, Elizabeth Bishop, Susan Sontag, and Toni Morrison. Recent issues feature conversations with Salman Rushdie, Joan Didion, Stephen King, Norman Mailer, Kazuo Ishiguro, and Umberto Eco. (A complete list of the interviews is available at www.theparisreview.org.) In November 2008, Picador will publish the third of a four-volume series of anthologies of *Paris Review* interviews. The first two volumes have received acclaim. *The New York Times* called the Writers at Work series "the most remarkable and extensive interviewing project we possess."

The Paris Review is edited by Philip Gourevitch, who was named to the post in 2005, following the death of George Plimpton two years earlier. Under Gourevitch's leadership, the magazine's international distribution has expanded, paid subscriptions have risen 150 percent, and newsstand distribution has doubled. A new editorial team has published fiction by Andre Aciman, Damon Galgut, Mohsin Hamid, Gish Jen, Richard Price, Said Sayrafiezadeh, and Alistair Morgan. Poetry editors Charles Simic, Meghan O'Rourke, and Dan Chiasson have selected works by Billy Collins, Jesse Ball, Mary Jo Bang, Sharon Olds, and Mary Karr. Writing published in the magazine has been anthologized in *Best American Short Stories* (2006, 2007, and 2008), *Best American Poetry*, *Best Creative Non-Fiction*, the Pushcart Prize anthology, and *O. Henry Prize Stories*.

The magazine presents two annual awards. The Hadada Award for lifelong contribution to literature has recently been given to William Styron, Joan Didion, Norman Mailer, and Peter Matthiessen in 2008. The Plimpton Prize for Fiction, given to a new voice in fiction brought to national attention in the pages of *The Paris Review*, was presented in 2007 to Benjamin Percy and to Jesse Ball in 2008.

The Paris Review won the 2007 National Magazine Award in photojournalism, and the *Los Angeles Times* recently called *The Paris Review* "an American treasure with true international reach."

Since 1999 *The Paris Review* has been published by The Paris Review Foundation, Inc., a not-for-profit 501(c)(3) organization.

The Paris Review is available in digital form to libraries worldwide in selected academic databases exclusively from EBSCO Publishing. Libraries can contact EBSCO at 1-800-653-2726 for details. For more information on *The Paris Review* or to subscribe, please visit: www.theparisreview.org.

Contributors

J. Brooks Bouson is Professor of English at Loyola University in Chicago. She has published essays and book chapters on a variety of authors (including Dorothy Allison, Margaret Atwood, Saul Bellow, Emily Dickinson, Ted Hughes, Franz Kafka, Jamaica Kincaid, Toni Morrison, Edwin Muir, George Orwell, Richard Russo, and Christa Wolf), and she is the author of five books—*Embodied Shame: Uncovering Female Shame in Contemporary Women's Writings* (forthcoming), *Jamaica Kincaid: Writing Memory, Writing Back to the Mother* (2005), *Quiet As It's Kept: Shame, Trauma, and Race in the Novels of Toni Morrison* (2000), *Brutal Choreographies: Oppositional Strategies and Narrative Design in the Novels of Margaret Atwood* (1993), and *The Empathic Reader: A Study of the Narcissistic Character and the Drama of the Self* (1989).

Karen Carmean is Charles A. Dana Professor of English at Converse College in Spartanburg, South Carolina. She is the author of *Toni Morrison's World of Fiction* and *Ernest J. Gaines: A Critical Companion*.

Earl G. Ingersoll is a Distinguished Professor and Distinguished Teaching Professor Emeritus at SUNY College at Brockport. He is the author or editor of a dozen books, including *Margaret Atwood: Conversations* and *Waltzing Again: New and Selected Conversations with Margaret Atwood*.

Jascha Hoffman has written for *The New York Times* and *Nature*. He lives in Brooklyn.

Lisa Jadwin, who received her Ph.D. from Princeton in 1989, is Professor of English at St. John Fisher College. Her publications include articles and books on nineteenth- and twentieth-century literature, including *Charlotte Brontë Revisited* (1997). She is currently completing a study of the ritual work of detective fiction titled *Over Her Dead Body*.

Dominick Grace is Associate Professor of English at Brescia University College. His research interests are eclectic; his publications range from work on Chaucer and Shakespeare to work on contemporary literature and popular culture.

Matthew J. Bolton is an English teacher and the academic dean of Loyola School in New York City. He earned his Ph.D. in English literature in 2005 from the Graduate Center of the City University of New York, where he wrote his dissertation on Robert Browning and T. S. Eliot. He received the T. S. Eliot Society's Fathman Young Scholar Award for work related to his dissertation. In addition to his doctorate, Bolton holds master's degrees in teaching and in educational administration from Fordham University. His research and writing center on connections between Victorian and modernist literature.

Jennifer E. Dunn teaches English literature at the University of Oxford and the University of Oxford Department for Continuing Education. She has published articles on twentieth-century women writers, including Katherine Mansfield, Angela Carter, Emma Tennant, and Margaret Atwood. She has also lectured and published on modernism, postmodernism, and literary theory. Her current research focuses on rewriting and intertextuality.

Coral Ann Howells is Professor Emeritus at the University of Reading, where she was Professor of Canadian and English Literature. She also served as the chair of the Margaret Atwood Society. Her publications include *Love, Mystery, and Misery: Feeling in Gothic Fiction* (1978, 1995), *Private and Fictional Words: Canadian Women Novelists of the 1970s and 1980s* (1987), *Jean Rhys* (1991), *Narrative Strategies in Canadian Literature: Feminism and Postcolonialism* (with Lynette Hunter 1991), *Margaret Atwood* (1996, 2005), *Alice Munro* (1998), *Contemporary Canadian Women's Fiction: Refiguring Identities* (2003), and *The Cambridge Companion to Margaret Atwood* (2006).

Madonne Miner is Dean of the College of Arts and Sciences at Weber State University. Prior to taking that position she was a Professor of English at Texas Tech University, where she also served as the Associate Dean of the Arts and Sciences College. Her publications include the book *Insatiable Appetites: Twentieth-Century American Women's Bestsellers* (1984) and numerous articles in journals such as *Critique, Film and History, Studies in Short fiction*, and *Twentieth Century Literature*.

Shirley Neuman has taught at the University of Michigan and the University of Toronto, where she also served as Vice President and Provost. She has published several books, including *Gertrude Stein: Autobiography and the Problem of Narration* (1979), *Some One Myth: Yeats's Autobiographical Prose* (1982), *Mazing Space: Writing Canadian, Women Writing* (with Samaro Kamboureli, 1986), *Gertrude Stein and the Making of Literature* (with Ira B. Nadel, 1988), *Autobiography and Questions of Gender* (1991), *ReImagining Women: Representations of Women in Culture* (1993), and *Témoignages: Reflections on the Humanities* (1993).

Chinmoy Banerjee taught literature at Simon Fraser University and serves as secretary of the South Asian Network for Secularism and Democracy (SANSAD). He has published essays in *Ariel, Essays on Canadian Writing, Modern Fiction Studies*, and *Canadian Literature*.

Elisabeth Hansot taught at Stanford University. Her books include *Perfection and Progress: Two Modes of Utopian Thought* (1974), *Managers of Virtue: Public School Leadership in America 1820-1980* (with David Tyack, 1982), *Public Schools in Hard Times: The Great Depression and Recent Years* (with David Tyack and Robert Lowe, 1984), and *Learning Together: A History of Education in American Schools* (with David Tyack, 1990).

Danita J. Dodson taught at the University of Mobile. She has published essays in *Critique, Utopian Studies*, and *Obsidian II*.

Hilde Staels is Associate Professor at the University of Leuven. Her essays on Atwood's work have appeared in *English Studies* and *Modern Fiction Studies*.

Eleonora Rao is Associate Professor of English at the University of Salerno. She is the author of *Strategies for Identity: The Fiction of Margaret Atwood* (1994) and *Heart of a Stranger: Contemporary Women Writers and the Metaphor of Exile* (2002).

Karen F. Stein is Professor of English and Women's Studies at the University of Rhode Island, where she is also Director of the Women's Studies Program. She is author of *Margaret Atwood Revisited* (1999).

Joseph Andriano is Professor of English at the University of Louisiana, Lafayette. His books include *Immortal Monster: The Mythological Evolution of the Fantastic Beast in Modern Fiction and Film* (1999) and *Our Ladies of Darkness: Feminine Daemonology in Male Gothic Fiction* (1993, 2005). He has published essays in numerous edited volumes and journals, including *Indiana English* and *ATQ: 19th Century American Literature and Culture*. He has also published a number of short stories.

Acknowledgments

"Margaret Atwood" by Karen Carmean, Karen F. Stein, and Earl G. Ingersoll. From *Critical Survey of Long Fiction*. 3d rev. ed. Edited by Carl Rollyson. Copyright © 2010 by Salem Press, Inc. Reprinted with permission of Salem Press.

"The *Paris Review* Perspective" by Jascha Hoffman. Copyright © 2008 by Jascha Hoffman. Special appreciation goes to Christopher Cox and Nathaniel Rich, editors for *The Paris Review*.

"*The Handmaid's Tale*" by Coral Ann Howells. From *Margaret Atwood* (2005) by Coral Ann Howells. Copyright © 2005 by Palgrave Macmillan. Reproduced with permission of Palgrave Macmillan.

"'Trust Me': Reading the Romance Plot in Margaret Atwood's *The Handmaid's Tale*" by Madonne Miner. From *Twentieth Century Literature* 37, no. 2 (Summer 1991), pp. 148-169. Copyright © 1991 by Twentieth Century Literature. Reprinted by permission of Twentieth Century Literature.

"'Just a Backlash': Margaret Atwood, Feminism, and *The Handmaid's Tale*" by Shirley Neuman. From *University of Toronto Quarterly* 75, no. 3 (2006), pp. 857-868. Copyright © 2006 by University of Toronto Press. Special thanks to the Graduate Centre for the Study of Drama at the University of Toronto. Reprinted by permission of University of Toronto Press Incorporated (www.utpjournals.com).

"Alice in Disneyland: Criticism as Commodity in *The Handmaid's Tale*" by Chinmoy Banerjee. From *Essays on Canadian Writing* 41 (1990), pp. 74-93. Copyright © 1990 by ECW Press Ltd. Reprinted by permission of ECW Press Ltd.

"Selves, Survival, and Resistance in *The Handmaid's Tale*" by Elisabeth Hansot. From *Utopian Studies* 5, no. 2 (1994), pp. 56-70. Copyright © 1994 by Society for Utopian Studies. Reproduced by permission.

"'We Lived in the Blank White Spaces': Rewriting the Paradigm of Denial in Atwood's *The Handmaid's Tale*" by Danita J. Dodson. From *Utopian Studies* 8, no. 2 (1997), pp. 66-87. Copyright © 1997 by Society for Utopian Studies. Reproduced by permission.

"Margaret Atwood's *The Handmaid's Tale*: Resistance through Narrating" by Hilde Staels. From *English Studies* 76, no. 5 (1995), pp. 455-468. Copyright © 1995 by Taylor and Francis Ltd. Reprinted by permission of Taylor and Francis Ltd, http://www.tandf.co.uk/

"A Body in Fragments: *Life Before Man* and *The Handmaid's Tale*" by Eleonora Rao. From *Strategies for Identity: The Fiction of Margaret Atwood* (1993) by Eleonora Rao. Copyright © 1993 by Peter Lang Publishing, Inc. Reprinted by permission of Peter Lang Publishing, Inc.

"Margaret Atwood's *The Handmaid's Tale*: Scheherazade in Dystopia" by Karen F. Stein. From *University of Toronto Quarterly* 61, no. 2 (1991), pp. 269-280. Copyright

© 1991 by University of Toronto Press. Special thanks to the Graduate Centre for the Study of Drama at the University of Toronto. Reprinted by permission of University of Toronto Press Incorporated (www.utpjournals.com).

"*The Handmaid's Tale* as Scrabble Game" by Joseph Andriano. From *Essays on Canadian Writing* 48 (1992/1993), pp. 89-97. Copyright © 1992 by ECW Press Ltd. Reprinted by permission of ECW Press Ltd.

Index

Abortion rights, 25, 28, 30, 97, 141
Adorno, Theodor W., 153
African Americans, 201, 207, 214
Alienation, 12, 34
Ambiguity, 16, 55, 65, 101, 166, 190, 192, 268
American Dream, 196, 199
American Dreams (Parrington), 198
American history, 149, 196, 198-199, 202
Angel/whore dichotomy, 81
Angels (*The Handmaid's Tale*), 177
Atwood, Margaret; awards and prizes, 10, 42; on bigotry, 200; Canadian identity, 23, 27; commentary on *The Handmaid's Tale*, 4, 22, 26, 30, 46, 49, 94, 150; family, 11, 23; heroines, 12; poetry, 11, 153
Aunt Lydia. *See* Lydia, Aunt (*The Handmaid's Tale*)
Aunts (*The Handmaid's Tale*), 5, 30, 35, 81, 87, 93, 97, 156, 209, 227, 231, 264, 272
Austin, J. L., 155
Autobiography, 85, 91, 206, 208, 216, 246, 252, 259
Avison, Margaret, 11

Bacall, Lauren, 150
Backlash (Faludi), 150
Backlash against feminism, 64, 139, 143, 149-150
Banerjee, Chinmoy, 48, 151, 199, 216
Barber, Benjamin, 73
Benveniste, Emile, 262
Bergmann, Harriet F., 49, 276, 284
Betrayal, 16, 125, 127, 189

Bible, 3, 84, 157, 277; patriarchal narratives, 91; reading, 165
Biblical allusions, 6, 35, 84, 138
Bilhah (Bible), 6, 84, 138, 147
Biological determinism, 74, 147
Birkerts, Sven, 71
Birthing ceremony (*The Handmaid's Tale*), 82, 96, 147
Bloom, Leopold (*Ulysses*), 248
Bodily awareness, 74, 77, 104, 256-257
Bodily Harm (Atwood), 12, 91, 254
Bogart, Humphrey, 150
Boredom, 157, 210, 232
Bradbury, Ray, 59, 263
Brainwashing, 102, 264, 278
Brave New World (Huxley), 15, 21, 34, 59
Brent, Linda (*Incidents in the Life of a Slave Girl*), 208, 211, 213, 216, 220

Canadian border, 93, 227
Canadian identity, 12, 23, 27
Captivity narratives, 197, 203, 205, 208, 212, 216, 218
Carby, Hazel, 208
Carrington, Ildikó de Papp, 171, 260
Carter, Jimmy, 27
Cavalcanti, Ildney, 49-50
Ceaușescu, Nicolae, 25
Censorship, 93, 231, 233, 272
Ceremony (*The Handmaid's Tale*), 35, 162, 165, 210, 212
Chatterjee, Gopal (*The Handmaid's Tale*), 38
Chieco, Kate R., 45
Children of Ham (*The Handmaid's Tale*), 201, 207, 214

Index **311**

China, reproductive rights, 25
Chris (*Life Before Man*), 247, 256
Christian Coalition, 29
Christian fundamentalism, 3, 28, 138, 147, 149, 151, 155, 158, 227
Circle Game, The (Atwood), 23
Cixous, Hélène, 80, 102
Clockwork Orange, A (Burgess), 59
Clothing; colors, 81, 156; Handmaids' uniform, 62, 76-77, 253, 279; symbolism, 24
Code 46 (film), 15
Colonies (*The Handmaid's Tale*), 113, 156
Colonization, 231, 240
Colony of the Unwomen (*The Handmaid's Tale*), 209
Commander (*The Handmaid's Tale*), 6, 129, 227; identity, 242; at Jezebel's, 31, 121, 188; and Latin, 120; privileges, 78; Scrabble games, 35, 86, 112, 183, 236, 281
Commanders (*The Handmaid's Tale*), 6, 138, 201, 211
Communication, 262; Atwood's heroines, 12; illicit, 178, 187, 193, 265
Complacency, 75, 158, 218, 222
Confessional writing, 197, 205, 218, 220, 246, 258
Conservatism, 16, 25, 30, 227; government, 26; religious, 3, 31
Consumerism, 21, 66, 72
Containment, 118, 180, 199, 207
Contradictions, 13, 77, 182, 246, 254, 257
Control; by governments, 25, 34, 79, 84; of language, 86, 264, 273; of women's bodies, 7, 28, 64, 124, 204, 266

Cooke, Nathalie, 87
Cora (*The Handmaid's Tale*), 76
Crake (*Oryx and Crake*), 61, 66-69, 72
Crescent Moon, Maryann (*The Handmaid's Tale*), 37
Cultural relativism, 63
Culture; American, 12, 201; Canadian, 12; development, 69; mass, 153; women's, 96, 147, 213
Culture wars, 36

Darkness at Noon (Koestler), 22
Daughters (*The Handmaid's Tale*), 204
Daughters of the North (Hall), 15
Davidson, Arnold E., 36, 222
Davidson, Cathy, 201
Deconstruction, 269, 272, 274
Deer, Glenn, 218
Delany, Lucy, 206
Delegitimation of narrative, 86
De Man, Paul, 255
Denial, 196, 199, 205, 215, 219, 223, 235
De Papp Carrington, Ildikó. *See* Carrington, Ildikó de Papp
Depersonalization, 231
Discontinuity, 247, 255, 257
Displacement of narrative, 85
Dodson, Danita J., 33
Dogmatism, 243
Domestic violence, 141
Dominant groups, 175, 178, 202
Domination and the Arts of Resistance (Scott), 175
Dopp, Jamie, 49
Doubling, 165, 272
Drumgould, Kate, 206
DuPlessis, Rachel Blau, 85
Dystopia, 198, 244

Dystopian fiction, 3, 15, 21, 34, 45, 48-49, 52, 59, 72, 84, 92, 113, 138, 147, 154, 163, 169, 175, 191, 194, 199, 213, 227, 239, 246, 250, 262; *Oryx and Crake* (Atwood), 65; *We* (Zamyatin), 251

Ecological disaster, 5, 31, 113, 156, 159
Econowives (*The Handmaid's Tale*), 76, 81-82, 93, 156
Edible Woman, The (Atwood), 11, 23, 139
Egg imagery, 185, 238, 282
Ehrenreich, Barbara, 45, 47, 114, 133, 136
Eliot, T.S., 59, 72
Elite groups, 175, 177-178, 188, 191
"End to Audience?, An" (Atwood), 153
Enslavement, 6, 15, 196, 203, 205, 209, 218
Environmental pollution, 31, 66, 138, 156
Equal Rights Amendment, 28-29, 141
Essentialism, 30-31
Eugenics, 15
Euphemisms, 25, 35, 282
Evangelical Christians, 28
Executions, 35, 146, 157, 193
Eyes (surveillance force, *The Handmaid's Tale*), 79, 83, 93, 177, 190, 204

Fahrenheit 451 (Bradbury), 59, 263
Fairy tales, 128, 132, 135, 253
Faludi, Susan, 142, 150
Falwell, Jerry, 28, 141, 158
Family prayer meeting, 184
Family values, 28
Fascism, 155, 159

Feminism, 5, 31, 46, 48, 50, 52, 74, 87, 96, 102, 113, 139, 146, 149, 213, 218, 261, 272; backlash, 3, 44, 64; critique, 21, 56; opposition, 28, 37, 141, 204
Ferns, Chris, 46
Fertility, 5, 28, 113, 117, 176, 179. *See also* Infertility
Feuer, Lois, 31
Fiedler, Leslie, 205
Financial independence, 75
Flashbacks, 13, 75, 101, 144, 247, 263
Flint, Dr. (*Incidents in the Life of a Slave Girl*), 211, 213, 216
Flint, Mrs. (*Incidents in the Life of a Slave Girl*), 212
Flower imagery, 100, 116, 126, 167, 169, 236
Flower, Dean, 150
Foot imagery, 165, 185, 194, 232, 255
Forgiveness, 146
Foster, Frances Smith, 216
Fowler, Roger, 228-229
Fragmentation, 101, 182, 246, 255-256
Fred (*The Handmaid's Tale*), 6, 120, 210, 227, 242, 277, 280, 283. *See also* Commander
Freedom, 93, 206, 214, 219, 249, 254
Freibert, Lucy M., 128, 136
French, William, 44
Freud, Sigmund, 268
Frye, Northrop, 259
Fundamentalism. *See* Christian fundamentalism; Muslim fundamentalism; Religious fundamentalism

Gardens, 100, 105, 116, 168, 238
Gattaca (film), 15
Gender inequality, 74, 75, 87, 120, 150

Gender politics, 3, 30
Genetic engineering, 60, 67, 70
Genette, Gerard, 161, 173
Gibson, Graeme, 11, 23
Gilead (*The Handmaid's Tale*), 3, 54, 102, 132, 138, 151, 155, 159, 164, 183, 187, 193, 196, 200, 204, 218, 222, 230, 242, 261, 271, 278; culture, 118, 170; establishment, 15, 31, 43, 47, 61, 93, 143, 176, 202, 227; failure, 240, 280; patriarchy, 35, 50, 74, 91, 263; racism, 207; religious fundamentalism, 60, 65, 84, 211, 251; repression of communication, 86, 187, 206, 233, 265; women's roles, 5, 80, 96, 113, 124, 146, 212, 256, 269
Gileadean Bible, 7
Glendinning, Victoria, 45, 133
God, 60, 66, 68, 70
Godard, John, 149
Gothic fiction, 45, 56, 84, 164, 166, 169, 173
Gray, Paul, 44
Green, Lesje (*Life Before Man*), 12, 247, 249
Greene, Gayle, 43, 45, 214, 248, 259
Guardians (*The Handmaid's Tale*), 78, 80, 93, 177, 189-190
Gulliver's Travels (Swift), 34

Hales, Leslie-Ann, 199
Hall, Sarah, 15
Hammer, Stephanie, 267, 272
Hancock, Geoff, 49
Hand imagery, 194, 232, 234, 236, 257
Handmaids (*The Handmaid's Tale*), 93, 159, 201, 204, 208, 220, 227, 230, 232, 255, 269, 279; isolation, 181, 193, 263; names, 76; Particicutions, 146, 193; punishment, 194; resistance, 80, 176, 187; role in Gilead, 5, 77, 138, 156; suicides, 283; training, 35, 142, 182, 187, 237; uniform, 62, 169, 277
Handmaid's Tale, The (Atwood); awards and prizes, 42; critical interpretations, 43, 45, 50, 55; film version, 4, 42, 49, 92, 150; "Historical Notes," 7, 36, 48-49, 54-55, 63, 83, 85, 91, 101, 107, 118, 135-136, 170, 191, 203, 207, 221, 229, 240, 251, 255, 268, 283-284; initial responses to, 43, 46; inspiration for, 22, 34; opera version, 42, 92, 143, 146, 148; writing process, 7, 25, 94
Harper, Frances, 216
Hepburn, Katharine, 142, 150
"Herstory," 83, 86, 91
Hidden transcripts, 175, 177, 188, 191, 193, 222
"Historical Notes on *The Handmaid's Tale*" (epilogue), 7, 36, 48-49, 54-55, 63, 83, 85, 91, 107, 118, 135-136, 170, 191, 203, 207, 221, 229, 240, 251, 255, 268, 283-284
Hogsette, David, 37
"Hollow Men, The" (Eliot), 59, 72
Holy Rollers (*The Handmaid's Tale*), 279
Homosexuality, 142
hooks, bell, 204, 206, 210-211, 214, 218, 221
Howells, Coral Ann, 86, 114, 136
Human rights, 71, 93, 196
Humiliation, 6, 16, 27
Hutcheon, Linda, 262, 270
Hutchinson, Anne, 197
Huxley, Aldous, 15, 21, 59

"Icicle, The" (Sinyavsky), 260
Identity, 7, 91, 98, 181, 186, 189, 192, 194, 230, 233, 242, 246, 253, 256, 258, 260
Ignoring, 144, 218
Impenetrablity, 78, 186
Imperialism, 33, 196, 202-203, 205, 207, 211, 219, 221
Incidents in the Life of a Slave Girl (Jacobs), 206, 208, 212, 217
Individuality, 77, 91, 98, 103, 263
Indoctrination, 156, 177, 200, 230-231
Indoctrination centers, 178, 187
Industrialization, 32, 34
Infertility, 6, 15, 32, 65, 142, 227, 232
Intertextuality, 250, 253
Intimacy, 81, 94, 148
Intolerance, 73, 200, 203, 207
Iran, fundamentalism in, 23, 27
Isolation, 82, 176-178, 181, 193-194

Jackson, Marni, 43
Jacobs, Harriet Ann, 197, 206, 208, 210, 212, 216, 220
Janine (*The Handmaid's Tale*), 97, 100
Jealousy, 212
Jefferson, Thomas, 198, 202
Jewish Americans, 201
Jezebel's (*The Handmaid's Tale*), 79-81, 99, 121, 127, 129, 147, 178, 188, 204, 211, 216
"Jihad vs. McWorld" (Barber), 73
Jimmy (*Oryx and Crake*), 66, 68
Johnson, S. Anne, 218
Johnson, Tara J., 51
Joyce, James, 248
June (*The Handmaid's Tale*), 49, 98, 136, 234, 237, 241, 277, 280, 283-284. *See also* Offred (*The Handmaid's Tale*)

Kafka, Franz, 21
Kaplan, Amy, 196, 199
Kauffman, Linda, 206
Ketterer, David, 46
Khomeini, Ayatollah Ruhollah, 24, 27
Klarer, Mario, 206
Koestler, Arthur, 22
Kolodny, Annette, 203
Kristeva, Julia, 229, 239, 245

Lacan, Jacques, 256
Lacombe, Michele, 136, 267, 271
Lady Chatterley's Lover (Lawrence), 167
Lady Oracle (Atwood), 253
Laingen, Bruce, 38
Language, 12, 106, 239, 246, 261; Offred's, 92, 112, 131, 243; poetic, 229, 235; and power, 121, 128, 230, 262, 267, 271
Larson, Janet L., 46, 206
"Laugh of the Medusa, The" (Cixous), 102
Laughter, 104
LeBihan, Jill, 218
Leclaire, Jacques, 46
Letcher, Tina, 270, 272, 274
Lethargy, 219
Life Before Man (Atwood), 12, 246-247, 250, 256-257
Limbaugh, Rush, 142
Literacy, 206, 221
Literary Women (Moers), 84
Literature of Their Own, A (Showalter), 84
Logocentrism, 80
Love, 94, 102, 114, 118, 124, 128, 132, 137, 211, 235, 237, 249, 254, 265, 269
Luke (*The Handmaid's Tale*), 65, 75, 114, 118-120, 122-124, 126-127,

129, 131, 133, 135-136, 144, 168, 182, 189
Luker, Kristen, 28
Lydia, Aunt (*The Handmaid's Tale*), 78, 81, 87, 97, 137, 142, 148-149, 169, 194, 232, 236, 278

McCarthy, Mary, 43, 54, 119, 136, 150, 244
Macpherson, Jay, 11
MaddAddam (*Oryx and Crake*), 70
Major, John, 26
Malak, Amin, 46-47, 114, 133
Male/female binary division, 74, 80
Male gaze, 74, 78
Margaronis, Maria, 44
Marginalization, 83, 200, 205, 207, 209, 217, 263, 270
Marthas (*The Handmaid's Tale*), 5, 76, 81-82, 100, 156, 177, 187, 204
Mass culture, 153-154
Matrix, The (film), 15
May, John, 198
Mayday (*The Handmaid's Tale*), 80, 83, 102, 119, 130, 168, 189
Meditation, 104, 262, 265
Meese, Elizabeth, 139
Memory, 60, 65, 71, 91, 98, 103, 182, 232, 234, 239, 246, 257, 268
Metafiction, 53, 246, 250, 269, 274
Metaphors, 12, 86, 104, 116, 232, 237, 276
Michael, Magali Cornier, 54
Miller, Perry, 32, 96, 200, 202
Mind-style, 228-229, 236, 239, 241, 244
Miner, Madonne, 52
Mirroring, 164, 166
Mirrors, 231
Modernism, 246-247
"Modest Proposal, A" (Swift), 155

Modesty, 78, 185, 264
Moers, Ellen, 84
Moira (*The Handmaid's Tale*), 30, 51, 81, 85, 87, 97, 99, 102, 125, 166, 171, 187, 190, 218, 269, 278
Moral Majority, 28, 141
More, Sir Thomas, 33, 46
Mulvey, Laura, 78
Muslim fundamentalism, 23, 27
Mutilation, 31, 256
Mythology, 69

Names, 6, 76, 91, 98, 177-178, 187, 189, 194, 266, 276-277, 279
Narration, 156, 161-162, 164, 172, 232, 242
Narrative; discontinuity, 257; fragmentation, 256, 267; oral, 251
National Homeland One (*The Handmaid's Tale*), 207, 214, 221
Nature, 66, 68
Newspeak, 230, 244
Nick (*The Handmaid's Tale*), 51, 98, 106, 114, 118, 128, 132, 134, 136, 146, 150, 166, 171, 188-189, 194, 234, 253, 266, 269
Nineteen Eighty-Four (Orwell), 21, 25, 34, 36, 59, 84, 251, 263
Norris, Ken, 49
Nostalgia, 71-72
Nuclear accidents, 5
Nunavit (*The Handmaid's Tale*), 49, 191, 240

Oates, Joyce Carol, 24
Objectification, 78, 256
Objective time, 246-247
O'Brien, Tom, 48, 150
Offred (*The Handmaid's Tale*), 3, 6, 16, 36, 45, 48, 65, 74, 78, 85, 130, 138, 156, 162, 176, 197, 202, 205, 209,

227, 258, 260-261, 278; apathy, 219, 221; and Commander, 120, 124, 127, 184, 210, 265; complicity, 51, 218; contradictions, 254; daughter, 82; displacement, 250; film version, 44; isolation, 181, 186, 194; at Jezebel's, 80, 178, 188; and Luke, 75, 119; memories, 30, 97, 142, 148, 150, 182, 235, 272; names, 49, 70, 91, 136, 266, 276, 284; as narrator, 53, 55, 72, 99, 115, 158, 168, 192, 230, 233, 268; and Nick, 131; opera version, 144; resistance, 103, 180, 188, 215; Scrabble games, 35, 112, 283; and Serena Joy, 60, 190, 213, 238

Ofglen (*The Handmaid's Tale*), 51, 62, 80, 99, 115, 119, 130, 135, 145, 156, 163, 177, 185, 188, 236, 263, 279

Ofwarren (*The Handmaid's Tale*), 97, 100

"One child" policy (China), 25

Oppression, 33, 36, 63, 65, 70, 213, 221; of subordinate groups, 205; of women, 31, 51, 74, 83, 151, 156, 158, 197, 209, 212, 214, 217

Oral narrative, 206, 251

Ortner, Sherry, 204

Orwell, George, 21, 25, 34, 36, 59, 84, 263

Oryx and Crake (Atwood), 16, 60-61, 65, 70-71

Pahlavi, Mohammad Reza Shah, 27

Paradice (*Oryx and Crake*), 67-68

Paradigm of denial, 196, 199, 205, 215, 219

Paradise, 59, 65

Paradoxes, 262, 270, 273

Parrington, Vernon Louis, Jr., 198

Particicutions (*The Handmaid's Tale*), 35, 83, 95, 97, 100, 157, 170, 193

Passivity, 51, 80, 178

Passports, 124

Patriarchy, 5, 7, 16, 28, 32, 35, 74, 80, 87, 91, 102, 261, 266

Patronymic names, 6, 76, 91, 276, 280

Pease, Donald, 202

Perfectionism, 70, 136

Persecution, 201

Personal expression, 75-76

Personal speech, 231, 233, 265

Pessimism, 153, 166

Phillips, Howard, 95

Pieixoto, Professor (*The Handmaid's Tale*), 8, 37, 49, 55, 63, 83, 87, 108, 118, 140, 167, 202, 207, 242, 266, 283-284

Pigoon (*Oryx and Crake*), 66

Pinter, Harold, 4

Plato, 33

Poetry (Atwood), 10, 23, 153

Political action committees, 28-29

Polk, James, 11

Pornography, 6, 16, 64, 68, 78, 143, 148, 272

Positivism, 241

Postfeminist era, 6, 142

Postmodernism, 45-46, 48, 53-56, 101, 261, 274

Power, 147; creative, 243; Gilead government, 138; of language, 267, 271, 279; political, 3, 93; sexual, 159, 167; social, 261, 265

Prayvaganzas (*The Handmaid's Tale*), 35, 95, 135, 187, 278

Pregnancy, 65, 104, 157, 187, 190, 210

Prescott, Peter, 45

Present (time), 231, 235, 237

Private discourse, 264-265

Private space, 76

Procreation, 176, 230, 237

Index 317

Propaganda, 34-35
Prostitution, 31, 68, 81, 211
Protestantism, 201
Prynne, Hester (*The Scarlet Letter*), 77, 251, 253, 260
Pseudo-singulative mode, 162
Psychoanalytic theory, 246, 256
Public personas, 179, 184, 194
Public transcripts, 175, 178, 187, 191, 193, 222
Punishment, 31, 159, 178, 194
Punning, 46, 49, 53, 87, 261, 265, 267, 270, 274, 279, 282
Puritanism, 5, 93, 96, 197, 199, 201, 203-204, 207-208, 227, 251, 253

Rachel (Bible), 6, 84, 138, 147
Racism, 155, 207, 217, 219
Radical pessimism, 153
Raisins (*The Handmaid's Tale*), 201
Rape, 6, 30, 36, 100, 148, 212, 221, 264, 272
Rapunzel syndrome, 253, 259
Rationalism, 241
Reading, 35, 37, 112, 115-116, 118, 123, 133, 136, 153, 279, 283
Reagan, Ronald, 26, 29, 141, 149
Rebellion, 83, 251, 266, 278
Recollection, 268
Reconstruction, 91, 103, 132, 136, 171, 240, 251, 258-259, 268-269, 272, 274
Red Center (*The Handmaid's Tale*), 82
Red Shoes, The (film), 194
Reeducation centers, 6, 95, 138, 142, 261, 264
Reflexivity, 171-172
Religious conservatism, 3, 16
Religious extremism, 23, 25, 61
Religious fundamentalism, 21, 233, 277; Gilead, 31, 60-61, 113

Religious intolerance, 73
Religious Right, 3, 95, 147, 227
Rennie (*Bodily Harm*), 254
Repression; of individuality, 77; political, 159, 262; sexual, 87, 272; of women, 16, 44, 49, 63, 99, 272
Reproduction, 77, 138, 156, 208, 256
Reproductive rights, 64, 227; China, 25; Romania, 25, 141
Republic (Plato), 33
Republic of Gilead. *See* Gilead (*The Handmaid's Tale*)
Resistance, 80, 83, 91, 98, 102, 104, 153, 164, 166, 175-177, 180, 183, 187-188, 190-192, 215-216, 261-262
Re-vision, 84, 86
Rich, Adrienne, 84, 262
Rita (*The Handmaid's Tale*), 82, 120
Rituals, 6, 83, 95, 118, 177, 232, 264
Robertson, Claire, 212
Robertson, Pat, 29, 141, 158
Roe v. Wade, 28-29
Roemer, Kenneth, 198
Romance, 45, 51-52, 56, 130, 132, 134, 136
Romania, reproductive rights, 25, 141
Room of One's Own, A (Woolf), 74, 80
Rowlandson, Mary, 203
Rubenstein, Roberta, 208, 255
Ruders, Poul, 92
Rule, Jane, 173

Sacrifice, 61, 70
Sage, Lorna, 30
Salem witch trials, 204
Salvagings (*The Handmaid's Tale*), 35, 82, 157, 170, 187, 191, 193
Sands, Mr. (*Incidents in the Life of a Slave Girl*), 216

Sapir-Whorf hypothesis, 36
Satire, 46, 52, 55, 84, 87
Scarlet Letter, The (Hawthorne), 250, 253, 260
Scheherazade, 8, 261, 266, 273
Schlafly, Phyllis, 142, 150
Schloendorf, Elisabeth (*Life Before Man*), 247, 249, 256
Schloendorf, Nate (*Life Before Man*), 247-249, 256, 259
Schloendorff, Volker, 4, 92
Science fiction, 42, 46, 48; extrapolation, 47
Scott, James, 175, 177, 180, 191, 193
Scrabble (game), 35, 86, 104, 112, 119, 133, 146, 277, 279, 281, 284
Seduction, 183, 211, 216
Segregation, 207, 214, 218
Self, 246, 251, 255, 257, 260-261, 263, 265, 269
Self-affirmation, 231, 243
Self-awareness, 145
Self-expression, 233, 243
Selfhood, 77, 255
Self-knowledge, 246
Self-reflection, 231
Sensuality, 179, 181-182, 185, 189, 191
Serena Joy (*The Handmaid's Tale*), 60, 81, 100, 105, 116, 127, 142, 147, 165, 169, 212, 215, 227, 238, 253, 264
Sexism, 37, 49, 87, 118, 155, 171, 267, 277, 284
Sexual intercourse, 177
Sexual surrogacy, 138
Sexuality, 146, 208, 272; control of, 7, 176; freedom, 31; and power, 159, 167, 266; shame, 77; taboos, 86, 216
Shame, 74, 77
Shibboleth, 277, 284
Showalter, Elaine, 84, 262

Singulative mode, 161
Sisterhood, 82, 220, 253
Slave narratives, 84, 197, 205, 208, 212, 216, 218
Slaves, American South, 206, 210, 228
Slotkin, Richard, 198, 200, 203
Smith, Barbara, 214
Smith, Valerie, 217
Snowman (*Oryx and Crake*), 66-69, 72
Social engineering, 67, 70
Social status, 261, 267, 272
Solidarity among women, 82, 214, 221
Solitude, 186, 192-193
Sons of Jacob (*The Handmaid's Tale*), 201, 277
Sorisio, Carolyn, 212
Soul Scrolls (*The Handmaid's Tale*), 157, 279
Speculative fiction, 193
Speech, 229-230, 235, 243, 262; hidden transcripts, 178, 187, 189; restriction, 193, 233, 264; restrictions, 184
Spelling, 276, 278, 283
Spivak, Gayatri, 214, 222
Staels, Hilde, 55
Star Wars (film), 15
Status, social, 261, 267, 272
Stein, Karen, 202
Sterility, 5, 32, 138, 156-157, 167. *See also* Infertility
Stillman, Peter, 218
Stimpson, Catherine R., 43
Storytelling, 7-8, 85, 91, 97, 101, 262, 265, 268, 270, 273
Subjective time, 246
Subjectivity, 262-263, 272
Subordinate groups, 175, 177, 179
Superiority, 200
Suppression, 238; of information, 138, 221; of speech, 233; of women, 47, 93, 227

Surfacing (Atwood), 11-12, 254, 257
Surveillance, 32, 34, 60, 76, 79, 84, 138, 155, 177, 191, 193
Survival, 7-8, 84, 87, 175, 177, 180, 186, 190, 192, 206, 220, 222, 234, 243
Survival (Atwood), 200
Symbolic thinking, 69
Symposium on Gileadean Studies, 36, 101, 108, 191, 203, 207, 240, 251

Taboos, 24, 78, 86, 216, 265
Televangelism, 60, 141, 157
Testifying (*The Handmaid's Tale*), 264
Text, 255-256
Thatcher, Margaret, 26
Theocracy, 3, 5, 15, 23, 25, 27, 62, 138, 149, 155, 158, 227, 229-230, 232, 236, 243
Three Guineas (Woolf), 146
Time, objective and subjective, 246-247
Tituba, 197, 205
Tolan, Fiona, 52, 87
Tome, Sandra, 51, 53, 201, 222
Totalitarianism, 22, 24, 32-33, 60, 65, 227, 230
Treason, 91, 187
Tuveson, Ernest, 198

Underground Femaleroad (*The Handmaid's Tale*), 83, 221, 227, 232
Uniforms, 76, 79
Unpure Woman (*The Handmaid's Tale*), 216
Unwomen (*The Handmaid's Tale*), 113, 204, 209
Updike, John, 45, 147, 150
Utopia, 197
Utopia (More), 33
Utopian fiction, 46, 154
Utopianism, 70, 201

Victimization, 144, 151, 230, 240, 261
Victorian imagery, 76
Violence; against abortion providers, 64, 141; Gilead government, 138; as theme in literature, 198; against women, 6, 93, 141, 210, 212, 218

War, 24, 34
We (Zamyatin), 21, 34, 59, 250, 254
Webster, Mary, 96, 197, 200, 205
White supremacy, 207
Wilderness, 10, 12, 23
Wilford, Rennie (*Bodily Harm*), 12
Willed ignorance, 144, 146, 148
William (*Life Before Man*), 247, 249
Wilson, Harriet E., 216
Wilson, Sharon Rose, 42, 49
Winthrop, John, 198, 202
Witchcraft, 202, 204
Wives (*The Handmaid's Tale*), 5, 76, 81-82, 93, 97, 100, 156, 204, 212-213
Wolvog (*Oryx and Crake*), 66
Women; African American slaves, 206, 210-211; and language, 104, 271; roles in Gilead, 91, 93, 227; writing, 74, 83, 157, 262
"Women and Fiction" (Woolf), 83
Women's rights, 28, 64, 72, 139
Woolf, Virginia, 74, 77, 80, 83, 146
Wordplay, 104, 265, 269-270, 272, 274
Writing; confessional, 246, 258; restriction, 264; as subversion, 251; women, 262
Writing the self, 252

Yamamoto, Tae, 52

Zamyatin, Yevgeny, 21, 34, 59, 250, 254